THE ANALYSIS OF
SOCIAL INTERACTIONS:
Methods, Issues, and Illustrations

THE ANALYSIS OF SOCIAL INTERACTIONS:
Methods, Issues, and Illustrations

Edited by

ROBERT B. CAIRNS
*University of North Carolina
at Chapel Hill*

LEA LAWRENCE ERLBAUM ASSOCIATES, PUBLISHERS
1979   Hillsdale, New Jersey

DISTRIBUTED BY THE HALSTED PRESS DIVISION OF
JOHN WILEY & SONS
New York   Toronto   London   Sydney

Lawrence Erlbaum Associates, Inc., Publishers
62 Maria Drive
Hillsdale, New Jersey 07642

Distributed solely by Halsted Press Division
John Wiley & Sons, Inc., New York

Library of Congress Cataloging in Publication Data

Main entry under title:

The analysis of social interactions.

   1. Social interaction—Addresses, essays, lectures.
I. Cairns, Robert B., 1933–
HM131.A447   301.11   78-31939
ISBN 0-470-26662-7

Printed in the United States of America

Contents

Acknowledgments

The impetus for this review of interactional methods and analyses came from the Society for Research in Child Development. The Long Range Planning Committee of SRCD (Harold Stevenson, Chair) provided the support for a workshop/conference on the issues and methods of social interactions, with the aim of identifying problems of cross-disciplinary concern and possible guides for their resolution. This volume is an outgrowth of the discussions held in Chapel Hill and at the Quail Roost Conference Center. The participants and their major areas include: developmental disorders (*L. Kalverboer*, Groningen, The Netherlands; *D. Routh*, North Carolina); ethology (*M. Bekoff*, Colorado); animal behavior development (*M. West*, North Carolina); child psychopathology (*G. Patterson*, Oregon Research Institute); behavioral embryology (*G. Gottlieb*, North Carolina; *D. Miller*, North Carolina Department of Mental Health); social development (*R. Bell*, Virginia; *R. Parke*, Illinois; *A. Siegel*, Stanford; *C. Waxler*, NIMH; *M. Yarrow*, NIMH); infancy (*C. Eckerman*, Duke; *H. Rheingold*, North Carolina); language development (*C. Garvey*, Johns Hopkins; *A. Gordon*, North Carolina); and statistics (*M. Appelbaum*, North Carolina; *N. J. Castellan, Jr.*, Indiana; *R. Dawes*, Oregon Research Institute).

The preparation of this volume was facilitated by the efficiency and kind assistance of the editorial staff at Lawrence Erlbaum Associates, especially Ros Herion, production editor at LEA. James A. Green of the University of North Carolina assisted in the final editing and in the preparation of the index. Allan Hardin expertly typed the final versions of several of the chapters. I greatly appreciate the contributions of each of these persons.

My own activities relevant to this project have been supported by the University of North Carolina and by the National Institute of Child Health and Human Development (HD 08464). It is a pleasure to acknowledge the role that both institutions have played in the support of my research.

I must express a word of personal thanks to my colleague, Harriet L. Rheingold, for her help in the initial planning of this project. Her contributions to the matters covered in this volume have been manifold, and all of us who attempt to study social development are indebted to her for her scholarship and her insights.

Chapel Hill   ROBERT B. CAIRNS

THE ANALYSIS OF
SOCIAL INTERACTIONS:
Methods, Issues, and Illustrations

Social Interactional Methods:
An Introduction

Robert B. Cairns
University of North Carolina at Chapel Hill

Significant breakthroughs have been achieved within the past decade in the development of methodologies for the study of social interactions. It is the aim of this volume to describe the nature of these advances and to explore some of their implications. Progress has been made in virtually all aspects of methodology: in formulation, in design, in techniques for data collection, and in statistical evaluation. The new procedures provide the impetus for a fresh view of an old concept. In this chapter, we offer introductory remarks on the background issues, comment on what is meant by the concept of social interaction, and identify some common misunderstandings about interactional methods. We close with an outline of what is to come in the rest of the book.

SOCIAL DEVELOPMENT AND
SOCIAL METHODOLOGY

The core issues of social development—how social patterns originate, how they are regulated, how they evolve—have been central ones for psychology since its founding as a separate discipline a century ago. In *The Expression of the Emotions in Man and Animals*, Charles Darwin (1872) faced squarely the problem of whether social behaviors and emotions and consciousness were continuous from animals to man. The matter remains as provocative today as it was a century ago (witness the furor surrounding the publication of E. O. Wilson's *Sociobiology* in 1975). A mere generation after Darwin, Sigmund Freud (1905) provided the substructure for much of what is current in today's theories of personality and social development. These include areas of

1

content (aggression, attachment, sexual identification) and mechanisms of development (critical periods of behavioral arrest, psychological determination).

Even a highly abbreviated and selective list of the early intellectual forerunners for contemporary concepts of social development would be incomplete if we were to omit J. M. Baldwin. Baldwin, a nearly forgotten genius in the history of developmental thought, gave us the first comprehensive statement of the concept of social interaction and its implication that the child was a "social outcome not a social unit." Although the total impact of Baldwin's work has not put him into the same league with Freud and Darwin, he has been a seminal contributor for our contemporary understanding of both cognitive and social development. Baldwin's principal book on social interaction and reciprocity, *Social and Ethical Interpretations in Mental Development: A Study in Social Psychology* (1897), remains brilliant, challenging, and obscure, each in about equal measure.

In retrospect, the proposals of Darwin, Freud, and Baldwin provided in their time a wholly fresh perspective on ancient issues of social behavior. The ideas remain alive today, not as historical vestiges, but as vigorous proposals that seem to be riding on the front edge of the present intellectual *Zeitgeist*. The extended youth of the concepts testifies to their power and to the magnitude of the contribution of the pioneers of our discipline. It also speaks to a less happy state of affairs for the science. A continuing problem in the study of social development has been that empirical studies of the phenomena have not kept pace with theoretical insights on their nature. Hence, scientific evaluations have not provided, for the most part, adequate bases for accepting, rejecting, or revising the key proposals of the field.

Why not? One answer is that the study of social development is an extraordinarily complex and abstruse business. Hence, everyday insights that appear simple when proposed by parents and competent teachers may transcend precise operational formulation and resist analysis. On this score, the empirical progress made over the past century must be measured in the light of the enormity of the problem.

A second answer, not inconsistent with the first, is that the methods available have not been adequate for the task. Without appropriate tools, the progress of any science will be slowed. Worse, the science may be retarded by the adoption of fallible instruments that yield plausible but inaccurate findings. One of the most difficult messages to accept is that things may not be as they seem to be. Categories of experience can be misleading, despite their apparent validity and practical utility. The significant discoveries of natural science came about when methods were invented that permitted the researcher to "see" phenomena more precisely or from a different perspective than was achieved by the unaided eye or ear. This principle may be as relevant for behavioral scientists as it has been for our colleagues in physical and biological science.

In their excellent critique of the methods available for the study of child rearing, Yarrow, Campbell, and Burton (1968) observe that the methods that have been employed have not achieved notable success in unraveling the secrets of social development. Although these authors focused their attention on the use of retrospective interviews with parents, a similar case can be offered against most of the other procedures that have been employed over the past 30 years in studies of social development. There has been a succession of "promising" techniques, but few have fulfilled their promise. After enjoying near-epidemic levels of acceptance, the techniques tend to fade from the scientific scene. So went the "F" scale for the study of the development of the authoritarian personality, the "marble drop" apparatus for assessing social reinforcement, the "manifest anxiety" test for the study of susceptibility to stress, in addition to the interview procedure for probing child-rearing antecedents of personality. Although judgments about the contemporary scene are risky, candidates for retirement in the foreseeable future include "moral dilemma" questionnaires and various short-term demonstrational experiments for assessing the power of imitation, attachment, and aggression-induction.

Why do procedures fall from favor, and what then happens to them? Those questions bring us to one of the reasons for preparing this volume. At this juncture, we can note that research techniques can rarely be described with profit in absolute terms as "good" or "bad" and "valid" or "invalid." Such judgments are relative to what dimensions are used to evaluate the procedures, when they are evaluated, and the aims that the investigator has in employing the methods. Hence, procedures that were once discredited can be legitimately resurrected, if the requirements for analysis change or the goals of the research are modified. So it has been with two of the first procedures that were employed for the study of social development: observational methods and rating scales. After dominating the study of social phenomena in the early years of research (notably in the 1920s and early 1930s), both procedures faded from the literature. They have been recently restored to favor and applied to the study of social interactions. Accordingly, one of our subsidiary aims in this volume is to undertake a detailed examination of these procedures at the time of their resurgence: their strengths and pitfalls, and their areas of application and misapplication.

Our more general concern is with the problem of how available methodologies, including designs, assessment techniques, and analytic strategies, can be employed to understand the interactive nature of social development. At this point, we should clarify briefly what is meant by conceptions of social interation.

CONCEPTIONS OF SOCIAL INTERACTION

The key idea of social interaction is that social acts and personality cannot be understood independently of the social context in which they are embedded because of the ongoing "dialectic" or interchange between the person and his surrounds. J. M. Baldwin (1902) captured the idea when he wrote that "we are members one of another" and that "the development of the child's personality could not go on at all without the constant modification of his sense of himself by suggestions from others. So he himself, at every stage, is really in part someone else, even in his own thought of himself [p. 30]."

In Baldwin's dynamic view of social development, a "dialectic of personal growth" constitutes the key mechanism of modification and change. Imitation in an interactive sense permits the child to learn from others and, in turn, permits others to be influenced by the child. The child's behaviors and attitudes become gradually formed by the dominant social influences to which he is exposed in a given social system: He becomes both a factor and a product of the social organization.

Baldwin's concept of social interactions and how they develop appears to have been most influential in the theoretical formulations of symbolic interactionism that were proposed by G. H. Mead and C. H. Cooley. Leonard Cottrell (1942, 1969), in turn, elaborated these concepts of interactional analysis in sociology. The essential ideas entered the mainstream of developmental thought by the efforts of R. R. Sears (1951), and they have recently been expanded in the work of several contemporary authors (see Part II, *Illustrations*, this volume).

The concept of the embeddedness of behavior in a social context has been independently discovered in other areas, including those stimulated by Darwin and Freud. That outcome should not be surprising, because the essential notion was implicit in the Darwinian descriptions of social patterns (and expanded by Tinbergen, 1972, and Hinde and Spencer-Booth, 1967). Similarly, few readers acquainted with Freud's description of the mother–infant relationship will find the contemporary post-Freudian emphases on filial interactions to be novel or inappropriate. H. S. Sullivan's interpersonal theory of psychiatry and John Bowlby's model of attachment share a common parentage and emphasis on interactions, despite obvious differences in content.

In sum, the concept of social interaction points attention to the properties of the feedback process by which organisms influence each other. One does not merely act in a social relationship; one reacts. And the reaction may have been stimulated, in part, by one's own earlier actions and the repercussions that the actions produced. Hence, Sear's (1951) conclusion that "unidirectional" or monadic concepts of personality have outlived their usefulness.

For many workers, the concept of social interaction has proved to be a powerful and intuitively attractive idea. There has been, nonetheless, a significant gap between theory and research. To the extent that feedback from application and assessment has not been forthcoming, the ideas themselves seem to have been arrested in growth. The chasm between concepts and methods may have also been partly responsible for the failure of interactional approaches, until the recent past, to bring about significant changes in our understanding of social and personality processes.

MISCONCEPTIONS OF SOCIAL INTERACTIONS

Misconceptions about what interactional methods involve have proved to be almost as important for their application as conceptions. Three kinds of misunderstanding have been so pervasive that they require mention at the outset of this volume (subsequent chapters deal with the matters in detail). One issue concerns the belief that the procedures that have been proposed for the study of interactions are too "molecular" and that they necessarily destroy the inherent integrity and organization of the behavior-to-be-explained. A second issue follows from the belief that interactional methods have set for themselves an impossible task because "everything interacts with everything else." Hence, it has been sometimes accepted that there must be an inevitable confusion between social effects and social determinants. A third issue concerns the relation between theory and method.

Molecular or Molar?

Consider first the belief that interactional procedures are too elementaristic. The criticism—which is sometimes justified—is that researchers becomes trapped by the capabilities of their equipment for analyzing the minutia of behavior. Even though slow-motion playback videotape recorders can produce a tolerable picture each 16–18-*thousandth* of a second, why do it? Can anything of value be discovered by such fine-grained analyses that greatly exceed the capabilities of children to recognize changes in the acts of others and to react to them? The same criticism can also be applied to slightly longer time intervals (5–6 seconds) when it is recognized that behavior can be organized in much more complex and coherent patterns. The problem, then, is one of segmentation and a fear that the integrity of the action pattern will be disrupted or destroyed by methods that involve very precise but very brief intervals.

Is there any foundation for the fear? The answer is clearly "yes" if one assumes that the methods must capture, at the first level of analysis, the "wholeness" of the phenomena under investigation. It is also the case that some investigators implicitly assume that there is an isomorphic relationship between the precision of their methods and the structure of the phenomena that they are investigating.

Both assumptions are misconceptions. Even highly "organized" patterns of activity or systems of social regulation can often be profitably studied by the use of exceedingly precise techniques that measure segmented elements of the system. In such cases, the burden lies with the investigator to keep in focus the essential coherence of the system while, simultaneously, dissecting its parts.

To illustrate, precise interactional methods have been used in psychobiology to identify mechanisms that account for intricate and interlocked patterns of social organization. T. C. Schneirla (1966) carried out an elegant series of observational and experimental interactional studies to account for the migratory pattern of the army ants of Central America. He found that the "raiding" patterns of insects were triggered by development-paced changes in the activity level of the new brood of offspring. The activity of the workers, in turn, stimulated changes in the reproductive state of the queen, which eventually led to the production of eggs and a new crop of young. The methods of Schneirla were elementaristic, but the social organization that he studied was molar and organized. By employing both molecular and molar interactional procedures, and observational as well as experimental designs, Schneirla accomplished what preceding generations of investigators had failed to do: He described and explained the social organization of this "most social" species (Wilson, 1975).

The general lesson is that there is not a necessary relationship between the level of the analysis employed and the nature of the phenomena to be explained. To identify the processes controlling social development— whether of ants or children—it is sometimes necessary to employ techniques that outreach the child's own capabilities to observe, analyze, and discriminate. But the problem for the researcher then becomes one of determining how the system can be put back together again—hence, the need for the researcher to be capable of operating at multiple levels of analysis, not merely molar or molecular ones.

Too Complex?

This brings us to a second misconception about interactional methods and to the "systems" analysis of which they are a part. The problem is simply that these methods may appear overly complex. Would it not be better to start out by trying to understand the activities of a single child, acting alone, before trying to deal with the complexities of his interchanges? Otherwise, is one not in the danger of coming to the conclusion that "everything must interact with everything else" and end up explaining nothing at all?

The misconception here is that studies of interchanges are inherently more complex than studies of children in social isolation. In this regard, some of the biggest problems surrounding social development have come about because generalizations to everyday life have been based on studies of children observed individually in "controlled" laboratory settings. Accordingly, it may be more complex to *omit* the sources of variance that may be attributed to the actions of other persons and the context than to include them. Nor does the simultaneous analysis of multiple sources of variance constitute an escape from precise analysis. Such measures may be required to determine which sources of control to focus upon in matters of theory construction and practical application, and which to ignore.

It is ironic that these two major misconceptions about interactional methods refer to the same problem, but from opposite perspectives. On the one hand, interactional procedures have been cast as being too molecular and unable to capture the essential integrity and organization of social development. On the other hand, they have been seen as being too complex and "system" oriented, so that precise antecedent–consequent relations will not be possible. Neither outcome is a necessary one. The hazards are clearly present in interactional methods, but no more so than in other methods available for the study of social development.

Theory or Technique?

Are interactional procedures necessarily bound to a given theory, such as Baldwin's or his modern counterparts, Kohlberg (1969), Patterson (Chapter 5, this volume), or Sullivan (1940)? The question supplies its own answer. The catholicity of the theories that have arisen concerning interactions tells us that the idea is an orientation to social phenomena, not a theory about them. To be sure, the proposal that social acts are embedded in a social matrix has implications for how one might go about understanding the nature and determination of social patterns and personality. But whether one proposes that the organization is appropriately conceptualized in terms of the self (as did Baldwin) or in patterns of antecedent–outcome relations (as does Patterson) is a matter for the theorist, not the methodologist.

But, on another level, we can observe that new theoretical formulations may be permitted by interactional methods. The procedures are "biased" to identify sources of control that have been typically ignored or overlooked by procedures that focus only upon individuals and their inherent dispositions. To the extent that behaviors of others, the features of social organization, and the nature of the context act upon the child—and the child acts upon these features of his environment—interactional methods will yield different results than noninteractional ones. Although interactional procedures do not require a particular theoretical model, they do permit the development of models that take into account the dynamics of interchanges and reciprocal controls.

WHAT IS TO COME

In the past decade, interactional methods have become increasingly prominent in the work of investigators concerned with issues of social development. They have been employed in studies of diverse problems, from developmental semantics and family therapy to aggressive development and maternal–infant patterns. In view of the potential significance of the methods, and the pitfalls that they present, it seemed timely to prepare an assessment of the procedures, along with illustrations of their use and guidelines for their application.

The content and organization of this volume represents an attempt among some current users of interactional methods to provide such an assessment. Part I, *Design, Techniques, and Analysis*, is concerned with the methods themselves. Part II, *Illustrations*, deals with how the methods have been applied to different areas of social development, including aggressive family systems, the ontogeny of play, and the origin of social interactions. Part III, *Summary and Conclusions*, consists of a single chapter in which some guidelines for interactional research are proposed; this chapter represents a summary of many of the ideas covered in the rest of the volume.

The appendix to this volume contains two shorter contributions. Appendix A was prepared because of the recent controversy surrounding the relative advantages of rating scales versus direct observations in the study of interchanges. Appendix B is an introductory statement on statistical analysis for persons who have had no prior experience with interactional findings or their descriptions.

A final comment is in order on the dangers inherent in preparing a methodological critique and guide. Despite our intentions to the contrary, the work might serve to discourage the use of the procedures that we discuss. Why might this outcome occur? First, the potential user may feel overwhelmed by the number of issues to be considered and may conclude that it would be easier to try other methods or to stay with the ones that are more familiar. Second, the user may show a *too* rigid adherence to the guides and fail to extend the methods in more creative and innovative directions. Perhaps it is because of such hazards that most critiques appear in *post mortem*, after the procedures have been discredited and are about to pass (temporarily) from the scene. But, unless we misread the current direction of research, interactional methods are not about to fade away in the immediate future. Hence, we hope to communicate the potential, the vigor, and the power of the procedures while, simultaneously, helping to identify some of their problems.

REFERENCES

Baldwin, J. M. *Social and ethical interpretations in mental development: A study in social psychology* (3rd ed.). New York: Macmillan, 1902. (1st edition published in 1897.)

Cottrell, L. S. The analysis of situational fields in social psychology. *American Sociological Review*, 1942, *7*, 370–382.

Cottrell, L. S., Jr. Interpersonal interaction and the development of the self. In D. A. Goslin (Ed.), *Handbook of socialization theory and research.* Chicago: Rand McNally, 1969.

Darwin, C. R. *The expression of the emotions in man and animals.* London; John Murray, 1872.

Freud, S. *Drei Abhandlungen zür Sexualtheorie.* Vienna: Deuticke, 1905. (Translated as *Three essays on the theory of sexuality*, 1962.)

Hinde, R. A., & Spencer-Booth, Y. The behavior of social living rhesus monkeys in their first two and half years. *Animal Behaviour*, 1967, *15*, 169–196.

Kohlberg, L. Stage and sequence: The cognitive-developmental approach to socialization. In D. A. Goslin (Ed.), *Handbook of socialization theory and research.* Chicago: Rand McNally, 1969.

Schneirla, T. C. Behavioral development and comparative psychology. *Quarterly Review of Biology*, 1966, *41*, 283–302.

Sears, R. R. A theoretical framework for personality and social behavior. *American Psychologist*, 1951, *6*, 476–483.

Sullivan, H. S. Some conceptions of modern psychiatry. *Psychiatry*, 1940, *3*, 1–117.

Tinbergen, N. *The animal in its world: Explorations of an ethologist.* London: Allen & Unwin, 1972.

Wilson, E. O. *Sociobiology: The new synthesis.* Cambridge, Mass.: Harvard University Press, 1975.

Yarrow, M. R., Campbell, J. D., & Burton, R. V. *Child-rearing: An inquiry into research and methods.* San Francisco: Jossey-Bass, 1968.

I DESIGN, TECHNIQUES, AND ANALYSIS

With the recent introduction of a variety of new "ecological" and "naturalistic" research designs, questions have arisen as to which are the most powerful and appropriate models to adopt. What, for example, are the relative advantages and disadvantages of studies of interactions in unconstrained settings as opposed to controlled "laboratory" circumstances? On still another dimension is the problem of manipulation and control, and how interactional experiments may be conducted outside the laboratory (the "field") as well as in prearranged laboratory settings. To what extent does the context (for example, the playground or the classroom, the home or the laboratory) have elicitation properties of its own and thereby present a "special" view of the interchange? Since an implicit assumption of interactional analysis is that the content does make a difference, the properties of the observation context itself seem worthy of direct analysis. The task of clarifying the interactional designs available was taken up by R. Parke (Chapter 1). Here one finds, among other guidelines, a clear statement on the need to employ more than a single design in disentangling interactional phenomena.

The several issues of "observing behavior" are addressed in Chapter 2 by M. R. Yarrow and C. Z. Waxler. Of particular importance for the potential user of interactional techniques are the issues of observer reliability and what contributes to interobserver agreement and disagreement. A thoughtful consideration of these issues indicates that the conventional assumption that one need only demonstrate "category reliability" is in error. As Yarrow and Waxler point out, agreement is a relative and variable property of observation; it is not a static index. It depends, in part, on the skills and characteristics of the observer as well as who is observed. This chapter, taken in conjunction with other treatments of the problem (see especially Patterson and Reid, 1976), suggests that some of our concerns about the observation process have been misplaced. For example, recent studies cited by Patterson and Reid (1976) indicate that the effects of "observer bias" and the "effects-of-being-observed" may have been overemphasized as problems. However, other sources of error have been overlooked, including "observer drift" (i.e., an idiosyncratic redefinition of categories over time), properties of the observer and those who are observed, and the interaction between categories and the persons to whom they are applied. Chapter 2 also suggests a powerful but little used or recognized adjunct to traditional reliability assessments—namely, the independent statistical analysis of the results obtained by different observers.

But these issues of interactional observations are not problems just for child psychologists. In Chapter 3, M. Bekoff reminds us that investigators of animal behavior have been concerned with such matters for as long as have child psychologists. The analyses developed in ethology are in many respects parallel to those in psychology, although not in all. This chapter provides another perspective on the issues of interactional observation and underscores again the relativity of the coding system to the aims of the investigator. Chapter 3 also emphasizes the first principle of animal observation, which can be stated succinctly as "know the phenomena." This principle applies with equal force to observations of child interactions.

After solving the problems of design and data collection, those who aspire to analyze interchanges are then faced with a formidable task of description and statistical analysis. Few graduate training programs—whether psychological, educational, sociological, or zoological—prepare their students for this assignment. A major purpose/concern of this volume is to identify what kinds of solutions are available and how they can be applied.

N. J. Castellan has performed a significant service for the area by clarifying in Chapter 4 how one might conceptualize interactional data in contingency analyses. Chapter 4 provides explicit guides on how one might deal with the dynamics of interchange patterns (i.e., where the acts of one person may change in their control properties during the course of the relationship). This proposal is an important one, because most descriptions of interchanges have an implicit assumption of "stationarity" (i.e., that the acts of one person have invariant and stable control properties for the other). In addition, Castellan offers a solution to the problem of how one might legitimately combine across dyads, and how one might assess the gains in prediction when one has precise information about the actions of the "other" member of the dyad.

Happily, the description and analysis of interactions has recently attracted the attention of a number of investigators and statisticians. In addition to the chapters in this volume, some excellent technical sources have recently become available. The references that appear to be most helpful to interactional researchers are noted in Chapter 4 and the two appendices of this volume.

The first appendix is addressed to special issues of assessment—namely, the relative merits of rating scales and behavior observations in the analysis of interchanges. A matter that has troubled some researchers concerns the apparent "unreliability" of behavior observations, despite their precision. This problem is taken up by R. Cairns and J. Green, along with a consideration of the assumptions underlying the procedures and their implications for application. The second appendix was prepared for students and investigators for whom the statistical evaluation of interchanges is a novel assignment. The note by R. Bakeman, R. Cairns, and M. Appelbaum was designed to serve as an introduction to the issues, hence its inclusion as an appendix to this volume. Reference to relevant statistical sources will be found in both notes.

REFERENCE

Patterson, G. R., & Reid, J. B. Methodological issues and psychometric properties. In J. B. Reid (Ed.), *A social learning approach to the treatment and study of families. II. Observation manual and observer procedures. Oregon Research Bulletin,* 1976.

1 Interactional Designs

Ross D. Parke
University of Illinois

INTRODUCTION

The complexities of social interaction are revealed through a variety of research strategies, in a range of different contexts, and through a host of data collection techniques. The purpose of this chapter is to discuss the ways in which both experimental and nonexperimental approaches can be effectively utilized in the study of social interaction. No single strategy will be advocated; rather, the advantages and limitations of a variety of approaches will be discussed. A multistep strategy, which involves the use of nonexperimental, descriptive, as well as experimental, designs will be advocated for the study of social interaction.

A HISTORICAL OVERVIEW

To appreciate our current problems in the study of social interaction, a brief historical overview will be helpful. The choice of strategy for the study of social interaction has undergone a variety of periodic shifts in fashion. In the 1930s and 1940s, social development was examined through the use of field-based observational procedures (e.g., Dawe, 1934; Goodenough, 1930; Parten, 1932). This era was also characterized by the occasional use of field experimental approaches (e.g., Chittenden, 1942; Jack, 1934; Page, 1936).

In spite of the urging of Sears (1951) for the direct study of social interaction, the 1950s were characterized by nonobservational approaches, particularly by the use of interview techniques. Moreover, the era had a distinctively noninteractional flavor. Its guiding assumption, which was largely derived from the Freudian–Hullian heritage, was that social development of children could be best understood by an analysis of parental child-rearing practices. Implicit in this approach was the assumption that the influence process was unidirectional, whereby the parent influences the child; the child's contribution was rarely recognized. In the early 1960s, there was a major methodological shift to the laboratory experiment as a primary methodological tool for understanding social development (e.g., Bandura & Walters, 1963). The adoption of this strategy brought developmental psychology into the main stream of psychology and advanced our knowledge of developmental processes of perception, learning, and social development. However, it continued the distinctively noninteractional flavor of the 1950s; the passive child in the parent–child paradigm was replaced by the passive subject in the experimenter–child relationship; a variety of factors that altered social behavior were examined, but social interaction between partners was rarely studied.

The late 1960s and the early 1970s was a period of questioning and re-orientation and the re-emergence of the direct investigation of social interaction. Two concerns are noteworthy. First, there was an increasing concern about the limited ecological validity of the laboratory paradigm, the *sine qua non* of the child developmentalist. One of the earliest critics was Baldwin (1967), who accused child development researchers, particularly social learning theorists, of building a "mythology of childhood" in which a set of effects obtained in the laboratory is assumed to actually take place in naturalistic socialization contexts and be an accurate account of how the child is socialized. As a result, there has been a confusion of necessary and sufficient causality: The laboratory experiments may tell us only that certain variables are potential contributors to the child's development. However, the extent to which these processes are, in fact, necessary or are actual contributors to socialization is left unanswered. Others expressed similar concerns about our heavy reliance on the laboratory experiment (Bronfenbrenner, 1974; Hartup, 1973; Parke, 1972, 1976) and set the stage for a broadening of our methodological strategies.

This second shift was theoretical. Traditionally, most approaches to social development assumed a unidirectional model, whereby the parent influences the child's development; the child's contribution to his own socialization was rarely recognized. Under the influence of Bell's (1968) classic paper, the historical imbalance was corrected, and the infant's contribution to his own socialization became widely accepted. In part, this shift came about during the 1960s, because of the experimental demonstration of a broad range of infant and child competencies. Infants and children were shown to have the capacities that would permit an active role in social interaction. A third phase is now being increasingly recognized. In our enthusiasm to correct a historical imbalance, we focused on the child's impact on the parent instead of the more appropriate focus on the reciprocal nature of the interactive process. The current zeitgeist, however, has clearly shifted to a study of the reciprocity of interaction and the ways that individuals mutually regulate each other during the course of interaction (Parke, 1978a).

The combination of the disenchantment with the laboratory–experimental approach and the increased recognition of the centrality of the interaction concept has led to an endorsement of alternative methodologies and designs in social development. Specifically, in both developmental and social psychology, there has been a movement toward the examination of social interaction in naturalistic contexts. In fact, there has been a tendency to draw sharp dichotomies between field and lab approaches. Rather than endorse this trend, this chapter outlines the ways in which social interaction can usefully be examined in both field and lab settings.

Specifically, it will be argued that neither laboratory nor field approaches are sufficient; instead, each can play a unique and distinctive role in understanding social interaction. Paradigms, that illustrate the ways in which laboratory and field approaches can be intermeshed will be described and evaluated in terms of their advantages and limitations in addressing different types of interaction questions.

SOME RECENT CONFUSIONS OF TERMS IN THE LABORATORY/FIELD DEBATE

Dichotomies, such as the current lab/field controversy, often arise not out of legitimate disagreement but due to misunderstanding and confusion concerning the meaning of certain scientific distinctions. A number of independent dimensions—such as (1) the setting in which the research will be executed, (2) the type of research design that will be employed, and (3) the kind of data collection system that is selected—are often treated as nonindependent. Due to the frequent co-occurrence of certain types of settings, designs, and data collection systems, the erroneous assumption is often made that these combinations are logically necessary. The most common error is to equate the laboratory context with an experimental design and to link a field setting with a nonexperimental strategy. Similarly, it has been fashionable to equate observational data collection procedures with naturalistic research contexts.

One purpose of this chapter is to illlustrate that these procedures, contexts, and data collection systems can vary independently of each other and that progress will be facilitated greatly by exploring the variety of ways in which these dimensions can interact in yielding new approaches to the study of social interaction.

THE FIELD–LABORATORY DISTINCTION:
A CONTINUUM OF NATURALNESS

Any research context can vary in the degree to which it approximates the child's naturalistic environment in three distinct features: (1) the large-scale physical setting; (2) the immediate stimulus field; and (3) the social agents available in the setting.

In defining naturalness, one approach is to revive the Brunswikian concept of probability, whereby the representativeness of each facet is determined by a sampling of a variety of environments, with a degree of naturalness being defined for a particular species in terms of the probability of occurrence in relation to certain functions or activities.

The Physical Setting

The physical setting that is chosen for the study of social interaction can vary along a continuum of naturalness (Thoman, Becker, & Freese, 1978). At one extreme is the naturalistic environment, which is selected as representative for the species under investigation. No attempt to alter the physical aspects of the environment is made, whether it be the home, classroom, or playground. Under the influence of environmental psychology (cf. Ittelson, Proshansky, Rivlin, & Winkel, 1974; Proshansky, Ittelson, & Rivlin, 1970), there has been a growing interest in describing the physical features of the environment, such as physical space available, arrangements of furniture in the space, lighting, and noise level of the environment. A number of studies have examined the impact of the naturalistic physical environment on social interaction patterns in both animals and humans (e.g., Barker & Gump, 1964; DeVore, 1963; Moos & Insel, 1974; Smith, 1974; Sommer, 1969).

Moving along the continuum of naturalness, one could fix the extreme opposite end as the laboratory setting in which the physical context is artificially arranged. For example, Porges et al. (Porges, Walter, Korb, & Sprague, 1975) placing of children in a mock space-ship in order to study their learning represents an extreme alteration of the child's usual physical environment. However, there are several variations along this continuum that represent degrees of deviation from the natural physical context. The setting itself can be retained, such as a playground, and the impact of introducing new kinds of play equipment on social interaction can be measured. Alternatively, the natural setting can be simulated by the experimenter. In the early 1930s, Gesell arranged a simulated home environment, in which the main features of a home context were represented in a laboratory setting. More recently, a playroom setting in which parent–infant interaction can be studied has been used by infancy researchers (e.g., Ainsworth & Bell, 1970;

Lewis, & Lee-Painter, 1974). Each of these settings can be described in terms of their physical arrangements and placed on a continuum of naturalness.

The Immediate Stimulus Field

The immediate stimulus field can be distinguished from the physical environment in which the social interaction takes place. For example, for the child in a home setting, the toys within reach may be part of his immediate environment, whereas those that are available in the home but removed may constitute part of the child's potential but remote physical environment. For example, the description of the child's home environment, including the size, shape, and color scheme of his room, needs to be distinguished from stimuli with which he is currently interacting (Parke, 1978b). A mobile located above the head of an infant resting in a crib or a T.V. program that is capturing his attention both would be part of his immediate stimulus field. On the other hand, toys that are available in the home but in another room would constitute part of the child's general physical environment.

Just as the physical environment can be described along a continuum of naturalness, the immediate stimulus field can be similarly described. To illustrate, consider the ways in which the mass-media stimuli can vary in terms of their degree of naturalness. In the studies of the effects of mass media on soical interaction patterns, one extreme is the use of uncut commercial films (Parke, Berkowitz, Leyens, West, & Sebastian, 1977) or the use of unaltered television programs (Eron, 1963; Friedrich & Stein, 1973). Variations of this include the introduction of specially prepared versions of T.V. programs that are still viewed in a naturalistic environment (Milgram & Shotland, 1973). More common is the use of clips or scenes from full-length films (Berkowitz & Geen, 1967) or from T.V. programs (Liebert & Baron, 1972). Finally, experimentally produced films and videotapes that are designed to satisfy a particular experimental requirement are often used (e.g., Bandura, Ross, & Ross, 1963). Next, we consider variations in the social composition of the setting.

Social Agents

On the social side, the main participants in each setting need to be described; for example, the parents, sibs, and other potential interactive agents are part of the home environment, and teachers, nurses, and doctors may be part of the social scene of a school or hospital setting.

Agents, as well as environments, can be represented along the continuum of naturalness. For example, degree of familiarity of the agent is one way to conceptualize this aspect; the mother may represent the most familiar, with a grandmother or other part-time caretaker representing a moderate degree of familiarity, whereas a female and male stranger represent extreme discrepancies. Naturalness can vary in terms of behavior as well as familiarity of the person. For example, Brazelton, Tronick, Adamson, Als, and Wise (1975) instructed the mother to behave in an unusual or unexpected manner (i.e., to be nonresponsive) in order to assess the impact of novel behavior patterns of familiar agents or infant behavior.

In summary, both the physical and social environment can vary in terms of the degree of naturalness. Moreover, a wide range of variations can be generated by combinations of physical and social manipulations, where familiar social agents are placed in increasingly unfamiliar contexts or where strange agents are introduced in contexts of differing degrees of naturalness. The principal conclusion of this section can be restated briefly: No simple dichotomy should be drawn between field and laboratory; rather, the variations in naturalness of the physical setting, the immediate stimulus field, and the social agents should be recognized and described.

INTERRELATIONSHIPS ALONG
THE CONTINUUM OF NATURALNESS

There are a variety of designs that can be employed by the investigator; these can be imposed upon the continua of naturalness that were described previously. In this section, a series of designs are outlined, including nonexperimental field studies, natural experiment approaches, field experiments, and laboratory experiments, as well as a variety of hybrid designs, which involve combinations of field and laboratory assessments.

A series of questions can be asked of each type of design. First, what function or purpose does each design serve? Second, at what point in the development and testing of theory should a particular type of design be used? Third, what are the advantages and disadvantages of each type? Fourth, what types of statements can be legitimately drawn from each type? Finally, are there ethical limitations that guide the choice of one type of design versus another? Fifth, what role can statistical and analytic models play in increasing the range of statements that can be inferred from different types of design?

NONINTERVENTION DESIGNS

Field Study

First, the naturalistic field study generally involves the description of ongoing social interaction patterns; no manipulation is introduced, and an attempt is made to minimize the impact of the agent, usually the observer, on the interaction patterns. All assessments take place in the natural environment. Generally, this approach is employed at the early stages of theory development and may provide the basis for generating hypotheses that can then be more rigorously tested in an experimental design. However, as noted later, recent advances have made it possible to engage in hypotheses testing in a field setting. A variety of issues concerning the selection of code and categorical schemes, and breadth of the categories, the role of prior theory in dictating the range of phenomena that are observed, and the level of analysis (molecular versus molar) have been discussed elsewhere. (See Chapter 2, by Yarrow & Waxler, and Chapter 3, by Bekoff, this volume; Rosenblum, 1978.) Examples of this type of approach are plentiful, although the level of analysis, the scope of the observational scheme, and the extent to which theory is guiding the observations clearly differs.

In the 1930s, the field study approach was very popular, but reviews of these early field studies (Wright, 1960) suggested a very narrow conceptual framework. Not only did the subjects consist primarily of preschool chidren, but often only a single setting was sampled (i.e, nursery schools). The data were frequency counts of molar behaviors, such as neurotic symptoms (Olson, 1930) or trait behaviors (Goodenough, 1930). As Wright (1960) notes, such descriptive data lent themselves only to a limited set of hypotheses. The form in which these data were collected lent itself to testing a few hypotheses about such individual difference variables as sex and age of child, stability of event sampling, or setting differences. Occasionally, there were investigators (e.g., Dawe, 1934) who went beyond simple descriptions of frequencies and focused on sequences of behavior. In the Dawe (1934) study of children's quarrels, information concerning the antecedents (hitting, dispute over toys, etc.) of the social behavior were provided. However, this type of study was clearly an exception.

Undoubtedly, much of the impetus for the New Look in field study methodology came from the efforts of Roger Barker and his colleagues (Barker, 1968; Barker & Wright, 1951, 1954; Willems & Raush, 1969). The power of this approach was based largely on the emphasis upon sampling of *both* setting variables and the child's behavior. The sequential form of these data made it possible to provide correlational tests for some long-standing hypotheses [e.g., the relation between frustrations and aggression (Fawl, 1963)]. It was also clear from these studies that settings did indeed exert powerful constraints upon the *kind* of behavior a child displayed (Gump, Schoggen, & Redl, 1963).

Recent field studies of the 1970s have moved beyond the Barker tradition by refinements in both methodology and statistical analyses. In terms of methodology, improvements have been made in the technology of gathering data in naturalistic settings. The introduction of portable videotape and camera equipment has made possible the collection of permanent records of social interaction in a wide range of natural settings. New technological advances in recording devices, such as the DataMyte Keyboard System (e.g., Bakeman & Brown,1977; Parke & Sawin, 1975; Vietze & Strain, 1975) and its variations (Holm, 1978; Sackett, Stephenson, & Ruppenthal, 1973), permit the acquisition and storage of fine-grained observational data and make them readily available for computerized analysis.

Accompanying these advances in technology are important advances in the application of sequential analyses models to observational data. These statistical advances provide the opportunity to test functional relationships between social agents in interaction contexts.

Excellent examples of this approach can be found in Patterson's work with aggressive children and their families (Patterson, Chapter 4, this volume; Patterson & Cobb, 1971), in Cairns' work with aggressive exchanges in rodents and children (Cairns, 1973; Cairns & Scholz, 1973; Hall, 1973), and in Lewis' (Lewis & Lee-Painter, 1974) and Stern's (Stern, 1974, 1977) examinations of mother–infant interaction patterns. Although these investigators have generally employed some variations of Markovian analyses, a variety of alternative techniques for the analyses of interaction sequences are available, including sequential lag technique (Sackett, 1974; Sackett, Holm, & Landesman-Dwyer, 1975) and time-series analysis (Campbell & Stanley, 1966; Glass, Willson, & Gottman, 1975). For a fine illustration of the application of time-series to parent–infant interaction data, see Thomas and Martin (1976).

Finally, techniques such as interrupted time-series (cf. Glass et al, 1975; Gottman, McFall, & Barnett, 1969) and cross-lag (Campbell, 1969; Clarke-Stewart, 1973; Eron, Lefkowitz, Huesmann, & Walder, 1972) can be employed to draw at least suggestive causal inferences from natural field studies. The interrupted time-series design assesses the impact of a naturally occurring event on the ongoing interaction patterns. For example, Gottman, McFall, and Barnett (1969) examined the effect of naturally occurring changes in teacher behavior or teacher absence on the classroom interaction patterns of children. Clarke-Stewart (1973) effectively used cross-lag techniques to study the effects of variations in mother–infant interaction on infant development.

The importance of these recent advances in field study methodology is that they not only serve to provide a better empirical basis for identifying the exact nature of events in the natural ecology that serve to accelerate and decelerate social behaviors, but in addition these techniques highlight the reciprocal nature of social interaction in which both participants—the infant or child as well as the adult socialization agent—are recognized as playing an active role in the socialization process.

Finally, the principal advantage of the field study stems from the generalizability of the findings; in contrast to more artificial approaches, there are fewer problems in generalizing the results to the natural habitat. Similarly, to the extent that participants have been informed that observations are being undertaken, ethical problems are minimal.

Natural Experiment

Second, the *natural experiment* needs to be noted; in this design, the investigator capitalizes upon a change in the environment that was *not* instituted by the investigator. For example, Gerard and Miller (1975) measured the impact of integration on racial relations by taking advantage of the government instituted busing program. The forced busing served to institute the integration "manipulation," although the investigators themselves were not responsible for the manipulation. Other examples include the assessment of anxiety on social interaction patterns during a power failure in New York City (Zucker, Manosevitz, & Lanyon, 1968). A classic and well-known example of this type of design is the Skeels and Dye (1939) study of institutionalized children. In this investigation, one group of children were shifted to another type of institution, and a second group remained in the original rearing environment. This manipulation permitted the evaluation of the impact of different rearing conditions on the children's development.

The independent variable(s) as well as the dependent variables are *usually* but not necessarily located in a naturalistic context. Both the advantage and limitation of this type of design flow from the uniqueness of the independent variable. To the extent that it has not been arbitrarily introduced by the experimenter, the event may be more ecologically valid. The magnitude of the manipulation may often exceed the levels that could ethically be introduced by an experimenter, thus permitting tests of extreme conditions. This is well illustrated in the Skeels and Dye (1939) study. On the other hand, the uniqueness of the event makes replication very difficult. Second, the specification of the exact nature and boundaries of the independent variable(s) is often difficult. Third, the selection of comparable control and comparison groups is also very difficult and serves to limit the usefulness of this type of design.

INVESTIGATIVE-CONTROLLED
MANIPULATIVE DESIGNS

In contrast to the two approaches outlined in the preceding section, there are a series of designs that involve varying degrees of investigator control over the independent variable. Generally, these approaches also more readily yield causal statements than nonintervention approaches. There are a variety of ways in which experimental intervention can be implemented; it is helpful to organize this discussion around the location of the independent and dependent variables in either a laboratory or field setting. It is recognized, of course, that these designations of field and laboratory serve merely to describe polar points along a continuum of settings. By combining the two dimensions—(1) setting (field–lab); and (2) type of variable (independent–dependent)—a heuristically useful 2 × 2 matrix emerges:

		Locus of Independent Variable	
		Field	Laboratory
Locus of Dependent Variable	Field	1	2
	Laboratory	3	4

Design # 1:
Field Experiment: Field–Field Relationship

The distinction between the *natural experiment* and the *field experiment* involves the control exercised by the investigator in the implementation of the independent variable. A field experiment involves the deliberate manipulation of an independent variable *in a naturalistic setting* and generally involves the assessment of this impact on the ongoing behavior patterns in this field context. Some examples are in order. Parke et al. (1977) investigated the impact of exposure to violent and nonviolent films on the social behavior of adolescent boys. The film manipulations (types of movies) were introduced in the natural setting in which the boys lived, and the dependent measures, the amount and type of aggression, were assessed in this same setting. In this case, the manipulations were imposed on an already established social system in which the relationships among the participants was already established. In another use of the field experiment, Sherif (1956), in his classic studies, effectively utilized field experimental techniques to study the processes by which group formation occurs. After experimentally establishing groups, Sherif then imposed a variety of further manipulations (e.g., competition) in order to explore the impact of these variables on intergroup relationships.

In the case of the field experiment, the usual agent in the environment is occasionally trained to serve as the carrier of the experimental manipulation. For example, Brown and Elliot (1965) trained teachers to ignore aggressive acts and to positively reinforce cooperative behavior in a nursery school setting. Similarly, Hawkins, Peterson, Schweid, and Bijou (1966) retrained parents to respond differentially to their children and to function as "home-based therapists." Peers have been experimentally trained to shape certain classes of peer behavior in a naturalistic environment (e.g., Wahler, 1967).

There are a variety of advantages to this approach. First, unlike the natural experiment, the investigator can control the timing (both onset and duration), the location, and the exact nature of the independent variable. Because both the manipulation and the assessment of the dependent measures are located in the natural environment, the ecological validity and the generalizability of the findings are enhanced. Several disadvantages should be noted as well. First, it is impossible to exercise the same degree of control over the independent variable in a naturalistic setting as the degree one is able to achieve in the laboratory. Second, on the dependent side, the disadvantage stems (a) from the possible inability to detect subtle effects due to the low base rate of occurrence of the target behavior or (b) from the difficulty of detection of the behavior in the multivariate network of relationships that are found in a naturalistic setting. Third, this approach is expensive in terms of time and money.

Design #2:
Field-Manipulation–Laboratory-Assessment Design

Our type #2 design involves the manipulation of the independent variable in a naturalistic setting while *measuring the dependent variable in a laboratory setting*. In the Parke et al. (1977) example cited previously, the investigators employed this strategy by assessing the impact of exposure to the films not only in the natural environment but also in a laboratory context. Specifically, the subjects were given the opportunity to deliver electric shocks to a confederate, as a way of assessing the effects of the film on aggressive behavior. This strategy overcomes one of the disadvantages of the field experimental design type #1; namely, the dependent behavior of interest may have a low base rate of occurrence, and therefore the impact of the manipulation may remain undetected.

Another example is Rheingold's (1956) study of the effects that extra "mothering" have on infant social responsiveness. In this study, infants were provided additional degrees of social interaction with an experimental caretaker in their usual institutional environment. The impact of the manipulations were systematically observed in response to a familiar caretaker as well as an unfamiliar adult. Observational procedures can, of course, play an important role in the execution of this paradigm. First, the implementation of the independent variable can often be usefully described in terms of observed interaction patterns; in the case of the Rheingold study, for example, replication potential was considerably enhanced by the detailed time-sampling description of the amount, timing, and type of impact directed toward the infant by the caretaker. Alternatively, on the dependent side, the impact of a field-anchored manipulation can often be usefully assessed by some type of structured interactional assessment, in which the interaction patterns are described the the employment of observational techniques.

Designs #3 & #4:
Laboratory-Manipulation–Field/Laboratory-Assessment Designs

In these two preceding paradigms, the independent manipulation always originated in a field setting with the location of the dependent variable shifting. However, in Designs #3 and #4, the reverse relationships between field and lab are explored. In the third and fourth paradigms, the independent variable is manipulated in the laboratory setting. However, the dependent variable is assessed in the field in the case of the third design which is a relatively underutilized strategy. In the final and familiar design, the dependent as well as the independent variables are assessed in the laboratory context. Variations, in terms of naturalness continuum, can be noted in this fourth design type. Let us discuss each of these designs.

Design #3. The third type of design can be illustrated by two examples. First, O'Connor (1969) exposed socially withdrawn nursery-school-age children to a film designed to increase their level of social interaction with their peers. The manipulation exposure to a film, was centered in a controlled laboratory setting, but the assessment of the impact of the films was assessed in the naturalistic context of the nursery school. Observers recorded shifts in the amount of social interaction on the part of the children as a function of the prior lab-based film manipulation. Sackett et al. (1975) has illustrated the use of this design in nonhuman primate research. Sackett et al. reared rhesus monkeys under different laboratory conditions, such as partial isolation and total isolation, and then examined the coping capacities of these differentially reared animals when they were returned to a naturalistic feral environment.

One advantage of this approach is the control over the independent manipulation by anchoring it in the laboratory. A second feature of this approach is the degree of generalizability of results. By locating the measurement of the dependent variable in the naturalistic environment—and presumably the target context for generalization of findings—the extrapolation issue that often confronts laboratory-based findings is minimized. The same disadvantages associated with field studies remain, such as the difficulty of detecting low base rate behaviors. However, this may be lessened in this type of design because the manipulation presumably alters the occurrence of the dependent behaviors.

Design #4. The final and fourth design is the most common one: namely, the laboratory experiment in which both the independent and dependent variables are centered in the laboratory context.

Social interaction can be studied in a variety of ways in the laboratory, with the degree of constraint imposed by the experimenter varying widely. At one extreme, manipulations are introduced in a free-play laboratory setting, and the social interaction patterns that may constitute the dependent variable are observed and coded similar to a field-based investigation (Rheingold & Eckerman, 1970). Although there is a degree of control over the specific patterns of interaction, a moderate degree of ecological validity is retained. At the other extreme, the social interaction may be under considerable experimental control by the use of a social interaction task, such as a cooperation task (Azrin & Lindsley, 1956; Shapira & Madsen, 1969) or some other type of highly constrained social game such as the Prisoner's Dilemma game (Zubin & Brown, 1975). In this case, the social interaction patterns of *both* partners can be under the experimenter's control.

In another variation, the experimenter may retain control over only one of the partners in a dyadic interaction. For example, Sawin, Parke, Kreling, and Harrison (1975) recently utilized a social interaction paradigm that involved interacting with an "individual" in another room via a T.V. monitor. This procedure permitted the behavior of one individual in the dyad to be experimentally controlled in order to examine the impact of reactions of one individual to another individual's social behavior. Specifically, an adult monitored and disciplined a child over a T.V. screen; in response to the adult disciplinary choices, the child's reactions (defiance, reparation, etc.) were systematically presented to the adult. In turn, the adult's subsequent treatment of the child was assessed over time as a function of different types of child reactions.

Both of these latter paradigms are high in their degree of control over the social interaction patterns but low in ecological validity. Moreover, deception is occasionally but not necessarily involved in the use of these paradigms and therefore of some ethical concern.

Another type of laboratory interaction situation is the "structured-interaction context." Well-known examples are the Hess and Shipman (1967) investigations of maternal teaching styles; in this case, parent and child interact in order to complete a task, such as a puzzle, and the parental teaching strategies are noted. Other examples include husband–wife marital decision-making studies, in which specific topics are set for resolution in a lab setting (Gottman, Markman, & Notarius, 1977). The clear advantage of these approaches is the retention of some degree of naturalness while at the same time overcoming the low base rate problem that plagues naturalistic assessments. A sample of relevant social behaviors can be achieved by arranging the situation. The laboratory context itself, however, does alter the behavior pattens of both parents (O'Rourke, 1963) and infants (Sroufe, Waters, & Matas, 1974), thus limiting the generalizability of findings from these types of structured-interaction studies. For example, O'Rourke (1963) found an increase in the expression of emotion by fathers and more active participation in decision making by mothers when the context shifted from the laboratory to the home.

Another variation on the structured-interaction theme involves the use of "natural" agents as experimenters. In this case, an agent with whom a subject already has a well-established relationship may be introduced into the laboratory as the medium through which a particular manipulation is channeled. One common example involves the use of parents (cf. LaVoie, 1973; Patterson, Littman, & Hinsey, 1964; Stevenson, 1965) or peers as experimental agents (cf. Hartup, 1964). In semi-experimental contexts, such as the Ainsworth strange situation, the mother is programmed to act in predetermined ways in order to assess the child's reaction (Ainsworth & Bell, 1970).

Less common, but nevertheless a potentially powerful paradigm, involves the use of the parents as dependent variables in a laboratory context. A recent study by Gewirtz and Boyd (1975) illustrates this approach. Parents were presented with experimenter-controlled presentation of their infant's smiles and vocalizations, and the impact of these variations in infant social responsiveness on parental behavior were noted. The importance of this paradigm lies in the control exercised over the infant behavior in the laboratory setting, which, in turn, permitted an assessment of the effect of the infant on the parent. Moss (1974) used a similar approach in assessing the controlling value of infant crying behavior on the parent.

FIELD ASSESSMENTS AS ADJUNCTS TO LABORATORY MANIPULATONS

Field-based assessments can often be used to supplement laboratory-based investigations; in this case, an aspect of social behavior is assessed in a field setting without any manipulation. In turn, this information is used as a way of ordering the individuals along a social dimension between levels of this dimension and responsivity to an experimental manipulation.

Although this approach is commonly employed by investigators of personality in order to investigate the interaction between individual differences in personality trait and situational variables, direct assessment of social behavior by naturalistic observation is less common. For example, Bandura, Ross, and Ross (1963) measured aggression in the classroom and divided their subjects into high- and low-aggressive groups; the children were then exposed to film-mediated aggressive models, and the impact of these manipulations on children of differing degrees of aggressiveness could be noted.

Another variation on this theme is illustrated by the Hartup and Coates (1967) investigation. Children were observed to determine the frequency of social reinforcement delivered and received in a nursery-school setting. Each child was then assigned to a model who was similar or different from the subject in the subject's typical level of social reinforcement. In this case, information derived from field observations was utilized to pair children in order to vary experimental conditions. Other studies in which popular and unpopular peers have served as peer reinforcing agents illustrates a similar approach (Hartup, 1964).

The importance of these types of combined field–laboratory designs stems from the often stated but rarely tested proposition that the child's prior social history is an important determinant of his reactions to current social cues.

Just as field-based assessments of individual differences in social behavior may aid in understanding laboratory-centered results, the assessment of the operation of various types of social-influence procedures in naturalistic contexts may yield insight into their impact in a laboratory setting. Consider a study of Paris and Cairns (1972) that combined naturalistic and laboratory methods in attempting to understand the relative effectiveness of positive and negative social reinforcement. Observations were made of the way in which positive (e.g., "good, ok") and negative (e.g., "wrong, no") social reinforcers were used in classrooms. These observations revealed that positive evaluations were used more frequently and indiscriminately and were less contingent upon children's behavior than negative comments. When these same positive and negative comments were used in a two-choice discrimination learning task, it was found that negative comments after incorrect responses greatly facilitated learning, whereas positive comments after correct responses had little effect. The information yielded by the field assessments—namely, that positive feedback was used in an ambiguous fashion in the naturalistic environment—was extremely valuable in understanding the pattern of laboratory results. Other examples of this strategy of assessing the manner in which a tactic is used in the natural environment as an adjunct to the examination of this tactic in the laboratory are appearing increasingly (cf. Dweck, 1976).

A MULTISTEP STRATEGY FOR STUDYING SOCIAL INTERACTION

It is clear that no single approach is sufficient; a variety of strategies are necessary at this stage of our understanding of social interaction. One strategy that is frequently employed involves beginning with observations in the naturalistic environment; this early stage is the "search" phase, in which one generates hypotheses about child behavior and isolates meaningful variables. The increased use of detailed, sequential data-collection strategies, which characterizes the new look in observational methodology, leads to greater likelihood of generating hypotheses concerning the functional relationships between variations in either the physical or the social environment. In addtion, the correlations (among events) provide a means of screening hypotheses to select those that are most worthy of further testing; similarly, sequential probability statements provide a further and even more finely tuned guide to the selection of testable relationships. The next stage is to test these hypotheses experimentally by systematic manipulation of the isolated variables in a more controlled context. The next step, however, need not necessarily be the laboratory; a field-based manipulation may be undertaken, and changes in the dependent variable(s) assessed. For example, Eron (1963) established a set of correlational relationships between viewing aggressive T.V. programs and interpersonal aggressive behavior; through longitudinal analyses and a cross-lag correlational model, Eron et al. (1972) demonstrated that the probable direction of causality flowed from T.V. viewing to social behavior rather than vice-versa. Friedrich and Stein (1973) later confirmed this suggested relationship in a field experiment in which children were exposed to either aggressive or neutral T.V. programs. The next step involved a series of laboratory experiments in which specific aspects of the aggressive films were systematically tested to determine the *critical* aspects of the film manipulations that were responsible for the modifications in viewer aggression.

A pair of recent studies of the impact of infant cues on parent behavior illustrates this stepwise strategy as well. In earlier field observational studies, Moss (1967) established correlational relationships between infant crying and maternal responsivity. Based on these findings, Moss (1974) then proceeded to explore experimentally the impact of crying and fussing on parental responsiveness.

A similar strategy was employed by Gewirtz and Gewirtz (1969), who first established through sequential probability analyses of caretaker–infant interaction that infant smiling and vocalizing elicited reciprocal social behavior in the adult caretaker. In a recent investigaton, Gewirtz and Boyd (1975) experimentally evaluated whether in fact these infant cues were capable of modifying caretaker behavior. They arranged a situation in which mother and infant interacted but in which the experimenter controlled the infant's behavior. The infant and mother were on opposite sides of an observation window, and the mother was unaware that she was responding not to her own infant but rather to a simulation of an infant turning his head and vocalizing. Through this experimental arrangement, Gewirtz and Boyd were able to confirm their earlier field-derived hypotheses—namely, that infant vocalizations can modify caretaker behavior.

A CONCLUDING NOTE

The field will be served by firm commitment to a full range of research designs and strategies in our future investigations of social interaction. Both laboratory- and field-based approaches can be usefully and effectively employed in furthering our understanding of this area. Hopefully, more use will be made of strategies that combine field and laboratory approaches in future research.

ACKNOWLEDGMENTS

Preparation of this chapter was supported by the following grants: Office of Child Development Grant OHD 90-C-900, and NICHD Training Grant HD 00244. Thanks to Robert B. Cairns and Gerald R. Patterson for their comments on this chapter, and to Brenda Congdon for her assistance in the preparation of the manuscript.

REFERENCES

Ainsworth, M. D. S., & Bell, S. M. Attachment, exploration, and separation: Illustrated by the behavior of one-year-olds in a strange situation. *Child Development*, 1970, *41*, 49–67.

Azrin, N., & Lindsley, O. The reinforcement of cooperation between children. *Journal of Abnormal and Social Psychology*, 1956, *2*, 100–102.

Bakeman, R., & Brown, J. Behavioral dialogues: An approach to the assessment of mother–infant interaction. *Child Development*, 1977, *48*, 195–203.

Baldwin, A. *Theories of child development.* New York: Wiley, 1967.

Bandura, A., Ross, D., & Ross, S. A. Imitation of film-mediated models. *Journal of Abnormal and Social Psychology*, 1963, *66*, 3–11.

Bandura, A., & Walters, R. H. *Social learning and personality development.* New York: Holt, 1963.

Barker, R. G. *Ecological psychology: Concepts and methods for studying the environment of human behavior.* Stanford, Calif.; Stanford University Press, 1968.

Barker, R. G., & Gump, P. V. *Big school, small school.* Stanford, Calif.: Stanford University Press, 1964.

Barker, R. G., & Wright, H. F. *One boy's day.* New York: Harper & Row, 1951.

Barker, R. G., & Wright, H. F. *Midwest and its children.* Evanston, Ill.: Row, Peterson, 1954.

Bell, R. Q. A reinterpretation of the direction of effects in studies of socialization. *Psychological Review*, 1968, *75*, 81–95.

Berkowitz, L., & Geen, R. G. Stimulus qualities of the target of aggression: A further study. *Journal of Personality and Social Psychology*, 1967, *5*, 364–368.

Brazelton, T. B., Tronick, E., Adamson, L., Als, H., & Wise, S. Early mother–infant reciprocity. In M. A. Hofer (Ed.), *Parent–infant interaction.* Amsterdam: Elsevier, 1975.

Bronfenbrenner, U. Developmental research, public policy and the ecology of childhood. *Child Development*, 1974, *45*, 1–5.

Brown, P., & Elliot, R. Control of aggression in a nursery school class. *Journal of Experimental Child Psychology*, 1965, *2*, 103–107.

Cairns, R. B. Fighting and punishment from a developmental perspective. In J. K. Cole & D. D. Jensen (Eds.), *Nebraska Symposium on Motivation: 1972.* Lincoln: University of Nebraska Press, 1973.

Cairns, R. B., & Scholz, S. D. Fighting in mice: Dyadic escalation and what is learned. *Journal of Comparative and Physiological Psychology*, 1973, *85*, 540–550.

Campbell, D. T. Reforms as experiments. *American Psychologist*, 1969, *24*, 409–429.

Campbell, D. T., & Stanley, J. C. *Experimental and quasi-experimental designs for research.* Chicago: Rand McNally & Co., 1966.

Chittenden, G. D. An experimental study in measuring and modifying assertive behavior in young children. *Monographs of the Society for Research in Child Development*, 1942, *7*(Serial No. 31).

Clarke-Stewart, K. A. Interactions between mothers and their young children: Characteristics and consequences. *Monographs of the Society for Research in Child Development*, 1973, *38*(Serial No. 153).

Dawe, H. An analysis of two hundred quarrels of preschool children. *Child Development*, 1934, *5*, 139–157.

DeVore, I. Mother–infant relations in free ranging baboons. In H. L. Rheingold (Ed.), *Maternal behavior in mammals*. New York: Wiley, 1963.

Dweck, C. S. Children's interpretation of evaluative feedback: The effect of social cues on learned helplessness. *Merrill-Palmer Quarterly*, 1976, *22*, 105–109.

Eron, L. P. Relationship of T.V. viewing habits and aggressive behavior in children. *Journal of Abnormal and Social Psychology*, 1963, *67*, 193–196.

Eron, L. P., Lefkowitz, M. M., Huesmann, L. R., & Walder, L. Does television violence cause aggression? *American Psychologist*, 1972, *27*, 253–263.

Fawl, C. L. Disturbances experienced by children in their natural habitats. In R. Barker (Ed.), *The stream of behavior*. New York: Appleton-Century-Crofts, 1963.

Friedrich, L. K., & Stein, A. A. Aggressive and prosocial television programs and the natural behavior of preschool children. *Monographs of the Society for Research in Child Development*, 1973, *38*(Serial No. 151, No. 4).

Gerard, H. B., & Miller, N. *School desegregation*. New York: Plenum, 1975.

Gewirtz, H. B., & Gewirtz, J. L. Caretaking settings, background events and behavioral differences in four Israeli child-rearing environments: Some preliminary trends. In B. M. Foss (Ed.), *Determinants of infant behavior: Vol. IV*. London: Methuen & Co., 1969.

Gewirtz, J. L., & Boyd, E. F. *The infant conditions his mother: Experiments on directions of influence in mother–infant interaction*. Paper presented at the meeting of the Society for Research in Child Development, Denver, March 1975.

Glass, G. V.; Willson, V. L., & Gottman, J. M. *Design and analysis of time-series experiments*. Boulder: Colorado Associated University Press, 1975.

Goodenough, F. L. Inter-relationships in the behavior of young children. *Child Development*, 1930, *1*, 29–47.

Gottman, J., Markman, H., & Notarius, C. The topography of marital conflict: A sequential analysis of verbal and nonverbal behavior. *Journal of Marriage and the Familiy*, 1977, *39*, 461–477.

Gottman, J. M., McFall, R. M., & Barnett, J. T. Design and analysis of research using time-series. *Psychological Bulletin*, 1969, *72*, 299–306.

Gump, P., Schoggen, P., Redl, F. The behavior of the same child in different milieus. In R. Barker (Ed.), *The stream of behavior*. New York: Appleton-Century-Crofts, 1963.

Hall, W. M. Observational & interactive determinants of aggressive behavior in boys. Unpublished doctoral dissertation, Indiana University, 1973.

Hartup, W. W. Friendship status and the effectiveness of peers as reinforcing agents. *Journal of Experimental Child Psychology*, 1964, *1*, 154–162.

Hartup, W. W. Social learning, social interaction and social development. In P. J. Elich (Ed.), *Social learning*. New York: Western Washington Press, 1973.

Hartup, W. W., & Coates, B. Imitation of a peer as a function of reinforcement from the peer group and rewardingness of the model. *Child Development*, 1967, *38*, 1003–1016.

Hawkins, R. P., Peterson, R. F., Schweid, E., & Bijou, S. W. Behavior therapy in the home: Amelioration of problem parent–child relations with the parent in a therapeutic role. *Journal of Experimental Child Psychology*, 1966, *3*, 99–106.

Hess, R., & Shipman, V. Cognitive elements in maternal behavior. In J. P. Hill (Ed.), *Minnesota symposia on child psychology* (Vol. 1). Minneapolis; University of Minnesota Press, 1967.

Holm, R. A. Techniques of recording observational data. In G. P. Sackett (Ed.), *Observing behavior* (Vol. II). Baltimore, Md.: University Park Press, 1978.

Ittelson, W. H., Proshansky, H. M., Rivlin, L. G., & Winkel, G. H. *An introduction to environmental psychology.* New York: Holt, Rinehart & Winston, 1974.

Jack, L. M. An experimental study of ascendant behavior in preschool children. *University of Iowa Studies in Child Welfare,* 1934, *9*(No. 3).

La Voie, J. C. Punishment and adolescent self-control. *Developmental Psychology,* 1973, *8,* 16–24.

Lewis, M., & Lee-Painter, S. An interactional approach to the mother–infant dyad. In M. Lewis & L. A. Rosenblum (Eds.), *The effect of the infant on its caregiver.* New York: Wiley, 1974.

Liebert, R. M., & Baron, R. A. Short-term effects of televised aggression on children's aggressive behavior. In *Television and social behavior.* Rockville, Md.: U.S. Department of Health, Education and Welfare, 1972.

Milgram, S., & Shotland, R. L. *Television and antisocial behavior: Field experiments.* New York: Academic Press, 1973.

Moos, R. H., & Insel, P. M. (Eds.). *Issues in social ecology.* Palo Alto, Calif.: National Press Books, 1974.

Moss, H. A. Sex, age and state as determinants of mother–infant interaction. *Merrill-Palmer Quarterly,* 1967, *13,* 19–36.

Moss, H. A. Communication in mother–infant interaction. In L. Kramer, P. Pliner, & T. Alloway (Eds.), *Advances in the study of communication and affect, Vol. 1, Nonverbal communication.* New York: Plenum Press, 1974.

O'Connor, R. D. Modification of social withdrawal through symbolic modeling. *Journal of Applied Behavior Analysis,* 1969, *2,* 15–22.

Olson, W. The incidence of nervous habits in children. *Journal of Abnormal Social Psychology,* 1930, *35,* 75–92.

O'Rourke, J. F. Field and laboratory: The decision making behavior of family groups in two experimental conditions. *Sociometry,* 1963, *26,* 422–435.

Page, M. L. The modification of ascendant behavior in preschool children. *University of Iowa Studies in Child Welfare,* 1936, *12*(No. 3).

Paris, S. G., & Cairns, R. B. An experimental and ethological analysis of social reinforcement with retarded children. *Child Development,* 1972, *43,* 717–729.

Parke, R. D. The socialization process: A social learning perspective. In S. B. Sells & R. G. Demaree (Eds.), *U.S. Office of Education: Child socialization task force report* (Res. Rep. No. 72-9). Institute of Behavioral Research, Texas Christian University, 1972.

Parke, R. D. Social cues, social control and ecological validity. *Merrill Palmer Quarterly,* 1976, *22,* 111–118.

Parke, R. D. Parent–infant interaction: Progress, paradigms and problems. In G. P. Sackett (Ed.), *Observing behavior* (Vol. 1). *Theory and applications in mental retardation.* Baltimore, Md.: University Park Press, 1978(a).

Parke, R. D. Children's home environments: Social and cognitive effects. In I. Altman & J. Wohlwill (Eds.), *Human behavior an environment* (Vol. 3). New York: Plenum, 1978(b).

Parke, R. D., Berkowitz, L., Leyens, J. P., West, S., & Sebastian, R. The effects of movie violence on juvenile delinquents. In L. Berkowitz (Ed.), *Advances in experimental social psychology* (Vol. 10). New York: Academic Press, 1977.

Parke, R. D., & Sawin, D. B. *Infant characteristics and behavior as elicitors of maternal and paternal responsivity.* Paper presented at the biennial meeting of the Society for Research in Child Development, Denver, April 1975.

Parten, M. B. Social participation among preschool children. *Journal of Abnormal and Social Psychology,* 1932, *27,* 243–269.

Patterson, G. R., & Cobb, J. A. A dyadic analysis of "aggressive" behavior. In J. P. Hill (Ed.), *Minnesota Symposia on Child Psychology* (Vol. V). Minneapolis: University of Minnesota Press, 1971.

Patterson, G. R., Littman, R., & Hinsey, W. C. Parental effectiveness as reinforcers in the laboratory and its relation to child-rearing practices and child adjustment in the classroom. *Journal of Personality*, 1964, *32*, 180–199.

Porges, S. W., Walter, G. F., Korb, R. J., & Sprague, R. L. The influences of methylphenidate on heart rate and behavioral measures of attention in hyperactive children. *Child Development*, 1975, *46*, 727–733.

Proshansky, H. M., Ittelson, W. H., & Rivlin, L. G. *Environmental psychology*. New York: Holt, Rinehart & Winston, 1970.

Rheingold, H. L. The modification of social responsiveness in institutional babies. *Monographs of the Society for Research in Child Development*, 1956, *21*(No. 63).

Rheingold, H., & Eckerman, C. The infant separates himself from his mother. *Science*, 1970, *168*, 78–83.

Rosenblum, L. A. The creation of behavioral taxonomy. In G. P. Sackett (Ed.), *Observing behvior* (Vol. II). Baltimore, Md.: University Park Press, 1978.

Sackett, G. P. *A nonparametric lag sequential analysis for studying dependency among responses in observational scoring systems*. Unpublished manuscript, University of Washington, 1974.

Sackett, G. P., Holm, R., & Landesman-Dwyer, S. Vulnerability for abnormal development: Pregnancy outcomes and sex differences in macaque monkeys. In N. R. Ellis (Ed.), *Aberrant development in infancy*. Hillsdale, N.J.: Lawrence Erlbaum Associates, 1975.

Sackett, G. P., Stephenson, E., & Ruppenthal, G. C. Digital data acquisition systems for observing behavior in laboratory and field settings. *Behavioral Research Methods Instrumentation*, 1973, *5*, 344–348.

Sawin, D. B., Parke, R. D., Kreling, B., & Harrison, N. *The child's role in sparing the rod*. Paper presented at the annual meeting of the American Psychological Association, Chicago, September 1975.

Sears, R. R. A theoretical framework for personality and social behavior. *American Psychologist*, 1951, *6*, 476–483.

Shapira, A., & Madsen, M. C. Cooperative and competitive behavior of kibbutz and urban children in Israel. *Child Development*, 1969, *40*, 609–617.

Sherif, M. Experiments in group conflict. *Scientific American*, 1956, 54–58.

Skeels, H. M., & Dye, H. A study of the effects of differential stimulation in mentally retarded children. *Proceedings and Addresses of the American Association on Mental Retardation*, 1939, *44*, 114–136.

Smith, P. Social and situational determinants of fear. In M. Lewis & L. Rosenblum (Eds.), *The origins of fear*. New York: Wiley, 1974.

Sommer, R. *Personal space*. Englewood Cliffs, N.J.: Prentice-Hall, 1969.

Sroufe, L. A., Waters, E., & Matas, L. Contextual determinants of infant affective responses. In M. Lewis & L. Rosenblum (Eds.), *The origins of fear*. New York: Wiley, 1974.

Stern, D. N. Mother and infant at play: The dyadic interaction involving facial, vocal and gaze behaviors. In M. Lewis & L. Rosenblum (Eds.), *The effect of the infant on its caregiver*. New York: Wiley, 1974.

Stern, D. *The first relationship*. Cambridge, Mass.: Harvard University Press, 1977.

Stevenson, H. W. Social reinforcement of children's behavior. In L. P. Lipsitt & C. C. Spiker (Eds.), *Advances in child development and behavior* (Vol. 2). New York: Academic Press, 1965.

Thoman, E. B., Becker, P. T., & Freese, M. P. Individual patterns of mother–infant interaction. In G. P. Sackett (Ed.), *Observing behavior: Theory and applications in mental retardation* (Vol. 1). Baltimore, Md.: University Park Press, 1978.

Thomas, E. A. C., & Martin, J. A. Analyses of parent–infant interaction. *Psychological Review*, 1976, *83*, 141–156.

Vietze, P. M., & Strain, B. *Contingent responsiveness between mother and infant: Who is reinforcing whom?* Paper presented at the annual meeting of the Southeastern Psychological Association, Atlanta, March 1975.

Wahler, R. G. Child–child interactions in free field settings: Some experimental analyses. *Journal of Experimental Child Psychology*, 1967, *5*, 278–293.

Willems, E. P., & Raush, H. L. (Eds.). *Naturalistic viewpoints in psychological research.* New York: Holt, Rinehart & Winston, 1969.

Wright, H. F. Observation child study. In P. Mussen (Ed.), *Handbook of research methods in child development.* New York: Wiley, 1960.

Zubin, J. Z., & Brown, B. R. *The social psychology of bargaining and negotiation.* New York: Academic Press, 1975.

Zucker, R. A., Manosevitz, M., & Lanyon, R. I. Birth order, anxiety and affiliation during crisis. *Journal of Personality and Social Psychology*, 1968, *8*, 354–359.

2 Observing Interaction: A Confrontation With Methodology

Marian Radke Yarrow
Carolyn Zahn Waxler
National Institute of Mental Health

INTRODUCTION

Observing behavior is remarkably difficult if one demands the same standards of good measurement that are required of other scientific tools. Observing is a human process; the information about behavior that is essential in the behavioral and biomedical sciences depends heavily on the observing person. Even though mechanical devices can aid in registering behavior, the translation or coding of behavior at molar levels turns on the skills of the observer. Though exceedingly practiced, the human observer, by many criteria, is a poor scientific instrument: nonstandard, not readily calibrated, and often inconsistent or unreliable. Counterbalancing these failings are the human capabilities of extraordinary sensitivity, flexibility, and precision. The challenge is to discover how to conduct disciplined observing while making full use of the discriminations of which the human observer is capable.

The purpose of this chapter is to examine the observing process and some of the consequences of different conditions and different techniques of observing for the nature of the data obtained. The domain of research in which we will be examining observations is the behavior of children in interaction with their environments of people and things. This domain involves a great range of demands as research questions require different kinds of data: the detection of minute, concrete, and momentary changes in an infant's orientation, the tracking of emotional and cognitive changes in a family undergoing psychotherapy or in a child receiving drug treatment, the documentation of bidirectional influences in interactions between child peers, and so on. The skill of the investigator lies in matching the questions of the research with the most appropriate data modes and in obtaining data of the highest fidelity. When the results of research are truly "elegant" and stable, one can be quite certain not only that the research question was meaningful but also that the methods by which the data were derived had a worthy level of precision or sensitivity. When, more frequently than we wish, research findings are untelling or unstable, we become aware that shortcomings in the methods may well have played a major role. Such bruised confidence lends incentive to find solutions to longstanding methodological obstacles to better behavioral data.

This chapter is addressed to a number of issues relating to observational methods:

1. some perspectives and assumptions about behavior and about observing it
2. veridicality and reliability of observations
3. the behavior sample
4. observers and the observed
5. research on techniques

Although discussion is oriented to an examination of problems encountered in obtaining observational data, this is not to suggest a low regard for the data of direct observation. It is to render explicit some of the obstacles that are "out there" with which one needs to deal in arriving at the best measures. We are drawing upon our own research experiences supplemented by those of our colleagues at NIMH. Most of the studies on which our discussion is based involve infants and young children and mothers and teachers in benign and relatively predictable environments of nursery school, home, and experimental situations.

SOME PERSPECTIVES AND ASSUMPTIONS ABOUT BEHAVIOR AND OBSERVING IT

Behavior is a special kind of phenomenon to deal with scientifically because of our everyday familiarity with it. Most everyone can interpret behavior and interactions sufficiently to predict, control, and communicate with others—to a degree. Why, then, do scientists encounter difficulties in trying to describe behavior and find in it an order and predictability? Is it possible that scientific study of behavior at molar levels is of doubtful realization? It is too early to accept this conclusion. It should be possible to develop methods of observing interaction that preserve the integrity of behavior yet cut through to its essential dimensions to answer specific research questions.

Because behavior appears to have face validity, it is tempting to proceed directly to the technology of its measurement without giving thought to the nature of behavior per se. Yet certainly assumptions are made, implicitly if not explicitly, as we transform behavior into categories, frequencies, relations, antecedents and consequences, sequences and conditional probabilities.

The properties of behavior, specifically of social behavior and of interaction, that seem to us of first line importance in decisions of measurement are the following: Behavior is continuous. Identification of its parts is difficult for the reason that an act or sequence of acts in a stream of behavior has (simultaneously) different defining characteristics or properties. The particular properties in terms of which one chooses to view behavior impose their organization or system of units. There is not, therefore, a unique system of units for the continuing behavior. Interconnections in the stream of behavior, whether in the behavior of the individual or in the interactions among individuals, are complex: Overt actions are likely to be multiply determined, and they often carry multiple (and inconsistent) messages. Further, with few exceptions, molar behavior is expressed, measured, and interpreted in the language of the observer. This means that observers bring a large amount of built-in structure to the observing process. This point was made long ago by Kurt Lewin and Roger Barker—namely, that when observers look at behavior, they perceive a person, not an arm or a mouth or a solid mass moving through space. Added to the built-ins that are inherent in being human are the special built-ins from the cultures and subcultures of the observers, including the "culture" of the discipline.

The particular research question increases or diminishes the salience of various behavioral properties. But with the essential properties always in mind, we stand a better chance of seeking and obtaining data that are least distorting of behavior and that optimally address the research question.

VERIDICALITY? RELIABILITY?

Plain and homely though it may be, the issue of the reliability of data draws the attention of serious investigators. In the context of the present discussion, reliability of observational data is a question of agreement on what is "registered" in independent observational records. This is an admittedly ambiguous formulation allowing the inclusion of many kinds of correspondence: between observers, between methods, between observer and another criterion of reality. Here we are not "taking on" a general examination of the issues of veridicality and reliability. We are reporting, instead, on research experiences, bad and good, in achieving, reproductability of behavioral data, through independent pairs of eyes. Our own research provides our case materials.

Our initial interest, in 1965, in pursuing direct observations of child–adult interaction was with the hope that such data would provide more veridical and more reliable information than had been obtained through the traditional methods of "child-rearing research"—namely, the interview method, and often the retrospective method. It was with the hope that one could observe and report the actions and interactions of a single object or a single child–adult dyad, preserving the intact behavior. The formula for the observational record was therefore narrative reporting of behavior and context in temporal order, in descriptive detail, and at low levels of inference and conceptualization. This should allow the full gamut of analyses: of the presence and frequency of singled-out responses, of the nature of chains of responses, and of the interconnections of responses.

Successive research experiences provide an account of decisions and experimentations with the boundaries on what was to be observed, the level of detail that was to be used, how little or how much of the psychological substrates of overt action was to be reported, and how behavior was to be sliced or unitized. Here we are discussing these experiences in relation to the criterion of observer agreement.

The first project was a naturalistic study of interactions in a nursery school.[1] Thirty-three children were observed independently by pairs of observers for a 30-minute sample of behavior. Prior to observing, 85 descriptive categories, presumably an inclusive system covering the range of interpersonal behaviors of children and teachers in this setting, were developed. The categories were organized atheoretically as positive, neutral, and negative, or in verbal and physical terms. Each observer subsequently coded her own dictated narrative protocols. Interobserver agreement $[A/(A + D)]$ required a matching of coded behavior units in the order of occurrence. The result was severely disappointing. Percent agreements ranged from a low of 9% on "threatening gestures" to a high of 77% on "crying." On more than three-fourths of the categories, agreement was less than 50%. More experience and other observers brought similar results. There were low agreement levels despite the fact that the uncoded protocols of the independent observers sounded very similar. The categories of behavior that were most and least observed were examined. The 10 with highest agreement were crying, praise, verbal threat, noninteraction, temper tantrums, physical aggression, gives rewards, destroys an object, cuddles, helps. The 10 with the lowest agreement were gestural threats, negative facial gestures, patting or holding hands, scolds, pushes away, commands, sauciness, nervousness, smiling, reasoning. There is perhaps some suggestion

---

[1]Roger Burton and John Campbell participated in planning and early phases of this study.

of common qualities among the items with the best agreement. They have less inherent ambiguity in them; they are the less subtle interactions; they may have more definite beginnings and endings than the behaviors for which there is lowest agreement.

We found that the greatest and most unyielding source of difference in coded observations was the "extra" or "missed" behaviors. In some instances this was a matter of one observer reporting behavior that the other observer had not seen. Also, some observers consistently see more, or see in more detail than others. But as often, and perhaps more often, "missed" or "extra" entries were a consequence of differences in observers' narrative styles, or more exactly, differences in the telescoping and separating and linking of behaviors. This can be illustrated in a trivial example of frequency and unit differences such as the following:

Observer A: "Come on Johnny." Johnny slows his pedaling of the trike he is riding. More insistently, "Come John, let's chase Bobby." Johnny frowns. "Aw, come on." With this command Johnny jumps off the trike and chases after Bobby with Bart.

Observer B: Bart calls urgently to Johnny, "Come on , come on, let's chase Bobby." After some hesitation, Johnny gets off his trike and runs to join Bart, follows after him, after Bobby.

It is not that the observations are grossly different, but, in an action-by-action coding system, the two records diverge.

With the data from this project, we then asked a different question—namely, how well do pairs of observers agree on the total frequencies of given behavior codes for individual children? For this purpose, an arbitrary time unit of 30 seconds was imposed on the dictated records, and the child's total frequency score was based on the number of units in which a given code appeared. Further, behavioral codes were combined into conceptual categories, By this assessment, the same observational records that had failed in the test of exact matchings across observers were now "reliable." For example, for adult behaviors of affection, giving praise or reward, rewarding child's attention seeking, interobserver correlations ranged from .70 to .85. The results are similar for the child behaviors ($r = .89$ for attention seeking, and $r = .88$ for compliance.) The total frequencies express each observer's sampling and unitizing of a child's behaviors. Even though observers sample in different ways or at different rates, the relative positions of different children on given categories are quite similar across observers. However, when reliabilities are based on the sum of occurrences of a given behavior, one had very little basis for concluding anything about agreements on the exact behaviors in sequential relation to one another. Because many research problems involve questions of exact sequence and dyadic interchange, the assurances provided by correlations are not always adequate. In subsequent studies, therefore, various changes in procedure were made in efforts to increase interobserver correspondence. Improved agreement, on an exact basis, was accomplished by narrowing the universe to be observed: Behaviors of one member of a dyad were programmed (Yarrow, Scott, & Waxler, 1973), or number of interactors was decreased to a single dyad (Waxler & Yarrow, 1975; Yarrow & Waxler, 1971), or situations were standardized along some dimensions (Yarrow & Scott, 1972), or specific subsets of variables and sequences were singled out for observations (Waxler & Yarrow, 1975; Yarrow & Waxler, 1976), or different observers were assigned different subsets of data or different actors (Yarrow & Scott, 1972). When narrative reporting was used in these circumstances, percents of agreement on individual variables in exact temporal order were, on the average, 20% higher than in the 1965 study. For example, on acts of physical affection, observer agreement increased from 44% to 77%; on acts of coldness, agreement improved from 41% to 77%. The observing demands in these studies seem to be close to the limits of the observers' capacities, at least for the behaviors involved.

The improved exact temporal agreements with the more circumscribed observing mission made possible studies involving questions of sequence. For example, maternal modeling and child imitation under close-to-natural conditions were investigated (Waxler & Yarrow, 1975).

For this kind of research questions, it is essential to have reliability on ordering of events. Observer agreement on modeling was 86%; on child's repetition of mother's acts it was 87%, and on mother's response to child's imitation it was 78%. Also, it is necessary to have the data in narrative form. What the mother does with the toys, or with the child, or by herself is done idiosyncratically. If one is to judge correctly the similarities in the child's responses, information is required in the observation record on the specific details of mother's and child's acts. If one is to be able to detect or follow a system of interaction or reciprocal interactions (which may not occur without the appearance of intervening events) a continuing behavioral account is needed. It can be concluded from the experience in the seminaturalistic modeling study that one can attain reasonably good reliability from observations in the form of the free flow of behavior, provided the observer's task is somehow restricted in scope. However, there is still a gap between reasonable reliability and high reliability.

Because we have turned first in our discussion of observation to the examination of observer agreement, we have, as it were, begun with the product and not the process of observing. Theoretically, interobserver reproducibility of the fine grains of behavior is important—essential for some research problems though not necessarily for all. However, an overemphasis in this direction runs the parallel dangers of neglecting sensitivity to the properties of behavior and allowing observer agreement to become an end in itself. The second problem first: Observer agreement is often achieved by coding systems that are modified to serve agreement. Codes are generally defined in context-free, sequence-free terms (smiles, attends, approaches, asserts). In the service of developing agreements, coders establish conventions for determining the boundaries of each code, and for handling the ambiguous events. Conventions can become too foolproof with everything fitted neatly into a set of categories. When small pieces of behavior are coded as if each carries its own stable message, this forces a literalness on the coder, suppresses ambiguities, and does not allow for different meanings and different connections in the behavior to be preserved. Although a good deal of uncertainty often accompanies coding, even though agreement exists, once coding is accomplished, feelings of uncertainty about possibly miscalled behavior begin to subside. Statistical evidence brings assurance; significant relations are forthcoming, and findings appear. But has the behavior been represented by this procedure as well as it should be? Probably not.

We would suggest that an emphasis on this kind of reliability takes investigators partly "off course." The issue of observer correspondence might profitably be considered as an issue of replication of research findings; that is, independent observations would be performed as usual (with all due monitoring and even item-by-item assessment) on the entire data-gathering process. Analyses and interpretations of results would be carried out separately on the data from each of the independent observers. One could thus assess to what degree the *findings and research conclusions* from one data gathering source are reproduced in the findings of a second source. This approach could have a very salutary effect on observers who would, by this means, be more motivated and oriented to veridicality than to the often trivial features that they anticipate will influence their agreement with a second observer.

LEVELS OF CODING

The process of coding behavior is, after all, a product of one's view of behavior. Hence, we need to look again at behavioral properties and codes in conjunction. In doing so, it is our feeling that significant characteristics of interaction do not always fit well with the structures imposed by our research needs for quantifiable analytic form. The misfit that we have sensed derives most strongly from the ambiguities, double messages, and multiple levels of meaning and function inherent in behavior. One cannot proceed very far in interactional analyses without encountering behavior that has different consequences for different persons at the very same moment of time, or behavior that expresses more than one motive on the part of the doer, or behavior the integrity of which is modified by the context or that modifies the context in which it appears. Some excerpts from our protocols serve as references:

1. Mother and father are standing in an affectionate embrace. Jenny (their 15-month-old child) runs up to them, wedges herself between them, and holds their legs tightly. (Is the child joining in their embrace or pushing them apart?)

2. Several 8-year-olds are playing at the swimming pool. Child A hits child B, whereupon child C "rescues" B by pushing A away, into the pool. (The multiple messages from A seem obvious.)

3. Charlie and Louise are both trying to get on the swing. Louise pushes Charlie to the ground and yells "Dummy!" Whereupon Charlie's mother comes to Charlie's rescue, scolding, shaking her finger at Louise, "Don't ever do that again." Later, Louise is seen with her younger sibling who has spilled his milk. She is scolding, shaking her finger and yelling "Don't ever, ever, ever." (Louise is imitating, is caretaking, is angry. Each meaning has an integrity of its own.)

4. Five-year-old Brad is playing with a somewhat battered toy when he notices that the teacher is holding another similar but new toy. Brad hurriedly offers another idle child the toy, then goes to the teacher and asks if he may play with the new toy. (Here, generosity and manipulation "share" the same behavior.)

There are implications for observational procedures in what we have been emphasizing in ambiguities, embeddedness, and multiple consequences. One of the reasons why observational research has moved away from dealing with ambiguity is undoubtedly the unspeakable difficulties that the latter creates for analyses. First, at the level of coding, one of the consequences of this kind of restructuring would be that opposites could be coded from the same pieces of behavior—for an act that is both aggressive and kind, for an act that is both competent and incompetent. Also, researchers might find themselves confronted with different conclusions depending on the level of inference. These are not easy difficulties to resolve. But reporting behavior with more complexity does not necessarily mean that analysis becomes more difficult. It is just possible that data that are more psychologically veridical may make psychological analyses easier. At least it is worth reconsidering the procedures we have adhered to, allowing ourselves to experiment with other guidelines. Observation might proceed in the direction of an expanded standard language system. Observers might *explicitly* sort out different *levels* of behavior: crisp, physical detail of space and motion; low-level psychological inference, alternative conceptual frameworks, a referencing of behavior to its contexts, and so on.

The flight some years ago from highly interpretive "clinical" observing procedures brought a healthy systematic approach to observing. With the cumulative knowledge gained from these experiences, it should now be possible to begin to move away from highly mechanistic procedures toward procedures that recognize and assess interaction by retaining some of the fundamental complexity of behavior, when such complexity is a very relevant part of the research questions being addressed. Fortunately, there are also areas of interaction in which one can feel justifiably comfortable with the very "clean" and simple observational measures. The goal is for the appropriate match of measure and research question.

In the following discussions, the data from observational research methods are examined first from the view point of sampling, and second as products of interaction between the observer and the observed.

THE BEHAVIOR SAMPLE

A sample of interaction is adequate by what standards? A small and select slice of the child's behavior becomes the data base in research no matter how extensive the investigation. Although theoretical considerations should determine the necessary properties of the sample, in reality such determinations are difficult to specify. Is it sufficient to observe a child's behavior for an hour a day over a week to establish a base line against which to test the effects of a treatment? Does one gain a representative measure of mother–child communication and interaction from three, six, or 20 observations in mealtime, playtime, or work settings, etc.? Can one arrive at a valid assessment of model influences in planned situations of saturated demonstrations by models? What shall be the sample boundaries in time and space in investigations of reciprocal influences between child and parents? If one looks for answers in the research literature, one is disappointed to find that for almost all of us the behavior samples that we use tend to be based on best guesses as to what will provide a reasonable assessment, on what the practices of the discipline will support, and what seems feasible under constraints of various sorts.

Nevertheless, in choosing a sample, we are making assumptions, whether or not explicitly, about representativeness, adequacy of opportunities for the behaviors to appear, absence of factors disturbing to the phenomenon being observed, generalizability of observed interactions, and so on. Thus, by creating a small distress (one child's equipment is not operating well) in the midst of children's play, and by observing their helping or ignoring or moralizing responses to the child caught in the difficulty, the researcher would like to assume that the responses observed are representative of what would occur in the normal course of children's daily activities. Or, by observing mother and child together for 10 minutes in a strange room supplied with toys, the investigator again assumes something about the reasonableness of this time and context for studying the particular mother–child interactions in which (s)he is interested. If the investigator turns to natural settings and taps into different activities under varied conditions over hours or days, obviously other assumptions are being made about sampling requirements. It is all too evident that the behavior captured in research is the creature of specific frames of time, contexts, and instruments.

Behavior Sampling Defined by Time

Time appears to have a kind of magic for researchers, as if it imposes an impeccable standardization and basis for quantification. Time is a primary emphasis in sampling and analysis: frequency of behavior in relation to time, looking at and looking away from behavior in a given time rhythm, cutting interaction into arbitrary time units (10, 20, 30 seconds) to mark the occurrence or nonoccurrence of the behavior, sampling in time blocks (e.g., 15 minutes of play, 15 minutes of structured teaching, etc.). What does (should) the researcher do about time as (s)he plans research?

Barker (1963) was among the earliest to call attention to an uncritical reliance on time as the chief basis for sampling behavior. The arguments put forth for the "stream of behavior" and for the "setting" of behavior are well known, and no attempt is made here to restate this position. We need to remind ourselves that the behaviors that we investigate generally do not have a simple relation to time. Behaviors are not distributed regularly along time; they are linked to time in various ways. Their density, rhythms, and cyclical or sporadic character are variable; events, individual states, and demands and constraints in the situation have significant bearing on their distribution. Thus in studying mother–child interaction, one might expect behavior such as a child's requests for attention or physical contacts with mother to have reasonably regular distributions along time under specified conditions, and one might feel some confidence in assessing a more or less continuous dimension such as a child's activity level in a simple time sample of behavior. The same could not be said for many other variables. If behaviors are cyclical, time sample and cycle have to be synchronized. Sampling is particularly difficult for behaviors that are sporadic (tantrums, aggressive outbursts) or unpredictable (impulsive acts) or sensitive to stimulus changes that are not readily controlled or recognized. How well do time blocks serve as the bases for sampling behaviors that are discontinuous in time (a child's strategies for coping with grief) or behavior for which equivalent units consume different amounts of time (kinds of reinforcements)? For many reasons, then, a less brittle dependence on time alone as a basis of sampling would seem to be indicated.

Even when one is accepting a diminished importance of time per se, one must still address the issue of how time units shape the information that is obtained. At least two questions are involved: The first is how one observes and records in relation to arbitrary time units (e.g., 10-second or 30-second intervals); the second is a matter of the total time of sampled behavior. The latter question concerns us here. When popular paradigms favor short time samples, and when there are no external checks on the adequacy of the period of observation, we ought to be at special pains to be certain that the time span of observation is carefully chosen to suit the particular variables and the research question. The question seems very much open whether we as investigators have good criteria for deciding on samples of time for many kinds of research questions.

An initial research investment that can help in arriving at a good behavior sample is the obtaining of preliminary frequency profiles of the behaviors to be studied. How much observing time is needed (in a given setting and for a given kind of research participant) in order to secure a distribution of scores that represents the individual child and variability among children? Such profiles were obtained on 4-year-olds' interactions in indoor and outdoor play. Behavior was sliced in units of 15 seconds and was sampled in four 10-minute periods, for a total of 160 units. We found that, on the average, social exchanges occurred in 95 of the units, with children distributed across a wide range of different kinds of social behaviors. The average number of units for any specific type of social interaction, however, was very much smaller: Children's seeking out of adults occurred, on the average, in 10 units; aggression, in 13 units; and cooperative interaction, in 22 units. Our interest was particularly in sympathetic and helping acts. The average was only between two and three units. Thus this particular time sample was certainly the lower limit of time for a naturalistic study of the latter kind of behavior. A much heavier investment of time would seem desirable.

The frequency scan in the foregoing sample has implications not only for investigation of this low-frequency response in naturalistic designs. There is a companion message for laboratory designs as well. Because few children respond to every opportunity for giving help or sympathy, the common laboratory practice of a one-time test of a specific response may not be the best measure of a child's status on this low-probability class of responses. A larger sampling, a battery of experimental provocations, would seem to be indicated. This personal research example suggests that pretesting of the behavior sample is one means by which investigators can better arrive at sampling decisions and assess the consequences of their decisions.

A further comment on time sampling: One criterion for length of observation is whether the relative positions of children are stable from one to another time sample. The comparisons available to us on this point are all on a relatively short time scale but a time scale that is customary in research. Using studies in which it was possible to extract frequencies of behavior in adjacent periods of time within the same study, we obtained the correlations presented in Table 2.1. From these correlations it appears that only when the

TABLE 2.1
Consistency in Assessments Obtained With Time Samples of Differing Length

	Correlations Between Successive Samples					
	5 to 10 Minutes with the Following 10 to 30 Minutes		*20 Minutes with 20 Minutes Several Weeks Later*		*60 Minutes or More with 60 Minutes or More 1 to 2 Weeks Later*[a]	
	Boys	*Girls*	*Boys*	*Girls*	*Boys*	*Girls*
Child Behavior						
Seeking adult attention	.43	.52[b]	.45[c]	.51[c]	.58[c]	.77[c] (indoors)
					.41[c]	.10 (outdoors)
Friendly peer contact		.32[c]	.53[c]	.19	.48[c]	.48[c] (indoors)
					.81[c]	.77[c] (indoors)
					.62[c]	.82[c] (outdoors)
Cooperation and helping	.18		−.03	.11		
Aggressive and	.62[c]		.39[b]	.28	.79[c]	.84[c] (indoors)
oppositional behavior					.82[c]	.81[c] (indoors)
					.07	.56[c] (outdoors)
					.33[b]	.38[b] (outdoors)
Maternal Behavior						
Contingent reinforcement						
for imitation	.28					
Nurturance	.58[c]	.68[c]				
Verbal punishment	.52[c]	.69[c]				
Range of Ns	17 to 77		35 to 42		35 to 125	

[a]Data contributed in personal communication with Frank Pedersen, NICHD, and Charles Halverson, NIMH.
[b]$p < .05$.
[c]$p < .01$.

samples being compared were an hour or more in length was there substantial stability in children's positions relative to one another on the variables studied (correlations of + .75 or more between successive samplings, columns 5 and 6). However, even samplings of this length are no guarantee of high correspondence. In all of the samples examined, whether 5 minutes or 60 minutes, there is tremendous fluctuation in correspondence, depending on the variable. The correlations in Table 2.1 remind us that we may often be using flimsy platforms of data from which to launch conclusions. The brief observation samples so characteristic of child behavioral research reflect an unfortunate reliance on the medical model. By drawing a drop of the patient's blood, it is possible to assess a host of conditions. A 5-minute drop of mother–child interaction or of child aggression fails to accomplish similar miracles. The uncertainty of good criteria for the choice of time dimension of a sample underscores the need for investigators to make more explicit the bases for their choices.

Behavior Sampling Defined by Context

We have been discussing sampling as time, without looking at what is "inside" the time. One hardly needs convincing, however, that behavior and therefore research data are significantly shaped by the settings or contexts. The question is whether the setting is itself of interest for a given piece of research or is simply a "neutral" or representative medium in which to study a phenomenon. Contexts in which children are observed may have been chosen on carefully considered theoretical grounds, but more often than not other considerations determine where children are studied. Researchers cannot be faulted for having in mind the availability of research participants, convenience, and even research tradition, but they have also to live with the limitations in generalizability that may result from contexts of convenience. This is especially the case when an entire literature is built of norms and relationships based on a single type of setting. Consider one example: Preschool-age children are likely to be studied in play settings in nursery schools. Mother and child are likely to be observed under similar planned play circumstances. Descriptions in journal articles of these settings now read like a well-rehearsed script. Although the settings are not unreasonable as research sites, they are very special. The nursery-school setting is special with respect to the ratio of children to adults, the age-homogeneity of the children, the saturation of the environment in toys and play equipment, the presence of skilled and trained adults with their full-time attention on the children. Certainly one would anticipate consequences for children's behavior from the opportunities, constraints, and demands in these circumstances and, hence, consequences for interpretation of research findings.

Behavior may be affected in a number of ways by contextual changes. Behavior of all subjects may be uniformly altered. In some settings, the possiblity for given behaviors may be limited; in others, the opportunities may be enhanced. Furthermore, settings may differentially influence the behaviors of different children. Obviously, there are implications for research findings. Data from the studies cited earlier provided some illustrations of setting effects.

Children and their teachers or mothers were observed in a number of settings in the nursery school (indoor play, outdoor play, lunchtime, group teaching). Frequencies on a variety of behaviors were obtained in each of the settings, and the subjects' relative positions were compared across settings. (See Table 2.2.) With few exceptions, correlations across settings are low. Although it is possible that the particular variables in these comparisons are

TABLE 2.2

Consistency of Behavioral Assessments from Samplings
in Different Settings in the Nursery School

Settings:	Play and Lunchtime		Play and Teaching		Lunchtime and Teaching		Indoor Play and Outdoor Play
Observers:	O_1	O_2	O_1	O_2	O_1	O_2	O_1
Child Behaviors							
Attention seeking	.05	.04	.08	.33[a]	.30	.23	.39[b]
Oppositional and aggressive	-.16	.04	.21	.14	.19	-.06	.50[b]
Positive peer interaction							.24
Cooperative and helping							.35[b]
Adult Behaviors							
Warmth	.15	.17	-.20	-.07	.24	.13	
Coldness	.00	.31[a]	-.05	.08	-.04	.09	
	$N = 33$		$N = 33$		$N = 33$		$N = 77$

[a] $p < .05$.
[b] $p < .01$.

unusally setting-bound, or that the samples in each setting are too brief, the instabilities are a reminder of the fragile nature of many assessments.

Research Instruments as Samples of Behavior

As a third dimension of sampling, we have considered the instruments through which observations are obtained. Instruments select their special samples of behavior, giving to findings a possible instrument-specific flavor. To explore this proposition, four different techniques of obtaining data on mother–child interaction were compared. The same subjects were assessed on the same variables, with reference to the same or similar periods of time. Definitions of variables were constant across instruments. The same team of investigators carried out the data collection.

Sixty preschool children (ages 3½ to 5) and their mothers (white, upper middle-class) were the participants. Each parent and child was observed in the home, on 2 days, for a total of 4 hours. Home observations covered periods of free play, teaching, mealtime, and bedtime, All mothers were asked to engage in the same teaching tasks—namely, showing the child how to use a tape recorder and how to play a game (pinning the tail on the donkey and the ear on the rabbit, with eyes closed). The game involved the obvious prohibition "don't peek," thereby providing a test of obedience.

Observations were made in stream of behavior fashion, dictated as the behavior occurred. The records were subsequently coded. Two dimensions of maternal behavior, warmth and restrictiveness, and three dimensions of child behavior, dependency on adult, compliance, and aggression were studied. Frequency scores were obtained on the total of maternal attentive and nurturing behaviors (an overall warmth measure) and on subsets of this dimension—namely acts of physical affection, praise and reward, and positive responding to child's dependent responses. Maternal restrictions and demands were measured in the context of the child's going to bed. The child's compliance was also measured in the same context. Resisting the temptation of "peeking" in the games was another measure of obedience. Assessments of dependency (seeking attention and/or comfort from the mother) and aggressive behavior were based on the entire observation periods.

A second kind of observational appraisal was made, approximating a "clinical" assessment: This was done after the second home visit but before the narrative records were consulted or coded. The observer rated both mother and child, generally on 5-point scales, on the variables indicated previously.

The third assessment was mothers' self-ratings of their children. At the close of the second home visit, the observer asked the mother to make ratings of what she had observed during the investigator's visit. The same variables and scales were used by mothers as had been used by the observers, except mothers were not asked to rate their own overall warmth.

TABLE 2.3
Correspondence in Assessments of Maternal and Child Variables
Derived from Different Research Procedures
[Kendall Tau Coefficients (Pearson Correlations in Parentheses)]

Paired Instruments	Maternal Variables				Child Variables			
	Warmth	Physical Affection	Use of Praise and Reward	Restrictiveness (at Bedtime)	Rewarding Attention Seeking	Attention Seeking	Compliance at Bedtime	Obeys Rules
1. Observed frequencies and observer's rating	.05	.26[a]	.18	—	-.08	.11	.27[a]	—
2. Observed frequencies and mother's rating	—	-.002	.24[a]	—	—	.14	.09	.44[b] (.41)[b]

3. Observer's rating and mother's rating	—	.34^b (.37)^b	.13 (.13)	.40^b (.47)^b	—	.37^b (.48)^b	.53^b (.61)^b	—
4. Observer's rating and interview	.48^b (.53)^b	.17 (.24)	.03 (.01)	.16 (.21)	—	.27 (.24)	.12 (.08)	—
5. Mother's rating and interview	—	.26 (.21)	−.14 (−.17)	.34^a (.39)^a	−.03 (.09)	.45^b (.57)^b	.11 (.11)	.27 (.27)
6. Observed frequencies and interview	−.26	.09	.28	—	.10	.14	.01	.11 (.06)

Note: One-tailed tests. *N*'s for mothers' interviews = 30, for home observations = 60.
$^a p < .05.$
$^b p < .01.$

53

The fourth research instrument was an interview. Two weeks prior to the home visits, 30 of the mothers were interviewed about current mother–child interactions. Interviews followed a Sears, Maccoby, and Levin (1957) format but were limited to the variables used in the observations. (Although interviewers were also the observers, a given mother was never interviewed and observed by the same person.)

One should expect that, in sampling the same parents and children, on the same dimensions, at very nearly the same time, with persons of the same training making the assessments, scores on the four instruments would be similar. This was not generally the case, however. The cross-methods comparisons are presented in Table 2.3. The paired techniques appear in the left-hand column in the order of their predicted agreement. We predicted that the narrative record, subsequently coded on specific acts, and the summary ratings of the same interactions (both records made by the same observer) would be in closest agreement. We anticipated that data from mothers' interviews prior to the home observations and observers' records might have the lowest agreement. These forecasts were only partly upheld.

Assessments based on mother's interviews and the observed frequencies in 4 hours of observation were not in close association. Tau coefficients range from –.26 to +.28 (row 6 of table). (This finding is consistent with published literature. Disagreement between interview and observations has been reported over the years [see Antonovsky (1959), Becker (1964), Bing (1963), and Lytton (1971)]. Smith (1958) is one investigator who reports somewhat more positive findings.) When the observer's method was a global rating instead of the observed frequency account (row 4), significant agreements appeared on the broadly defined dimension of warmth ($r = .53$). Other associations for other dimensions were again nonsignificant.

The two sets of scores based on the observer's assessments (one the frequency count and the other her ratings, row 1) were in poor agreement. This finding is not unique to this particular study. In an experiment by Scott, Burton, and Yarrow (1967) on the effects of positive social reinforcement in increasing the frequencies of positive peer interactions, the observers were unaware of changes in the child's behavior; in fact, they declared that no changes were occurring. However, the analyses of frequencies of behaviors over time based on the observers' daily narrative records indicated that the predicted changes were indeed taking place.

The closest agreements in paired scores across methods were between the observer's ratings and the mother's ratings (row 3) when observer and mother were referring to the same period of home observation, but even here agreement is far from perfect. Associations are significant (r's from .37 to .61), with the notable exception of ratings on use of praise and reward ($r = .13$). When frequency records and mothers' ratings were compared (row 2), there was little correspondence. The highest agreement was on a discrete bit of behavior (whether the child refrained from peeking), but there was only a

TABLE 2.4
Relations Between Maternal Warmth and Child Variables
Derived from Different Research Procedures

	Maternal Warmth and Child's Seeking Attention	Warmth and Compliance	Warmth and Obeys Rules	Warmth and Aggression
Interview ($N = 30$)	−.02 (−.08)	−.05 (.04)	.31 (.25)	.07 (.04)
Observation ($N = 60$)	.41[b]	.23[a]	(.11)	—
Observer rating ($N = 30$)	.34[b] .43[b]	.00 (.01)	—	−.01 (.01)

Note: Associations are Kendall Taus and, in parentheses, Pearson correlations.
[a] $p < .05$.
[b] $p < .01$.

correlation of +.41. Not only were mothers and observers providing unlike assessments, there were also systematic directional biases. Mothers were "harder" in their judgments of the children and "easier" in their judgments of themselves than were the observers.

Given the preceding disagreements, it is not surprising that relations between maternal and child variables are also seriously discrepant as one moves from one technique to another. The disparities in findings are seen in Table 2.4. For example, maternal warmth based on observations is associated with the child's seeking attention (Tau = +.41), whereas maternal warmth based on interview data and attention seeking are unrelated (Tau = −.02).

The purpose of this much detail on a given set of data is to provide a demonstration that we have yet a long way to go before we have sturdy measures of behavior, free of instrument idiosyncrasies. Instruments represent yardsticks that differ in many respects; these differences may be of as much consequence as any "treatment" condition under study. In summary, sampling of behavior (in terms of time, setting, and instrument) leaves many questions for the curious. Here we have chosen to highlight problems, to shake any complacencies that may exist about how briefly, easily, or surely one can arrive at valid indices of the innumerable variables subsumed under "interaction."

OBSERVER AND OBSERVED

Anyone who has observed children (or adults) over any length of time or variety of experiences will be almost certain to agree that observing is not only an exacting job but also one in which the observer is often "involved." Observation of human interaction is rarely a neutral occasion. How the observer and the observed react to each other and how these reactions effect the contents of the observational record are not well explored. Issues of this kind, as applied to the observers, are generally subsumed under the label of bias, which has some unfortunate connotations. From this perspective, the problem is seen as a set of prejudgments, which the observer brings to the task (that can be summed up in terms of sex or race or culture of the observer), that determine a stable kind of "screen" through which observing takes place. No doubt, such general biases operate. However, we would like to look at qualities or biases of the observer and of the observed as they interact with each other, assuming that these influences change in nature and magnitude, depending on the content of the research and the particular pairings of observer and observed.

We have explored from this point of view in the following questions:

1. As we all know, agreements in observations vary—considerably. Is some of the disagreement among observers consistent and predictable with respect to certain kinds of research *subjects*? Suppose, for the moment, that this is the case. It would be important to identify the kinds of subjects (given the kinds of observers) who are observed least reliably and to take the necessary steps to remedy or allow for the elevated error.

2. Observers are often themselves very aware of demands, difficulties, and fluctuations in their own observing. Can the self-reports of observers contribute to understanding the observing process?

3. Another set of considerations involves the *observed*: What does being observed do to the behavior of the observed?

4. Via personality and training differences, observers lend unknown variations to observational reports. Can some qualities of both be identified as "good" for observers?

Subject Differences in Observer Agreement

It goes without saying that one's degree of confidence in research conclusions is, in part, dependent on the extent to which the behaviors are reliably measured. Although some level of unreliability, or observer disagreement, has to be tolerated, relations in the data are influenced by this observer error. Johnson and Bolstad (1973, p. 17), commenting on the consequences of unreliability, remind us of the different implications that observer error has for positive and for negative findings. Other things being equal, if a positive finding appears even with considerable error in the measures, a relatively strong relation can be assumed. On the other hand, observer unreliability leaves one less certain as to what can be concluded from negative findings (i.e., from the absence of relations between variables).

Suppose, then, that certain groups of subjects are observed more or less reliably than other groups. Does this fact have a bearing on our research findings? More often than not, within a given study, analyses involve distinct subsamples (subjects of higher vs. lower education, males vs. females, depressed vs. nondepressed, aggressive vs. nonaggressive, and so on). Whatever the assessment of observer agreement, in most cases it has been ascertained on the entire sample, not on each of the subgroups used in analyses.

To follow up the obvious question, we have again used our "work horse" studies to examine reliabilities for different subgroups. Sex is an obvious subgrouping. In most studies of children, analyses are done separately for boys and girls, and frequently significant relations are found only for one or the other. Such findings may indeed represent the true relations between variables. We should not ignore another possiblity, however—namely, that in some instances differences in findings for boys and girls may result from differences in the ease with which one or the other sex is observed with respect to given behavioral dimensions. "Ease" is of various kinds: The responses of one sex with respect to a given variable may be consistently more ambiguous in meaning, less vigorous, less open, more rapid, etc., than the behavior of the other sex. Or ease may be related to how "fitting," or condemnatory, or usual the observer finds the behavior to be for each sex.

In our data we compared reliability assessments for boys and girls on a range of interaction variables: noninteraction, aggressive contacts with peers, prosocial acts, etc. For many behaviors the two sexes were observed with equal reliability, but there were some intriguing exceptions. In one study, nursery school teachers' cold or negative contacts with children were reliably observed when such acts were directed to boys ($r = .71$) but not to girls ($r = .11$) Similarly, in observing teachers' handling of children's attention seeking, observers were in better agreement for boys (correlations were .94 and .88 for reward and for punishment of attention seeking, respectively) than for girls ($rs = .66$ and .58, respectively). However, teachers' physical displays of warmth (acts of affection, attentiveness, comfort) were reliably assessed only when directed toward girls ($rs = .89$ for girls and .24 for boys).

How readily is aggression observed in each sex? We singled out aggression because of different expectations held by many regarding boys' and girls' propensities. In two different studies, aggressive acts were observed more reliably for boys ($rs = .95$ and .76, in the respective studies) than for girls (rs were .76 and –.19). In both studies, when relations between aggression and prosocial behavior were examined, the associations were significant only for boys. Perhaps these illustrations serve to alert us to the possiblity that when a relation "holds only for boys," the negative findings for girls may sometimes be confounded by unreliability. Such differences in reliability suggest the necessity for ascertaining reliability "inside" our samples in ways that correspond to the subsamples used in the analyses.

Having found these sex differences in observer reliability, one must next ask whether it is sex role stereotypes that are interfering with assessments of the two sexes, or whether the specific behavioral phenomenon is actually more ambiguous and less easy to observe in one sex than the other. Although the reliabilities on aggression fit sex-role expectations (boys' aggression is more clear-cut than girls'),not all of the sex differences appearing in our sampling are so easily interpreted. For example, the attention-seeking behaviors that are frequently stereotyped as more characteristic of girls were not found to be consistently more reliably observed in the "tender sex." In one study, the direction of difference was for higher observer correspondence for girls' attention-seeking than for boys' (rs = .92 and .75, respectively), but in another study the reverse was true (rs = .95 for boys and .61 for girls). Attempting to understand the sex differences in reliability is somewhat secondary at this point. In any investigation using analyses of subgroups, the first order of importance is the investigator's reporting of the reliability of information on each sex.

From the data available in our studies, we cannot address the issue of whether behaviors of one sex can *generally* be assessed with greater ease than behaviors of the other sex. Data supplied by a colleague (Charles Halverson, personal communication, 1975) bear on this problem. Reliability coefficients across 40 variables were obtained for each of 125 nursery-school children. Average reliabilities for boys and girls were compared. Reliability for boys was .67, for girls .62 (t = 1.84, df = 123, $.05 < p < .10$), suggesting that the boys were, in general, more reliably observed—at least by these teams of female observers.

As one would expect, systematic subject-related differences in observer agreement are not restricted to the sex of subjects. Moss and Jones (1977) provide an example in which social class of subjects makes a difference. They reported more significant associations between mothers' attitudes in pregnancy and their behaviors with their infants for middle-class mothers than for lower-middle-class mothers. In looking back at interobserver agreements for each class, reliabilities too were consistently higher for the middle-class than for the lower-middle-class subjects. Moss and Jones interpret this as possibly reflecting the observers' better understanding of those mothers who were most like themselves in class background.

Let us look at subjects' contributions to observation error in another way. Barker (1965) made the point that the observer's view of the subject may change over time. Observers develop an image of the subject, which may be consistent or may indeed change drastically. What do these images do to selectivity of observing? Consider a hypothetical example of observing highly aggressive children. Is it not difficult for observers to resist building up an expectation of aggression? Will this expectation progressively tune them in to the negative behavior categories? Will reliability on the dimension of aggression be higher for aggressive children than for less-aggressive children, for whom the expectation or sensitivity does not exist? Also, what are the influences of observers' theories of behavior on the reliabilities of interrelated variables? For example, how do observers' theories about the kinds of children who are aggressive or prosocial influence acuity in observing *other* specific behaviors that are viewed by the observers either as compatible or incompatible with aggressive or prosocial behavior?

We re-examined our data with these questions in mind. The sample was divided at the median in frequency of social initiations: children initiating many contacts with their peers, and children initiating few contacts. For each group, interobserver agreement was computed for two variables: One variable was an act of social intervention (namely, coming to someone's aid); the other was a passive act (being the recipient of a helping act). Interobserver correlations on children's helping acts were +.54 in the subgroup of outgoing children and +.29 in the subgroup of the more inactive children. On the other hand, when being the *recipient* of a helping act was the issue, observer agreement (by the same observers) was better for the relatively withdrawn children ($r = .89$) than for the more socially interactive children ($r = .55$). The hypothesis we are advancing is that the general expectation of observers was sensitizing them differentially to other behaviors that were congruent or not with their theories of behavior. Johnson and Bolstad (1973) have noted that high-frequency interactions tend to be more reliably assessed than low-frequency acts. In the examples just cited, higher and lower reliabilities are not accounted for by frequency differences in the subgroups. Observer agreement differences that are systematically related to subject differences (sex, demographic variables, behavioral dimensions, or whatever) thus would seem to have implications for the conduct and interpretation of research.

Observers' Self-Reports on Observing

Observers are generally taught an observing technique with the expectation that it will be applicable equally to all subjects. But, as just seen, subjects can have a substantial influence on the observing process, and this influence can, at times, be highly individualistic. In the preceding examples, we have been dealing with influences of which the observers were unaware. There are also influences that are very much in the awareness of good observers. The following are illustrations: An experienced observer reported finding herself peculiarly unable, as she observed a particular 4-year-old, to find the right words or codes to describe the child's behavior. On another occasion, one child in the group had a strong emotional impact on all observers. This was "little Benjy," who drew forth all the mothering instincts until, at almost the same junction of observing, each observer became aware of the child's all too obvious manipulative ways, at which time the consensual love was irrevocably lost. At another time, an observer commented that each time a certain mother was to be observed, the day was an especially easy one; she found herself ready to record the mother's actions almost before the events occurred. Another observer was distressed by her own strong feelings about a mother in the study, especially when she heard herself referring to the mother by a most uncomplimentary pseudonym.

This collection of observer insights was intended to raise questions of variability in quality of assessments of individual subjects, but it should be noted also that the illustrated differences in observability are themselves data about the children and mothers being observed: Thus, does the child of the mother who is observed with such ease and predictability experience similar predictability in relationships with that mother? Do the pervasive behavioral ambiguities in a child's behavior that confuse the observer also confuse those with whom the child interacts? Moss and Jacobs (personal communication, 1975), recognizing ambiguity as an observing issue, have had observers rate infants' behaviors in terms of "clarity of cues." This kind of rating could enable investigators to identify the nature and the consequences of such ambiguity.

To obtain evidence of the uniformity of observer agreement from child to child, records of pairs of observers were compared for each of 14 children on each of a number of interaction variables. The criterion of agreement was exact temporal correspondence in the report of designated acts. Percent of agreement varied widely from one child to the next, as can be seen in a representative example: On praise or reward from caretaker, observers agreed 25% and 30% for two of the children, and 100% for two others. A more substantial exploration of individual variation was available in data supplied by Halverson (personal communication, 1975): 125 nursery-school children were observed on 40 variables for a total observation time of more than 7 hours. A single correlation was obtained for each child representing observer correspondence on the frequencies for each of the 40 variables. Again, agreement on individual children varies widely. At the low end of agreement are children with interobserver correlations of +.35 and +.43; at the high end of agreement there are correlations of +.88 and +.90. Yet, on group estimates, the reliabilities of all of the variables are at acceptable levels. These data would seem to say with some authority that the person being observed is a special source of error in observational data and that more than likely the assessments of individuals in our usual samples vary considerably in veridicality.

Being Observed

Observation is invariably discussed from the point of view of the observers. The observed have provided far less in the dialogue on observing. Have you ever stood in a grocery check-out line and turned to find yourself looking into a little face appearing over the shoulder of the man who is standing just behind you? Your eyes meet those of the child and you look back and smile ever so slightly. You keep on looking. The child in arms begins to squirm. His head drops suddenly; then his eyes travel rapidly round in all directions. He turns his head away, but almost as soon he looks back to see if your eyes are still there. They are. He then digs his head into his father's shoulder and he begins to kick his feet. By now his father (unaware of you) reacts to the squirms and shifts Billy to his other shoulder, thereby giving grateful little Billy somewhere else to look. This little fellow knew that he was being observed, and it did something to him.

We have assumed a great deal of "toughness" in our subjects by assuming that observations do not affect them—that our experimental rooms, with marked floors and carefully placed toys, one-way mirrors, and TV cameras, and our trailing of subjects with tape recorders and notepads are only minor incidentals in their environments. Although *we* are very accustomed to our research ways of creating the architecture for interaction or injecting ourselves in the natural habitats and then spotlighting the behavior before us, it may not be altogether settled that the observed are equally accustomed.

Being observed is not necessarily unpleasant or distorting or disruptive. We can point to a great deal of experience to reassure ourselves that interactions in nursery schools, on playgrounds, in many school settings, and even sometimes at home do not seem to be materially altered by the presence of observers. In these settings, adults are part of the environmental equipment; hence, an additional adult changes things very little. Likewise, the tender participant approach of investigators in the Roger Barker tradition (and others as well) has greatly humanized the long observing that pursues the subject, though it may still influence how the subject behaves. Unfortunately, it is not an easy matter to ascertain what subjects' behaviors would have been had no observation occurred.

Unless truly unaware of being studied, research subjects must have images of why they are being studied. One can hardly imagine as many possible purposes as research participants sometimes conjure up: Does the observing mean being spied on, helped, tricked, a guinea pig for science, a peculiar, or a special, or a problem person, and so on? The more stringent requirements of informed consent by research participants will mean that the research purposes are more clearly understood. Explicitly declared objectives, though respecting the subjects' right to know and reducing ambiguities, have necessarily the effect of establishing a definition of the situation—and of the subject. Being observed as a "family at risk," as "gifted children," as children of divorced parents, as parents of boys, etc., puts quite different cloaks on the observed. It seems a reasonable hypothesis that these definitions can result, in some instances, in self-fulfilling prophecies, or they can tune up or down some of the indices that are important to the investigator. In the process of informing subjects about research purposes and findings, it is quite possible that subjects can tell the investigators some valuable things about the art of being observed and how, in their views, they did or did not change from the "usual" to the "observed." The effect on the observed of being observed is conditional; it can neither be assumed to be minimal on the general grounds of "good rapport," nor can it be anticipated as problematic solely because the observing appears to be intrusive. The reality of effects, therefore, needs to be examined in each investigation.

"Good" Observers

An observer is a good instrument to the extent that (s)he is able to carry the observing load that is required by the particular methods of recording. Because the loads are so varied, a single set of standards by which to identify good observers is likely to be inadequate. There are some general criteria, however: A good observer is one who can be trained to be constant within an observing framework, no matter what the particular schema. If the reporting is to minimize intent, if an identified conceptual interpretation is to govern reporting, if large (or small) chunks of behavior are the units, if precise temporal ordering is required, if feelings are to be tuned into the record, or whatever, the good observer is able to perform unerringly within specifications. Although this seems obvious, it is not readily obtainable, and failure in this regard is one distressing and recurring source of observer disagreement as well as loss of information.

An ideally good observer is one who has the wisdom or sensitivity to judge the goodness of fit of the data being recorded and the research purposes for which they are to be used. Observers are in closest contact (and are often the only persons in direct contact) with the phenomena under study. They are in a position to monitor research operations on an ongoing basis, and to pick up signs of problems of many kinds—not only in the mechanics of data gathering but in the interpretation of data as well. Good observers are not simply instruments for the investigator but extensions of the investigator. Therefore, their essential level of skill goes far beyond obtaining statistical agreement.

Because we have found that equal training does not always result in equal observer performance, we have become interested in pretraining qualities that are predictive of good observing. With impressions as our primary data, a number of attributes seem to be important in the selection of observers:

1. *Ability to sustain attention without early habituation.* Often the same or similar behaviors, with changing nuances, occur over and over in a subject's repertoire. The observer has to continue to see the same stimuli and changing stimuli with equal discrimination.

2. *Ability to take in a high load of environmental stimulation without confusion.* The kind of person whose daily functioning is in this mode has had practice for systematic observing.

3. *Compulsivity.* This kind of person finds details important and is aware of them. Although compulsivity and order may clash with the ambiguities and apparent disorder in behavior, a compulsive person can be trained to postpone "order" by recording conflicting or ambiguous behavioral signs in excessive detail, thus handling ambiguity compulsively.

4. *Insight into his or her own biases and theoretical commitments.* A neutral person is a myth. An observer best approximates a scientifically defensible instrument to the extent that (s)he can achieve detachment and distance when observed interactions and recognized personal values meet.

5. *"Intense," analytic, and introspective.* This kind of person has much practice in observing by virtue of his or her own life style. Observers are "principals" in any research, with findings only as stable and genuinely reflective of the behavioral phenomena being investigated as are the observers' records.

OBSERVATIONAL TECHNIQUES IN RESEARCH AND RESEARCH ON TECHNIQUES OF OBSERVING

This chapter has not been a "how to observe" report. It has presented a point of view about observing and has examined sources of problems and means of solving problems in observing. It has not been much concerned with the kind of research in which it is possible to so control the situation or focus on a response that observing is limited to one or several predictable and readily unitized behaviors. The focus has been on the research terrain in which the observations needed are of a kind that will (1) register continuities in behavior, and (2) cope with a high measure of behavioral variability and unpredictability, as well as with multiple behavioral events and actors. Many of the research experiences reported from our own files have been compromises between what is desired and what has been attainable in disciplined observations. These experiences have enabled us to pinpoint a variety of obstacles to good observations—in techniques of reporting and coding, samples of behavior, subjects being observed, and observers' capabilities—and to identify some ways of confronting them. And finally, growing out of these experiences are some thoughts about further research on observing procedures and approaches.

First, we would suggest that consideration be given to direct evaluations of controversial procedural issues. As long as we invest ourselves in given preferences and prejudices regarding ways of observing, we will remain ignorant about comparative gains and losses from observing procedures other than our own. Many present and future investigators would be grateful for careful studies comparing the consequences of differences in observational techniques for research results and conclusions. Specifically, how are results affected: (1) if reporting is in noninferential terms or in psychological terms; (2) if behavior is reported in one kind of unit rather than other; (3) if behavior is reported narratively or as behavior present or absent in a designated time period; (4) if the observer alternates looking for a period with recording for a period; and (5) if the observers are behind a mirror or moving about with the subjects or if a camera substitutes for the observer? There could be answers from methodological research. The logistics for such studies are somewhat staggering, but the findings would be most valuable.

A second wishful experimentation grows out of problems of inaccessibility of many interactions to direct observation by researchers. Inaccessibility limits the questions that we can hope to investigate and turns us to substitute methods. Inaccessibility really challenges the general value of direct observation: How well have we managed systematically to observe parental conditioning of child behavior, child–parent aggressions and affections, child problem behaviors, changes in behavior as the consequence of interventions, and so on? The extent of limitations makes a good case for breaking with some research conservatisms: Could one not do more to train "accessible" observers, such as parents or grandparents or child peers, or other "professionals" who are natural in the situation? Parents have been peculiarly maligned as incapable. There is no good reason, however, to rule them out for training for specific research purposes. Some fruitful interplay of experimental and parental designs might then be forthcoming. Also by this means, sampling of behavior could be extended from the usual contexts. The constraints of inaccessibility are the other side of our earlier discussion of readily accessible contexts in which behavior is routinely sampled.

A third suggestion grows out of the limits of observer capacities on the one hand and the inherent properties of behavior on the other. An observing overload is soon reached if, in reporting interactions, numerous behavioral dimensions, details, subtle cues, reciprocal exchanges, etc., are involved. The use of synchronized observers offers possibilities. Each observer is trained to use a different "lens" in observing. The lenses would be tailored to the needs of the research problem. Observers would focus on selected aspects of the interaction or the conditions of interaction. An observational system or set of codes that dwells on the particular must ignore the general, and vice versa; yet for the understanding of many issues of interaction, influence processes, and behavioral change, both the particular and the general are important. The greatest potential would seem to be in the synchronized reporting on the same interactions with differing levels of inference or kinds of conceptualization or kinds of units. Simultaneous observing with different lenses might help to retain or increase the clarity of the multiple messages inherent in behavior and interaction. Multiple observations could provide improved precision but not at the price of abusing behavior. Although such an abundance of data on any research question could bring overwhelming problems of analysis, experimentation outside the usual observational probes may be both healthy and wise.

ACKNOWLEDGMENTS

We wish to thank the following individuals who served as observers and/or data analysts: Janet Turnage, Barbara Strope, Marcia Judson, Jean Darby, Eleanor Monohan, Marilyn Pickett, Doris Hawkins, Frances Polen, Claire Horowitz, Thomas Padrick, David Eaton, and Ellen Nannis.

REFERENCES

Antonovsky, H. F. A contribution to research in the area of mother–child relationship. *Child Development,* 1959, *30,* 37–51.

Barker, R. (Ed.). *The stream of behavior.* New York: Appleton-Century-Crofts, 1963.

Barker, R. *Ecological psychology.* Stanford, Calif.: Stanford University Press, 1965.

Becker, W. C. Consequences of different kinds of parental discipline. In M. L. Hoffman & L. W. Hoffman (Eds.), *Review of child development research* (Vol. 1). New York: Russell Sage Foundation, 1964.

Bing, E. Effect of child rearing practices on development of differential cognitive abilities. *Child Development,* 1963, *34,* 631–648.

Halverson, C. F. Personal communication, 1975.

Johnson, S. M., & Bolstad, O. D. Methodological issues in naturalistic observation: Some problems and solutions for field research. In L. A. Hamerlynck & E. J. March (Eds.), *Behavior change: Methodology, concepts, and practice.* Champaign, Ill.: Research Press, 1973.

Lytton, H. Observation studies of parent–child interaction: A methodological review. *Child Development,* 1971, *42*(3), 651–684.

Moss, H. A., & Jones, S. J. Relations between maternal attitudes and maternal behavior as a function of social class. In P. H. Leiderman & S. R. Tulkin (Eds.), *Cultural and social influences on behavior in infancy and early childhood.* New York: Academic Press, 1977.

Moss, H. A., & Jacobs, B. Personal communication, 1975.

Scott, P. M., Burton, R. V., & Yarrow, M. R. Social reinforcement under natural conditions. *Child Development,* 1967, *38,* 53–63.

Sears, R., Maccoby, E., & Levin, H. *Patterns of child rearing.* Evanston, Ill.: Row, Peterson and Co., 1957.

Smith, H. G. A comparison of interview and observation methods of maternal behaviors. *Journal of Abnormal and Social Psychology,* 1958, *57,* 278–282.

Waxler, C. Z., & Yarrow, M. R. An observational study of maternal models. *Developmental Psychology,* 1975, *11,* 485–494.

Yarrow, M. R., & Scott, P. M. Imitation of nurturant and nonnurturant models. *Journal of Personality and Social Psychology,* 1972, *23,* 259–270.

Yarrow, M. R., & Waxler, C. Z. Child effects on adult behavior. *Developmental Psychology,* 1971, *2,* 200–311.

Yarrow, M. R., Scott, P. M., & Waxler, C. Z. Learning concern for others. *Developmental Psychology,* 1973, *8,* 240–260.

Yarrow, M. R., & Waxler, C. Z. Dimensions and correlates of prosocial behavior in young children. *Child Development,* 1976, *47,* 118–125.

3

Behavioral Acts: Description, Classification, Ethogram Analysis, and Measurement

Marc Bekoff
University of Colorado

It takes time for the eye to become accustomed to recognize differences, and once that has occurred the nature of the differences has to be defined in the mind by careful self-interrogation if the matter is to be set down on paper... The fact remains that an observer must empty his mind and be receptive only of the deer and the signs of the country. This is quite a severe discipline, calling for time and practice... It is necessary intellectually to soak in the environmental complex of the animal to be studied until you have a facility with it which keeps you as it were one move ahead. You must become intimate *with the animal... I would emphasize the importance of thinking of little else but the animal and its environment until one's intellectual complex has become "tuned in" on them. In this state the observer learns more than he realizes.*

—Darling (1937, pp. 24–26)

The hardest of all is that which seems the easiest—to see what is right in front of your eyes.

—By a German poet, translated by Lorenz (1969, p. 82)

The investigator of behavior is faced with a potential paradox in that categories of behavior must be formed ... but these categories are unlikely to be either homogeneous (i.e., indivisible) or mutually exclusive (i.e., functionally independent) on refined analysis. Stated briefly, and without much exaggeration, categories of behavior must be formed, *but the investigator* must not believe them!

—Fentress (1973, p. 163)

67

INTRODUCTION

The description, classification, and measurement of behavioral acts, as well as the compilation of as complete an ethogram (behavioral repertoire) as possible, represent the "backbone" of any study in which observed patterns of behavior form the raw data base. In this chapter, I briefly review some current literature in an attempt to provide a reference guide for workers interested in "making harder" what frequently is referred to as "soft" science (for complete reviews, see Sackett, 1977, 1978). As pointed out by Tinbergen (1951) and others, behavioral studies, when done with the rigor that they demand, are at least as difficult if not more so, than other scientific endeavors.

OBSERVATION AND DESCRIPTION

The first and most important stages of a behavioral study involve the careful observation of chosen subjects and the description of their behavioral patterns. Tinbergen (1951), Lorenz (1960, 1973), and other ethologists have stressed that keen observation and clear description is essential to all science, and this is especially true of the behavioral sciences in which the goal is to communicate in intelligible language and in a reliable, unambiguous, fashion *what* it is that an animal(s) is doing.

Observation and Sampling

Observational methods (as does all methodology) vary with the questions being asked. Eyes, ears, and to a lesser extent the nose and mouth are all used in "observation," usually along with equipment that increases our perceptual ability with respect to these senses and devices that facilitate recording on-going behavioral interactions (e.g., binoculars, spotting scopes, audio- and videotape, sonograms for physically describing sounds, gas chromatography for analyzing scents, keyboards, and event recorders (Dawkins, 1971; Stephenson, Smith, & Roberts, 1975; White, 1971). Ample equipment is readily available to aid in the observational stage of research. But a problem that often arises when a population of animals is being studied concerns the way in which group and individual behavior is sampled.

J. Altmann (1974; see also Dunbar, 1976) presents an "observer's guide" in which she discusses seven types of sampling methods that have been used in observational studies of social groups of animals (see Table 3.1). Focal-animal sampling, if it can be used, is the method of choice and may be used in conjunction with other methods depending on the question(s) being asked. The use of multiple sampling methods, if possible, is considered a good use of research time. Altmann categorizes behavior either as *events* or *states. Events*

TABLE 3.1

Seven Different Sampling Techniques That Can Be Used in Studies of Social Behavior[a]

Sampling Method	State or Event Sampling	Some Possible Biases and Limitations	Recommended Uses
Ad libitum: typical field notes.	Either	Assumes that all types of behavior have an equal probability of occuring and of being recorded; different individuals may be visible for different amounts of time; some behaviors and individuals are more readily observed than others.	Of limited use because of possible biases; rare events may be observed.
Sociometric matrix completion; data are cast into matrices in which rows and columns represent two interactants. These can be "winner" and "loser" or "groomer" and and "groomee", for example.	Event	No indications of duration; no biological interpretation can be given to the rows and columns; results not necessarily representative of nonbiased sampling.	Gives information on directionality and degree of one-sidedness in relations between pairs of animals.
Focal-animal sampling; all occurrences of specified (inter)actions of an individual(s) are recorded during each sample period, and a record is made of the length of each sample period, and for each focal individual, the amount of time during the sample period that individual actually is observed.	Either	Does not provide information about behavioral synchrony among individuals in a group.	Gives information about rates, duration, and spatial relations.

(continued)

TABLE 3.1 (continued)

Sampling Method	State or Event Sampling	Some Possible Biases and Limitations	Recommended Uses
Sampling all occurrences of some behaviors.	Usually event	Assumes that: (1) observational conditions are excellent; (2) the behaviors are sufficiently "attention attracting" so that all cases will be observed; and (3) the behavioral events never occur too rapidly to be recorded.	Gives information on rates, durations, and behavioral synchrony.
Sequence sampling; focus of observation is on interaction sequences regardless of who the interactants are.	Either	Difficult to define the beginning and end of a sequence.	Enables observer to obtain large samples of social behavior regardless of participants [the sequence may persist even if an individual(s) stops participating].
One-zero sampling; in each sampling period, the occurrence (one) or nonoccurrence (zero) of a behavior (not frequency) is scored.	Usually state	No information is provided concerning true frequency, rate, or duration; "frequency" actually means the number of time intervals within a sampling period that included any amount of time spent in that behavior.	None
Instantaneous and scan sampling; observer records an individual's current activity at preselected moments in time— when instantaneous sampling is performed on groups, it is called scan sampling.	State	Difficult to make an instantaneous recording, especially when there is more than one animal.	Can be used to obtain data from a large number of group members; also information on synchrony may be obtained; the percent of time that individuals devote to various activities may be estimated from the percent of samples in which a given activity was recorded.

[a]From J. Altmann (1974)

are instantaneous (the occurrence of the behavior is considered at a single defining instant or at the moment of its onset), whereas *states* have appreciable durations. For example, if we simply indicate that an animal "begins eating," we are recording an event; however, if we say that the individual "has been eating" for some period of time, we are recording a state. Altmann's timely paper is well worth reading because of the way in which she carefully analyzes the pros and cons of the various sampling methods.

Description

The importance of the descriptive stage of a behavioral study cannot be overstressed. It is essential that the motor behavior of an animal be precisely described in objective terms. As one's familiarity with a given species increases, an attempt should be made to compile as complete a behavioral inventory, or *ethogram,* as possible.

Criteria for Description

Robert Hinde (1959, 1970) provides excellent reviews of the ways in which behavioral acts may be described and classified. According to Hinde, one may describe behavior by: (1) *physical characters;* or (2) *consequence.* Although each system uses different criteria, they are not mutually exclusive. In the first method, *description by physical characters,* behavioral units are described by their spatiotemporal patterns of muscular contraction. Descriptions of postures, gestures, facial expressions, and reflexes may be presented in this manner. Usually, reference is made to gross patterns of limb or body movements, and typically it is not stated that a particular muscle contracted to a certain degree. However, electromyographic (EMG) records may be made from selected muscles to give a detailed description of movement patterns (A. Bekoff, 1976, 1978; A. Bekoff, Stein, & Hamburger, 1975; Hoyle, 1975; Seiler, 1973; Welker, 1971; Willows, Dorsett, & Hoyle, 1973a,b). One disadvantage to the use of this technique is that for complex behavior patterns such as those involved in fighting or predation, the physical description may be very cumbersome (i.e., a lot of muscles or different parts of the body are involved) or not provide enough detailed information.

The second method, *description by consequence,* does not make reference to patterns of muscular contractions. Rather, behavioral units are described with reference to an animal's orientation to objects or individuals in the environment, the results of which lead to the accomplishment of some task or produce some result. Examples include "retrieving eggs," "picking up nest material," "approaching," and "pouncing on prey." *Advantages* to this method of description include (Hinde, 1970):

1. One descriptive term may be used to refer to a variety of motor patterns. For example, "approaching" may include running, flying, swimming, or walking; "pouncing on prey" describes a motor pattern that is the result of the coordinated action of the entire body.

2. Units of behavior might be defined objectively in terms of changes in the environment. One would not dispute an observation that a rat presses a lever or a ring dove gathers nesting materials, because such descriptions do not involve anthing but recording *what* is done, regardless of the underlying causes.

3. When describing by consequence, attention may also be called to features of the environment or to the individual's (or group's) responsiveness to external stimuli. As with point 2, the report of an observed response to a detectable environmental stimulus usually would not be questioned. In addition to the description of the behavior in this manner, there also is information about what was "correlated" with it.

Disadvantages of description by consequence include:

1. Detail is lost by using a "catch-all" term such as "approaching," "preying," "fighting," etc. The researcher must decide when detail may be forfeited.

2. The way(s) in which the categories of behavior are described may have important effects on later hypotheses and research. For example, the "direction" of the consequence is critical. When animal *A* approaches animal *B*, it may also be withdrawing from animal *C*. When a mouse is placed in a maze and it successfully negotiates the turns, it can be said either that it "enters the goal box" or that it "escapes from the maze."

3. Over-interpretation of the data may occur if motivational causes or mechanisms are included in the description. Nothing about causation should be suggested when using description by consequence, although, as stated previously, correlational information is provided.

Criteria for Classification

After describing behavioral patterns, they usually are then classified into groups using one of three different criteria (Hinde, 1970): (1) *immediate causation;* (2) *function* (see Hinde, 1975); and (3) *history.* When classifying by causation, behavior units can be grouped together according to the factors that seem to be responsible for their appearance. For example, acts whose frequency or intensity of occurrence are affected by sex hormones may be called "sexual behaviors," whereas those behaviors that are elicited by infants may be called "parental behaviors." But not all behaviors that are elicited by sex hormones are necessarily directly related to procreation, and not all behavior that is directed to an infant is parental. In addition, morphologically similar motor patterns may be "caused" by different external or internal stimuli and not necessarily by only a specific set of circumstances. Also, dissimilar motor acts may be elicited by similar circumstances and can be "motivationally" interrelated. In the cichlid fish, *Pelmatichromis subocellatus kribensis*, eating, digging, and attack readiness are related to one another (Heiligenberg, 1965) in that readiness to attack by one fish may be decreased either by biting another fish or by biting the substrate in the form of digging movements.

When classifying behavior by *function*, behavioral units are clumped together according to the adaptive function (e.g., acquisition of food or mate or communicative significance) that they appear to serve. Using brain telestimulation procedures, Maurus and Ploog (1969, 1971) and Pruscha and Maurus (1975) have classified social signals in squirrel monkeys, *Saimiri sciureus*, according to function. The function of the signals was determined largely by the response of the recipient. Functional and causal classification systems often, though not necessarily, overlap.

Historical classification involves the grouping of behaviors according to one of two systems:

1. Patterns of behavior may be grouped if it is believed that they have a common phylogenetic origin or source (e.g., "fixed" or modal action patterns; see Barlow, 1968, 1977). The basic criterion used in this system is the similarity in the pattern of muscular contractions, as judged by the observed form of a behavior. The possibility that two (or more) unrelated species have converged to use similar actions (for example, flying by insects, birds, and mammals) must be considered in this type of classificatory scheme.

2. Patterns of behavior may also be grouped according to their "method of acquisition" (e.g., "learned," "ritualized," "innate"). Classification by acquisition often results in broad, vague groupings that provide little detail. However, the use of historical classification system 1 has yielded valuable results in studies of the origin of social signals (Eibl-Eibesfeldt, 1970; Lorenz, 1958; Morris, 1956; Moynihan, 1955; Tinbergen, 1960) and the evolution of predatory behavior (Eisenberg & Leyhausen, 1972).

It should be obvious that description should not be taken lightly. Interobserver consistency and agreement can be facilitated when clear descriptions of motor patterns are provided. Any level of analysis is permissible and is related to the questions being asked (Barlow, 1968; Bateson, 1976; Manning, 1976). All too often it is the descriptive part of a study that is given too superficial a treatment, when, in fact, this stage of the behavioral study can dictate future avenues of research and is far from being superfluous (Lorenz, 1973). As Hinde (1959) has written: "A constant awareness of the problems involved in description and classification is essential, for the future course of research may depend on the choice of units, and the criteria by which they are recognized become the bricks from which hypotheses are built [p. 568]."

ETHOGRAM COMPLETENESS ANALYSES

As mentioned earlier, the compilation of behavioral repertoires is one of the most important steps in a behavioral study. Besides careful description, it is important that a worker have some way by which to assess the completeness of a "working" ethogram based on strong quantitative measures (e.g., Fagen

TABLE 3.2
A Completeness Analysis on the Behavior Repertory of Three Canids

Species	Total Frequency of Acts Observed	Observed Repertory Size (Type of Acts)	Estimated Repertory Size[a]	Estimated 95% Confidence Intervals, Total Repertory Size (Chi-square; df)
Wolves (Canis lupus)	7134	50	50	50, 51 (8.7; 6)
Coyotes (C. latrans)	7733	49	49	49, 49 (8.9; 6)
Beagles (C. familiaris)	9408	47	47	47, 48 (6.1; 5)
Total	24,275	146	146	

Frequency Range	Number of Acts Falling in This Range		
	Wolves	Coyotes	Beagles
1	1	0	1
2	0	0	0
3–4	1	0	2
5–8	1	2	2
9–16	1	2	0
17–32	5	1	4
33–64	7	8	4
65–128	17	10	7
129–256	6	16	14
257–512	9	9	9
513–1024	2	1	4
Total	50	49	47

[a]Based on goodness-of-fit to the lognormal Poisson distribution; observations were conducted for infants 21–50 days of age; for details on the analytical method, see Fagen and Goldman (1977).

& Goldman, 1977; Wildenthal, 1965) and also to be able to estimate the amount of additional sampling needed to add a given number of new behavioral patterns to an existing repertory. Such measures have been developed by Fagen and Goldman (1977). Basically, their procedure for measuring the degree of completeness of an observed repertory involves analyzing the goodness-of-fit of the observed repertory size based on number of types of acts, to an expected repertory size based on the truncated lognormal Poisson distribution (for details, see Fagen & Goldman, 1977). As the total frequency of acts increases, the number of types of acts detected increases to a point at which the probability of adding a new type of act to the repertory becomes exceedingly small.

A representative completeness analysis for three infant canids is presented in Table 3.2. The ethogram is more fully described in M. Bekoff (1972, 1974, 1978). As can be seen, the observed repertory for all three canids is identical to the estimated repertory size based on the total frequency of acts observed. The width of the 95% confidence interval is equal to 1 for wolves and beagles; for the coyotes, there is no variation around the estimated repertory size. In addition, the majority of acts occurred between 65 and 256 times, with very few acts occurring fewer than 33 times. For all three canids, 23 types of acts accounted for over 85% of the total number of acts observed (M. Bekoff, 1978). Therefore, the remaining 24 to 27 types of acts occurred very infrequently. Because the observed repertory size and expected repertory size are in very close agreement with one another, it may be concluded that the probability of adding a new type of act is very low. In other words, the amount of additional sampling needed to add more types of acts would be large, and by using the repertory developed from our previous endeavors, one could perform observational studies on these three canids (and perhaps others) with the confidence that a relatively complete ethogram has been established.

THE PHYSICAL MEASUREMENT OF BEHAVIORAL PATTERNS

In any science in which quantification of results is necessary, the problem of measurement exists. With respect to behavior, there are some unique problems. For example, many motor patterns do not readily lend themselves to direct physical measurement. The difficulty with which various behavioral phenomena can be measured varies with the behavior being studied. Sonograms provide analyzable "pictures" of animal sounds. Scents may be analyzed as to their chemical composition using a variety of chemical techniques. Until recently, however, the signals to which we are very attentive—visual displays or acts—have been infrequently studied metrically (see Barlow, 1968, 1977; M. Bekoff, 1977a). It is well worth mentioning some recent advances in this aspect of ethology.

Visual behaviors such as postures, gestures, and facial expressions that do not lend themselves to easy metrical description have been quantified by using electromyograms or by doing film analyses by projecting the visual image on some type of grid on which the units of measurement are arbitrarily, but consistently, defined (see Baerends & van der Cingel, 1962; M. Bekoff, 1977a, b; Brown, 1964; Golani, 1969, 1973, 1976; Hausfater, 1977; van Tets, 1965; Wiley, 1975). Examples of the use of grid systems to describe quantitatively visual displays and movements are represented in Figs. 3.1 and 3.2. In his comparative study of communication in pelicans, van Tets (1965) measured tail elevations. He divided the possible range of tail movements into nine sectors and then calculated the frequency distributions of tail elevation in each of the sectors for different species while they performed different displays (Fig. 3.1).

A more detailed analysis has been used by Golani (1969, 1976; see also Fentress, 1978). Golani constructed a reference system for the movement of a

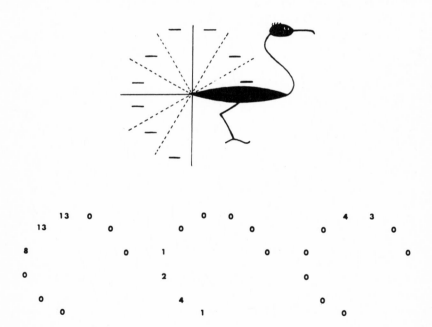

FIG. 3.1. *Top:* Diagram showing the nine 30-degree sectors that were used to measure the frequency distribution of tail elevations in a variety of *Pelicaniformes. Bottom:* The frequency distributions of tail elevations of three *Pelicaniformes* in the nine 30-degree sectors for (left to right): sky-pointing of *Sula sula,* wing-waving of *Anhinga anhinga,* and throw-back of *Phalacrocorax aristoelis.* (From van Tets, 1965, with permission of The American Ornithological Union.)

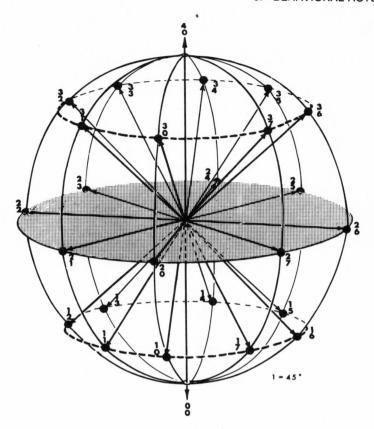

FIG. 3.2. A reference system for measuring body movements within a spherical system. The lower number indicates the horizontal coordinate, and the upper number the vertical coordinate. (From Golani, 1969, with permission of The Movement Notation Society, Tel Aviv; see also Golani, 1976.)

joint around a fixed point and also for the movement of a limb within a sphere (Fig. 3.2). Coordinate systems are used to define and measure various types of movements. Although Golani's method is rather complex and requires time-consuming detailed analyses of movie film or videotape, it is very precise. However, the temptation for "over-kill" must be resisted. First, it may be the case that other types of analyses will be more appropriate to the questions that are under study. Second, it may be the case that van Tets' and others' more "crude" measurements will provide equally important data, especially if the species under study is not able to dissect its own behavior to the same degree that the researcher does! The perceptual abilities of the animals must be considered. Experiments must be used to determine how fine a discrimination in movement the species actually is able to make (e.g., Hazlett, 1972).

CONCLUSION

Ethology basically is an observational science, regardless of whether or not experimental manipulations are resorted to. The observational and descriptive stages of a behavioral study must be given serious attention. In this chapter, different methods of sampling, describing, classifying, and measuring behavioral actions have been briefly discussed. It is hoped that precision in the description and measurement of observed patterns of behavior will not be pushed aside and will remain a primary consideration in studies in which the behavior of animals is being investigated.

ACKNOWLEDGMENTS

I thank Charles Fuenzalida and Harriet Hill for comments on an earlier draft of this chapter. Robert Fagen performed the completeness analysis. Nutan Pall typed the manuscript.

REFERENCES

Altmann, J. Observational study of behaviour: Sampling methods. *Behaviour,* 1974, *49,* 227–267.

Baerends, G. P., & van der Cingel, N. A. On the phylogenetic origin of the snap display in the common heron (*Ardea cinerea* L.). *Symposia of the Zoological Society of London,* 1962, *8,* 7–24.

Barlow, G. Ethological units of behavior. In D. Ingle (ed.), *The central nervous system and fish behavior.* Chicago: University of Chicago Press, 1968.

Barlow, G. Modal action patterns. In T. A. Sebeok (Ed.), *How animals communicate.* Bloomingotn, Ind.: University of Indiana Press, 1977.

Bateson, P. P. G. Specificity and the origins of behavior. *Advances in the Study of Behavior,* 1976, *6,* 1–20.

Bekoff, A. Ontogeny of leg motor output in the chick embryo: A neural analysis. *Brain Research,* 1976, *106,* 271–291.

Bekoff, A. A neuroethological approach to the study of the ontogeny of coordinated behavior. In G. Burghardt & M. Bekoff (Eds.), *The development of behavior: Comparative and evolutionary aspects.* New York: Garland, 1978.

Bekoff, A., Stein, P. S. G., & Hamburger, V. Coordinated motor output in the hindlimb of the 7-day chick embryo. *Proceedings of the National Academy of Sciences,* 1975, *72,* 1245–1248.

Bekoff, M. The development of social interaction, play and metacommunication in mammals: An ethological perspective. *Quarterly Review of Biology,* 1972, *47,* 412–434.

Bekoff, M. Social play and play-soliciting by infant canids. *American Zoologist,* 1974, *14,* 323–341.

Bekoff, M. Quantitative studies of three areas of classical ethology: Social dominance, behavioral taxonomy, and behavioral variability. In B. A. Hazlett (Ed.), *Quantitative methods in the study of animal behavior.* New York: Academic Press, 1977. (a)

Bekoff, M. Social communication in canids: Evidence for the evolution of a stereotyped mammalian display. *Science,* 1977, *197,* 1097–1099. (b)

Bekoff, M. Social development in coyotes and eastern coyotes. In M. Bekoff (Ed.), *Coyotes: Evolution, behavior, and management*. New York: Academic Press, 1978.

Brown, J. L. The integration of agonistic behavior in the Steller's jay *Cyanocitta stelleri (Gmelin)*. *University of California Publications in Zoology*, 1964, *60*, 223–328.

Darling, F. F. *A herd of red deer*. New York: Oxford University Press, 1937.

Dawkins, R. A cheap method of recording behavioural events for direct computer-access. *Behaviour*, 1971, *40*, 162–173.

Dunbar, R. I. M. Some aspects of research design and their implications in the observational study of behaviour. *Behaviour*, 1976, *58*, 78–98.

Eibl-Eibesfeldt, I. *Ethology*. New York: Holt, Rinehart & Winston, 1975.

Eisenberg, J. F., & Leyhausen, P. The phylogenesis of predatory behavior in mammals. *Zeitschrift für Tierpsychologie*, 1972, *30*, 59–93.

Fagen, R., & Goldman, R. N. Behavioural catalogue analysis methods. *Animal Behaviour*, 1977, *25*, 261–274.

Fentress, J. C. Specific and nonspecific factors in the causation of behavior. In P. P. G. Bateson & P. H. Klopfer (Eds.), *Perspectives in ethology* (Vol. 1). New York: Plenum, 1973.

Fentress, J. C. *Mus musicus:* The developmental orchestration of selected movement patterns in mice. In G. Burghardt & M. Bekoff (Eds.), *The development of behavior: Comparative and evolutionary aspects*. New York: Garland, 1978.

Golani, I. *The golden jackal*. Tel Aviv: The Movement Notation Society, 1969.

Golani, I. Non-metric analysis of behavioural interaction sequences in captive jackals (*Canis aureus* L.). *Behaviour*, 1973, *44*, 89–112.

Golani, I. Homeostatic motor processes in mammalian interactions: A choreography of display. In P. P. G. Bateson & P. H. Klopfer (Eds.), *Perspectives in ethology* (Vol. 2). New York: Plenum, 1976.

Hausfater, G. Tail carriage in baboons (*Papio cynocephalus*): Relationship to dominance rank and age. *Folia Primatologica*, 1977, *27*, 41–59.

Hazlett, B. A. Response to agonistic postures by the spider crab *Microphrys bicornutus*. *Marine Behavior and Physiology*, 1972, *1*, 85–92.

Heiligenberg, W. A quantititative analysis of digging movements and their relationship to aggressive behavior in cichlids. *Animal Behaviour*, 1965, *13*, 163–170.

Hinde, R. A. Some recent trends in ethology. In S. Koch (Ed.), *Psychology: A study of science* (Vol. 2) New York: McGraw-Hill, 1959.

Hinde, R. A. *Animal behavior*. New York: McGraw-Hill, 1970.

Hinde, R. A. The concept of function. In. G. Baerends, C. Beer, & A. Manning (Eds.), *Function and evolution in behaviour*. New York: Oxford University Press, 1975.

Hoyle, G. Identified neurons and the future of neuroethology. *Journal of Experimental Zoology*, 1975, *194*, 51–74.

Lorenz, K.Z. The evolution of behavior. *Scientific American*, 1958, *199*, 67–68.

Lorenz, K. Z. Methods and approaches to the problems of behavior. In *The Harvey Lectures*. New York: Academic Press, 1960.

Lorenz, K. Z. Innate bases of learning. In K. H. Pribram (Ed.), *On the biology of learning*. New York: Harcourt, Brace & World, 1969.

Lorenz, K. Z. The fashionable fallacy of dispensing with description. *Naturwissenschaften*, 1973, *60*, 1–9.

Manning, A. The place of genetics in the study of behaviour. In P. P. G. Bateson & R. A. Hinde (Eds.), *Growing points in ethology*. New York: Cambridge University Press, 1976.

Maurus, M., & Ploog, D. Motor and vocal interactions in groups of squirrel monkeys, elicited by remote-controlled electrical brain stimulation. *Proceedings of the Second International Congress of Primatology*, 1969, *3*, 59–63.

Maurus, M., & Ploog, D. Social signals in squirrel monkeys: Analysis by cerebral radio stimulation. *Experimental Brain Research*, 1971, *12*, 171–183.

Morris, D. The feather postures of birds and the problem of the origin of social signals. *Behaviour*, 156, 9, 75–113.

Moynihan, M. Remarks on the original sources of displays. *Auk*, 1955, 72, 240–246.

Pruscha, H., & Maurus, M. Classifying agonistic behavior patterns according to their function in the communication process. *Contemporary Primatology*, Proceedings of the Fifth International Congress of Primatology, 1975, 245–253.

Sackett, G. P. (Ed.). *Observing behavior* (Vols. 1 and 2). Baltimore, Md.: University Park Press, 1977 and 1978.

Seiler, R. On the function of facial muscles in different behavioral situations. A study based on muscle morphology and electromyography. *American Journal of Physical Anthropology*, 1973, 38, 567–572.

Stephenson, G. R., Smith, D. P. B., & Roberts, T. W. The SSR system: An open format event recording system with computerized transcription. *Behavior Research Methods and Instrumentation*, 1975, 7, 497–515.

van Tets, G. F. A comparative study of some social communication patterns in the Pelicaniformes. *Ornithological Monographs*, 1965, 2, 1–88.

Tinbergen, N. *The study of instinct.* New York: Oxford University Press, 1951.

Tinbergen, N. The evolution of behavior in gulls. *Scientific American*, 1960, 203, 118–130.

Welker, W. I. Ontogeny of play and exploratory behaviors: A definition of problems and a search for new conceptual solutions. In H. Moltz (Ed.), *The ontogeny of vertebrate behavior.* New York: Academic Press, 1971.

White, R. E. C. Wrats: A computer compatible system for automatically recording and transcribing behavioural data. *Behaviour*, 1971, 40, 135–161.

Wildenthal, J. L. Structure in primary song of the mockingbird (*Mimus polyglottus*). *Auk*, 1965, 82, 161–189.

Wiley, R. H. Multidimensional variation in an avian display: Implications for social communication. *Science*, 1975, 190, 482–483.

Willows, A. O. D., Dorsett, D. A., & Hoyle, G. The neuronal basis of behavior in *Tritonia*. I. Functional organization of the central nervous system. *Journal of Neurobiology*, 1973, 4, 207–237. (a)

Willow, A. O. D., Dorsett, D. A., & Hoyle, G. The neuronal basis of behavior in *Tritonia*. III. Neuronal mechanism of a fixed action pattern. *Journal of Neurobiology*, 1973, 4, 255–285. (b)

4 The Analysis of Behavior Sequences

N. John Castellan, Jr.
Indiana University at Bloomington

INTRODUCTION

In this brief chapter, several techniques are summarized that are useful in analyzing sequences of behavior. In recent years, increasing attention has been paid to the analysis of sequential behavior of two sorts—one dealing with dyadic behavior sequences, and the other dealing with the sequence of behaviors observed in a single subject. The former focuses on the behavior of dyads in which antecedent–consequent behavior pairs are observed over a period of time. Such pairs could be mother–infant behavior pairings, sibling–sibling behavior pairings, etc., and are often generically labeled *interaction sequences.* The latter focuses on the sequence of behavior of a single individual across time in which the behavior occurring at particular intervals is observed and coded. An example is the behavior observed when an organism is placed in a free-field situation and the transitions from behavior to behavior are coded.

Although there are a variety of techniques for analyzing such sequential data, there is one technique that is simple in its conception but powerful enough to capture many nuances of theoretical and practical interest in the sequences. The technique is called *contingency* or *frequency table analysis.* The analysis of contingency tables can be extended to cover a wide range of situations and hypotheses of interest in the analysis of sequences for which few parametric assumptions need to be made. A vast literature on the analysis of contingency tables exists, albeit often presented under different rubrics. Such papers range from the methodological and pedagogical (e.g., Bobbitt, Gourevitch, Miller, & Jensen, 1969; Hinde & Stevenson, 1969; Raush, 1965; and Slater, 1973) to statistical (Castellan, 1965; Chatfield, 1973; Kullback,

Kupperman, & Ku, 1962; and Maxwell, 1961). Over the years, L. A. Goodman and his associates have made many important and useful contributions to this literature. Recently, a systematic presentation of a large number of techniques for the statistical analysis of qualitative (frequency) data has become available (Bishop, Fienberg, & Holland, 1975). However, although many papers have been published on the techniques in general, or on specific tests for specific purposes, the aim of this chapter is to provide a systematic compilation of procedures that can be used in a comprehensive analysis of sequences of behavior.

In the analysis of sequences—whether of dyads or of single behavior strings—there are many questions that may be asked. In the case of behavior sequences, there are hypotheses concerning sequential dependencies in behavior transitions—that is, the extent to which the occurrence of a particular behavior is dependent on previous behavior. Examples of analyses of sequential dependencies may be found in the work of Delius (1969), who studied the maintenance behavior of skylarks, and Fentress (1972), who studied the grooming behavior of mice as a function of breeding characteristics. Hypotheses of interest in their studies included the degree of sequential dependency of the behaviors and the stability over time of both the behaviors and the sequential dependencies that occurred among behaviors.

In the examination of dyadic interaction sequences, hypotheses include the dependence of consequent behavior on the type of antecedent behavior. Hazlett and Bossert (1965) used procedures similar to those to be described in this chapter in a study of the aggressive behavior of hermit crabs. Lytton and Zwirner (1975) studied the effect of parent's verbal behavior upon the compliance of their children to their verbal statements. Steinberg and Conant (1974) studied the interactive behavior of male grasshoppers. In a study of the stability of interactions in group discussion, Lewis (1970) utilized some of the methods to be described here. In addition to concern about the stability of sequences and the nature of behavior dependencies, there is also the important problem of comparing the interactions and behavior sequences across individuals, dyads, and groups.

In reviewing the aforementioned empirical studies (and many others) on the applications of sequence analysis, the need for a systematic presentation of analytic techniques became clear. It would be very easy to cite examples of incomplete analyses. Moreover, it is easy to find that inappropriate and incorrect analyses have been done. Although the reasons for such problems are many, a principal one appears to stem from the uncritical use of a statistic that was employed in a similar study, which, while appropriate in the original work, was not appropriate to the later study. Thus analyses and techniques are applied by analogy—and very often the analogy is false. If such difficulties are found from one paper to the next, it is easy to see how the problems become compounded as one goes from primary to secondary to tertiary sources. Moreover, it is difficult for a researcher to review the original statistical literature appropriate to sequential analysis of frequency tables—in part because often it is not referenced in empirical studies, and in part because such references vary widely in their accessibility and intelligibility to the typical researcher. Therefore, the need for a systematic presentation of techniques together with the foundations and underlying assumptions is essential if researchers are to make effective use of the techniques.

This chapter summarizes some of the techniques relevant to sequential analysis. We begin by giving a general introduction to contingency table analysis in which the relevant background, models, and assumptions are presented. This is followed by a presentation of techniques for analyzing interaction sequences. Next, several models and techniques for analyzing single sequences are discussed. Finally, measures of the degree of relation between variables in interaction analysis are outlined. Such measures complement the hypothesis-testing procedures in the earlier sections and, with them, can provide useful insight into the underlying processes.

THE GENERAL CONTINGENCY TABLE

The analysis of dyadic interaction and behavior sequences involves a common framework for the description of behavior. This common framework arises in many situations that involve categories of behavior or variables about which frequencies of occurrence are observed. Data from such situations may be summarized in a frequency table, which is often called a *contingency table*. Because most of the hypotheses of interest concerning dyadic interaction and behavior sequences can be cast in terms of those for a contingency table, it is useful to begin with a general discussion of contingency tables.

In analyzing contingency or frequency tables, there are many hypotheses that may be considered. It is our purpose here to outline the various hypotheses and provide tests of them. We begin by considering the general two-way table and by developing the notation to be used throughout this chapter. In general, we observe the joint occurrence of two outcomes, one from each of two classes. These classes can be thought of as random variables, and the joint occurrence of the variables can be represented in a two-way table. We denote the row and column variables as A and B, respectively. An entry in the table is denoted as f_{ij}, which is the frequency of the joint occurrence of the variables A_i and B_j. In addition, let I and J be the number of mutually exclusive and exhaustive classes or categories for the variables A and B, respectively. Thus the general contingency table may be represented as

TABLE 4.1
The General Contingency Table

Variable A	Variable B						
	B_1	B_2	...	B_j	...	B_J	
A_1	f_{11}	f_{12}	...	f_{1j}	...	f_{1J}	f_1^A
A_2	f_{21}	f_{22}	...	f_{2j}	...	f_{2J}	f_2^A
$\vdots$	$\vdots$	$\vdots$		$\vdots$		$\vdots$	$\vdots$
A_i	f_{i1}	f_{i2}	...	f_{ij}	...	f_{iJ}	f_i^A
$\vdots$	$\vdots$	$\vdots$		$\vdots$		$\vdots$	$\vdots$
A_I	f_{I1}	f_{I2}	...	f_{Ij}	...	f_{IJ}	f_I^A
	f_1^B	f_2^B	...	f_j^B	...	f_J^B	n

illustrated in Table 4.1. The total number of observations is n, which is the sum of the frequencies of joint occurrences:

$$n = \sum_{i,j} f_{ij},$$

where $\Sigma_{i,j}$ denotes the sum over all of the row (i) and column (j) categories. In addition to the individual cell frequencies, we need to represent the marginal frequency of the A and B variables. The marginal frequencies are denoted as f_i^A and f_j^B, where f_i^A denotes the row marginal frequency of variable A_i, and where f_j^B denotes the column marginal frequency of variable B_j. [This follows the notation conventions used by Goodman (1970).] In general,

$$f_i^A = \sum_j f_{ij}, \quad \text{and} \quad f_j^B = \sum_i f_{ij}.$$

In specifying hypotheses about this table, we find that there are many different sorts of hypotheses that may be entertained. However, we here consider four basic hypotheses that comprise those encountered most frequently.

Hypothesis 1:
Fit of Frequencies to Specified Probabilities

In this case, it is assumed that there is some basis—theory or model—that allows one to specify the probability of occurrence of each pairing (A_i–B_j). Thus, we have an hypothesis that may be stated as follows:

H1:   The probability of the joint occurrence of the classification (A_i-B_j) is equal to p_{ij}.

In order to test this hypothesis, the expected frequency in each cell must be found. If there are n observations, and the probability of the (A_i-B_j) category is p_{ij}, then the expected frequency is given by

$$F_{ij} = np_{ij}.$$

The test statistic is then:

$$X^2 = \sum_{i,j} \frac{(f_{ij} - F_{ij})^2}{F_{ij}}$$

$$= \sum_{i,j} \frac{(f_{ij} - np_{ij})^2}{np_{ij}}, \tag{1}$$

which is asymptotically distributed as chi-square with $IJ - 1$ degree of freedom.[1] For example, if the hypothesis is that all joint categories are equally likely, then $p_{ij} = 1/IJ$ and $F_{ij} = n/IJ$.

Hypothesis 2:
Fit of Marginal Frequencies to Specified Probabilities

In this case, the joint frequencies are not of primary interest. Instead, the marginal frequency of occurrence of the categories—the A_i or the B_j—are tested for fit to some model or theory. Thus we have the following hypothesis:

H2:   The probability of occurrence of the row (or column) variable A_i (or B_j) is equal to $P[A_i]$ (or $p[B_j]$).

---

[1]Statistics of the form given in Eq. (1) to Eq. (11) are often called "Pearson chi-square" tests. Such tests asymptotically have chi-square distributions, which means that the sampling distribution of X^2 approaches that of the chi-square distribution as the sample size becomes large. It should also be noted that there are alternatives to the tests presented here. Some are based upon log-likelihood ratio distributions and others upon information-theoretic analyses. In virtually all such cases, the sampling distributions of the statistics are asymptotically chi-square. For many purposes, the tests can be considered equivalent. The Pearson chi-square test was chosen in this chapter because its interpretation and computation is more familiar, and because a recent study comparing several statistics (Larntz, 1978) suggests that the Pearson statistic is preferable for small samples.

For convenience and consistency, the marginal probabilities are denoted as:

$$P[A_i] = p_i^A = \sum_j p_{ij}, \text{ for rows, and}$$

$$P[B_j] = p_j^B = \sum_i p_{ij}, \text{ for columns.}$$

For hypotheses about marginals, it should be clear that there are two tests: One deals with the row variable or category, and the other deals with the column variable or category. The expected marginal cell frequencies are:

$$F_i^A = n\,p_i^A \quad \text{and} \quad F_j^B = n\,p_j^B,$$

for rows and columns, respectively. The tests for these hypotheses are

$$X^2 = \sum_i \frac{(f_i^A - n\,p_i^A)^2}{n\,p_i^A} \tag{2a}$$

for rows, and

$$X^2 = \sum_j \frac{(f_j^B - np_j^B)^2}{n\,p_j^B} \tag{2b}$$

for columns. These test statistics are asymptotically distributed as chi-square with $I - 1$ and $J - 1$ degrees of freedom, respectively.

Hypothesis 3:
Conditional Fit of Row (or Column) Frequencies
to Specified Probabilities

Whereas the first hypothesis is used to test the fit of joint frequencies, and the second hypotheses are used to test the fit of marginal probabilities, the third type of hypothesis is used to test the fit of observed frequencies to specified conditional probabilities. As with Hypothesis 2, there are two tests, one for rows and one for columns. The following discussion of "conditional" independence focuses on the row test. In this test, the conditional probabilities of occurrence for the pairs $(A_i - B_j)$ in each row are specified, but the probability of occurrence of the categories (the A_i) is either not known or not specified. (This conditional aspect is similar to specifying the effects of a treatment, but having no interest in, or information about, base rates.) In this case, the hypothesis is:

H3: The conditional probability of occurrence of the column (or row) variable given the row (or column) variable is equal to $P[B_j|A_i] = p_{j,i}$ (or $P[A_i|B_j] = p_{i,j}$).

Note that $p_{j,i}$ is the conditional probability that an observation will be in the (ij)th cell *given* that it is in the ith row. Put differently, $p_{j,i}$ is the probability that an observation falls in the jth column given that it falls in the ith row. When these *conditional* probabilities are specified, the expected frequencies are given by:

$$F_{ij} = f_i^A \, p_{j,i}.$$

For this hypothesis, the test statistic is:

$$X^2 = \sum_i \sum_j \frac{(f_{ij} - f_i^A \, p_{j,i})^2}{f_i^A \, p_{j,i}}, \tag{3a}$$

which is asymptotically distributed as chi-square with $I(J - 1)$ degrees of freedom. Thus it is a test that I distributions of J categories (columns) have specified population distributions.

If the test for conditional fit of the row variables given the column variables is desired, then the test statistic is:

$$X^2 = \sum_j \sum_i \frac{(f_{ij} - f_j^B \, p_{i,j})^2}{f_j^B \, p_{i,j}}, \tag{3b}$$

which is asymptotically distributed as chi-square with $J(I - 1)$ degrees of freedom.

There is an important variant of Hypothesis 3 that should be noted. Suppose that one does not know the conditional probabilities $p_{j,i}$ (or $p_{i,j}$) and wants to test the hypothesis that the conditional probabilities of the B_j given and A_i are equal to the marginal probabilities of the A_i; that is, that $P[B_j|A_i] = P[B_j]$ (or $P[A_i|B_j] = P[A_i]$). This hypothesis is that the rows (or columns) are proportional to each other and also is often called a *test of homogeneity*. In this case, the tests for Hypothesis 3 given in Eq. (3a) and (3b) are not appropriate because the probabilities must be estimated. We see shortly that this hypothesis is related to Hypothesis 4.

Hypothesis 4:
The A and B (Row and Column) Variables Are
Independent of One Another

This test is the most common test on contingency tables. In this test, no probabilities are known, but we are interested only in whether the variables are independent or not. More precisely, the hypothesis is:

H4: The observed behavior categories are independent, viz. $P[A_i, B_j] = P[A_i] \ P[B_j]$, $(p_{ij} = p_i^A \ p_j^B)$.

In this case, the expected frequencies are given by

$$F_{ij} = n \ p_i^A \ p_j^B.$$

However, the marginal probabilities are not known and must be estimated by $\hat{p}_i^A = f_i^A / n$ and $\hat{p}_j^B = f_j^B / n$. The cell frequencies are then estimated by:

$$\hat{F}_{ij} = n \ \hat{p}_i^A \ \hat{p}_j^B$$

$$= (f_i^A f_j^B)/n.$$

The test statistic is then given by the common formula:

$$X^2 = \sum_{i,j} \frac{(f_{ij} - \hat{F}_{ij})^2}{\hat{F}_{ij}}$$

$$= \sum_{i,j} \frac{[f_{ij} - (f_i^A f_j^B)/n]^2}{(f_i^A f_j^B)/n}, \tag{4}$$

which is asymptotically distributed as chi-square with $(I - 1)(J - 1)$ degrees of freedom. (It should be noted that if the marginal probabilities were known, then $p_{ij} = p_i^A p_j^B$, and the test for independence would be equivalent to the test discussed for Hypothesis 1.)

It was noted in the discussion of Hypothesis 3 that one might desire to test the hypothesis that the conditional probabilities between the rows (or columns) are homogeneous. The hypothesis may be stated more precisely as:

H4A: $P[B_j | A_i] = P[B_j]$, for rows, or

H4B: $P[A_i | B_j] = P[A_i]$, for columns.

That is, it is hypothesized that the conditional probabilities are equal to the corresponding marginal probabilities. But if the marginal probabilities are not known, they must be estimated. Thus,

$\hat{p}_{j.i} = \hat{p}_j{}^B = f_j{}^B/n$, for rows, and

$\hat{p}_{i.j} = \hat{p}_i{}^A = f_i{}^A/n$, for columns.

The expected frequency for the (ij)th cell is then

$$\hat{F}_{ij} = f_i{}^A\,\hat{p}_{j.i} = (f_i{}^A\,f_j{}^B)/n$$

for rows, and

$$\hat{F}_{ij} = f_j{}^B\,\hat{p}_{i.j} = (f_j{}^B\,f_i{}^A)/n$$

for columns. It should be noted that these expected values are the same whether testing the conditional probabilities for rows or columns. Moreover, the expected value for each cell is the same as that for the test for independence given by Eq. (4). Thus the test for independence and the test for homogeneity are equivalent. It should be noted, however, that although the tests are the same, the interpretation and the use of the tests are quite different. For example, H4 is appropriate when we take a random sample from some population and wish to test whether or not the variables A and B are independent. As a random sample, there is no effort to control marginals, and the inference to be drawn is about the independence of the variables in the population. On the other hand, suppose that we wished to test whether the distribution of some variable B is the same for all (or some) levels of another variable A. In this case, hypothesis H4A is to be tested. To accomplish this, one might take a random sample, or, more commonly, constrain the data collection to ensure particular numbers of observations in categories A_1, $A_2, \ldots, A_I$. For example, the variable A might be sex, and a sample of 50 males (A_1) and 50 females (A_2) might be used; the inference to be drawn is about the distribution of the variable for B for males and females and *not* about the independence of the variables in the population. Finally, it should be noted that for the test of independence, the categories of both A and B must be exhaustive, whereas for the test of homogeneity, the sampling of the controlled variable need not be exhaustive of the categories.

The four kinds of hypotheses are summarized in Table 4.2. Hypothesis Type 1 is that the observed frequencies follow some specified pattern (often equiprobable). Type 2 hypotheses test the marginals against a specified set of frequencies and ignore joint frequencies. Hypothesis Type 3 is that the categories of B (or A) are related to A (or B) in terms of specified conditional probabilities. This form is sometimes used to test the hypothesis that the B (or A) categories are equiprobable given the level of A (or B). Finally, Hypothesis Type 4 is the test of independence of the A and B categories, which is the common test applied to joint frequencies; Hypotheses Type 4A and 4B test

TABLE 4.2
Types of Hypotheses for the Two-Way Table

Type of Hypothesis	Expected Values	Degrees of Freedom	Fitted Marginals
1	np_{ij}	$IJ - 1$	all
2	np_i^A	$I - 1$	A
	np_j^B	$J - 1$	B
3	$f_i^A P_{j.i}$	$I(J - 1)$	$B\vert A$
	$f_j^B P_{i.j}$	$J(I - 1)$	$A\vert B$
4	$\dfrac{f_i^A f_j^B}{n}$	$(I - 1)(J - 1)$	A, B independent

the conditional independence that the categories of B (or A) are independent of A (or B). It should be noted that, common or not, the choice of test applied to a contingency table depends on the hypotheses one has about the relation between the variables. In the subsequent sections of this chapter, we consider several forms of dyadic and sequential data that are amenable to the general analytic methods outlined here.

AN INTERACTION ANALYSIS MODEL

Suppose that we have a sequence of observations of a behavior of a dyad. For example, the data could be a sequence of mother–infant behaviors, coded in terms of the pairing of mother behavior and infant behavior. Using the notation developed in the previous section, suppose that the data are coded such that variable A is the behavior of one member of the dyad (e.g., mother) and variable B is the behavior of the other member of the dyad (e.g., infant) in response to the behavior of the first member. We then have a contingency table, which might be called a *behavior transition matrix:*

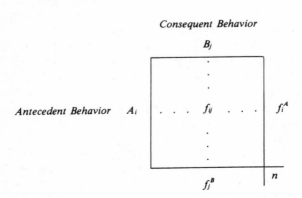

In this case, f_{ij} is the number of times behavior B_j *followed* behavior A_i. The marginal frequencies f_i^A and f_j^B are the frequencies of particular antecedent and consequent behaviors, respectively. The categories for A and B may differ in number and type.

Several hypotheses may be of interest, of which perhaps the most important is:

H: Consequent behavior is independent of Antecedent behavior.

More specifically, this hypothesis is that $P[B_j|A_i] = P[B_j]$, where the values of $P[B_j]$ are unknown and must be estimated. Referring to the previous section we see that the test is that of an Hypothesis Type 4A and Eq. (4) is appropriate.

Example

Consider a situation in which the response of a mother to a child's vocalizations was examined. The antecedent (A) behavior is whether the behavior of the child was a vocalization or not. The consequent behavior was the response of the mother—a smile or other behavior. A sequence of interactions was recorded and is summarized in Table 4.3. In the lower portion of the table, the conditional probabilities are listed. The hypothesis to be tested is that the two rows of conditional probabilities are the same. Using Eq. (4), the value $X^2 = 1501$ was calculated. Because the statistic X^2 is

TABLE 4.3
Example of Dyadic Interaction Sequence Summary

	Frequencies		
Antecedent Behavior of Child	*Consequent Behavior of Mother*		
	Smile	*No Smile*	*Total*
Vocalization	85	15	100
No Vocalization	15	2000	2015
Total	100	2015	2115

	Conditional Probabilities	
Antecedent Behavior of Child	*Consequent Behavior of Mother*	
	Smile	*No Smile*
Vocalization	.85	.15
No Vocalization	.01	.99

asymptotically distributed as chi-square with 1 degree of freedom, and reference to a table of the chi-square distribution indicates that the critical value of chi-square at the .001 significance level is 10.828, we may reject the hypothesis that the conditional probabilities are equal. That is, we reject the hypothesis that the conditional probabilities .85 and .15 are equal to the conditional probabilities .01 and .99, respectively. Thus, we infer that the mother's behavior is *not* independent of the child's behavior.

THE STABILITY OF SEQUENCES OF EVENTS

It is usually the case that the Antecedent–Consequent pairs are observed over time—that is, an (A_i-B_j) pairing is observed as part of an ongoing sequence of behavior. The frequencies in the contingency tables described in the earlier sections were obtained by collapsing the sequence of behaviors across time. Such collapsing may obscure behavior patterns that may change as a function of time. However, such temporal changes—or the lack of them—is often an important part of the substantive questions raised in an interaction analysis. In particular, are the transitions between Antecedents and Consequents constant across time? That is, are the behavior transitions stationary?

To test the hypothesis of constant transitions, it is necessary to group and code the data in terms of time. Let there be T time periods or blocks of time in which the behavior is observed. Recall that f_{ij} is the transition frequency of (A_i-B_j) pairs; let $f_{ij}(1)$ be the frequency of transitions from A_i to B_j in the first block, and $f_{ij}(t)$ to be the transition in block t. These transitions are in Table 4.4. Actually there are I such tables, one for each antecedent A_i. Before proceeding to the analysis model, it is appropriate to explain the concept of

TABLE 4.4
Transition Table for Antecedent A_i
Behavior for Various Time Blocks

Time Block	Consequent						
	B_1	B_2	...	B_j	...	B_J	
1	$f_{i1}(1)$	$f_{i2}(1)$	...	$f_{ij}(1)$	...	$f_{iJ}(1)$	$f_i^A(1)$
2	$f_{i1}(2)$	$f_{i2}(2)$	...	$f_{ij}(2)$	...	$f_{iJ}(2)$	$f_i^A(2)$
⋮	⋮	⋮		⋮		⋮	⋮
t	$f_{i1}(t)$	$f_{i2}(t)$	...	$f_{ij}(t)$	...	$f_{iJ}(t)$	$f_i^A(t)$
⋮	⋮	⋮		⋮		⋮	⋮
T	$f_{i1}(T)$	$f_{i2}(T)$	...	$f_{ij}(T)$	...	$f_{iJ}(T)$	$f_i^A(T)$

Note: There is one table like the above table for each Antecedent A_i.

time as it applies to the analysis of series of events. A time block may be comprised of units of equal time such as 5-second blocks, or 15-minute blocks, etc. However, in some cases it may be appropriate to organize the blocks in terms of behavior pairs. In the latter situation, if $100(A_i-B_j)$ behavior pairs were observed during the observation period, then there might be 5 "time" blocks, each containing $20(A_i-B_j)$ behavior pairs, the first block containing the first 20 pairs, the second block containing the next 20 pairs, and so on.

The hypothesis that the transition or conditional probabilities are constant across time (blocks) is:

$$H: \quad p_{j.i}(t) = p_{j.i}, \quad t = 1, 2, \ldots, T,$$

where $p_{j.i}(t)$ is the conditional probability of the behavior B_j, given behavior A_i in the tth block, and where $p_{j.i}$ is the marginal conditional probability computed across time blocks. It should be noted that $p_{j.i}$ is the conditional probability of Consequent B_j, given the Antecedent A_i described in an earlier section, and is referred to as either a *conditional probability* or *transition probability*. In the following test, it is assumed that $p_{j.i}$ must be estimated from the data, which is the case when one has no prior hypothesis about the value of the transition probabilities. Then the estimate is:

$$\hat{p}_{j.i} = f_{ij}/f_i^A,$$

and the estimated expected frequency of transitions in the tth block is then:

$$\hat{F}_{ij}(t) = f_i^A(t) \, (f_{ij}/f_i^A),$$

where $f_i^A(t)$ is the marginal frequency of A_i in the tth block. The test statistic is:

$$X_i^2 = \sum_{t=1}^{T} \sum_j \frac{[f_{ij}(t) - \hat{F}_{ij}(t)]^2}{\hat{F}_{ij}(t)}$$

$$= \sum_{t=1}^{T} \sum_j \frac{[f_{ij}(t) - f_i^A(t) \, (f_{ij}/f_i^A)]^2}{f_i^A(t) \, (f_{ij}/f_i^A)}, \tag{5}$$

which is asymptotically distributed as chi-square with $(T-1)(J-1)$ degrees of freedom. It should be noted explicitly that this test tests the stability for transitions from antecedent A_i only. Thus it corresponds to a test of those transitions depicted in Table 4.4. In order to test the hypothesis of constant transitions from *all* antecedents, it is necessary to apply Eq. (5) to each antecedent and sum the resulting X_i^2. That is, to test the hypothesis

H: $p_{j.i}(t) = p_{j.i}$, $t = 1, 2, \ldots, T$,
$\qquad\qquad\quad i = 1, 2, \ldots, I$,

we use the following statistic:

$$X^2 = \sum_i X_i^2$$

$$= \sum_i \sum_t \sum_j \frac{[f_{ij}(t) - f_i^A(t)\,(f_{ij}/f_i^A)]^2}{f_i^A(t)\,(f_{ij}/f_i^A)}, \qquad\qquad (6)$$

which is asymptotically distributed as chi-square with $I(J - 1)(T - 1)$ degrees of freedom. When subdividing sequences to test for stability, care should be taken not to use too many blocks. If too many blocks are used, the expected values become small and the test becomes less sensitive. If blocks are constructed by behavior transitions rather than time transitions, the number of transitions per block should be constant. In that way, the power of the test for stability is maximized. This capability of maximizing the power makes the subdivision by behaviors rather than by time a more useful technique. However, if one wants to test for changes in frequencies of *all* behaviors (i.e., collapse across the variable A) in terms of time, then time must be used as the blocking variable.

It should be noted that if the statistic computed using Eq. (6) is significant, it tells only that the conditional probabilities are not constant for at least one Antecedent–Consequent transition in at least one time period. By breaking the test into the components given in Eq. (5), there is more specific information concerning the specific Antecedents that gave rise to the differences found.

The importance of homogeneity of the behavior sequences to the validity of the tests about sequences pooled across time or blocks cannot be overstressed. Hintzman (1972) and Gardner (1976) have given some simple examples extant in psychological research in which inappropriate pooling of data can lead researchers to conclusions that are not only misleading but are exactly the opposite of what is actually true. This effect, known as *Simpson's Paradox*, seems to be rediscovered periodically in the methodological literature.

THE COMPARISON OF INTERACTION TABLES

In an earlier section, the analyses were outlined in terms of single dyads only. Suppose that we have observed Antecedent–Consequent behavior sequences from each of M dyads and that we wish to determine whether or not the dyads are homogeneous—that is, we would like to know whether the interaction tables from each of the dyads can be considered as samples from the same general population. In this situation, we denote the (A_i-B_j) behavior pair for the mth dyad as $(A_i-B_j)_m$. The hypothesis of homogeneity of dyads can be given explicitly as

$$H: \quad P_m[B_j|A_i] = P[B_j|A_i], \qquad m = 1, 2, \ldots, M,$$

where $P_m[B_j|A_i]$ is the conditional probability of Consequent B_j given Antecedent A_i for the mth dyad. If we let f_{ijm} be the frequency of the $(A_i-B_j)_m$ behavior pairs, and f_{im}^A be the marginal frequency of the occurrence of Antecedent A_i for the mth dyad, then the estimated expected frequency of $(A_i-B_j)_m$ pairs is

$$\hat{F}_{ijm} = f_{im}^A(f_{ij}/f_i^A).$$

Also note that, unlike the notation used in earlier sections, f_{ij} and f_{ij}^A are the frequencies summed across dyads—that is,

$$f_{ij} = \sum_{m=1}^{M} f_{ijm},$$

and

$$f_i^A = \sum_{m=1}^{M} f_{im}^A.$$

In this situation, there are two hypotheses. The first concerns the homogeneity of the conditional probabilities across dyads for a given Antecedent A_i, and the second combines the separate tests for each antecedent to give an overall test of homogeneity. The hypothesis that the transitions are constant across dyads is:

$$H: \quad P_m[B_j|A_i] = P[B_j|A_i] \quad \begin{array}{l} j = 1, 2, \ldots, J, \\ m = 1, 2, \ldots, M. \end{array}$$

The test statistic for the Antecedent A_i is:

$$X_i^2 = \sum_{m=1}^{M} \sum_{j} \frac{[f_{ijm} - f_{im}^A(f_{ij}/f_i^A)]^2}{f_{im}^A(f_{ij}/f_i^A)}, \tag{7}$$

which is asymptotically distributed as chi-square with $(M-1)(J-1)$ degrees of freedom. There is a test of this sort for each Antecedent. If the test statistic achieves significance, then the hypothesis that the conditional probabilities are the same for each dyad is rejected.

The hypothesis of homogeneity of dyads across all antecedents may be stated as:

$$H: \quad P_m[B_j|A_i] = P[B_j|A_i] \quad \begin{aligned} i &= 1, 2, \ldots, I, \\ j &= 1, 2, \ldots, J. \\ m &= 1, 2, \ldots, M. \end{aligned}$$

The test statistic is given by:

$$X^2 = \sum_i X_i^2 = \sum_{m=1}^{M} \sum_{i,j} \frac{[f_{ijm} - f_{im}{}^A(f_{ij}/f_i{}^A)]^2}{f_{im}{}^A(f_{ij}/f_i{}^A)}, \tag{8}$$

which is asymptotically distributed as chi-square with $I(M-1)(J-1)$ degrees of freedom. It should be noted that the tests given by Eqs. (7) and (8) test the conditional probabilities $P_m[B_j|A_i]$. Thus, because the tests do not compare the overall frequencies of behavior pairs, the fact that the observation sequence for one dyad may include 100 behavior pairs, and another may include 50 pairs, is neither relevant to nor tested by the statistic. Nonetheless, if the hypothesis of homogeneity of dyads is rejected, it is sometimes desirable to compare the dyads. In this case, one can compute a statistic that tests the conditional independence in each dyad (Hypothesis 4A) and compare the individual values of X^2 directly. However, if the number of observations for each dyad is different, and the hypothesis of independence is rejected, the X^2 values are affected by the number of observations. To remove this context effect so that the statistics may be compared, one may compute either X^2/n for each dyad, or the Cramér coefficient, V, which is discussed later.

THE ANALYSIS OF SINGLE SEQUENCES

The earlier discussion focused on the transitions between antecedents, A_i, and consequents, B_j. Suppose that intead of observing antecedent–consequent pairs, we observe a sequence of I behaviors $A_i(1), A_j(2), \ldots, A_k(t), \ldots$. An observation is made at each time period t, and we assume that the observed behaviors are mutually exclusive and exhaustive. Suppose further that observations are made on each of T time periods. Let f_{ij} be the frequency of transitions from state (behavior) i to state (behavior) j. Then there will be

TABLE 4.5
Transition Matrix of Behaviors

Behavior at Time $t-1$	Behavior at Time t					
	A_1	A_2	$\ldots$	A_j	$\ldots$	A_I
A_1	f_{11}	f_{12}	$\ldots$	f_{1j}	$\ldots$	f_{1I}
A_2	f_{21}	f_{22}	$\ldots$	f_{2j}	$\ldots$	f_{2I}
$\vdots$	$\vdots$	$\vdots$		$\vdots$		$\vdots$
A_i	f_{i1}	f_{i2}	$\ldots$	f_{ij}	$\ldots$	f_{iI}
$\vdots$	$\vdots$	$\vdots$		$\vdots$		$\vdots$
A_I	f_{I1}	f_{I2}	$\ldots$	f_{Ij}	$\ldots$	f_{II}

$n = T - 1$ transitions. These transitions may be recorded in a transition matrix like that in Table 4.5. In analyzing single behavior sequences, the transition table may be formed by taking time-based transitions or behavior-based transitions, as in the dyadic interaction analyses discussed earlier. However, a problem in analysis arises, because a transition between a behavior and itself is impossible when forming behavior-based transition frequency tables. That is, when the behaviors themselves form the basis of the transitions, transitions from $A_i(t)$ to $A_i(t + 1)$ are not possible. Thus the transition frequency table would have zeros on the diagonal. This constraint requires that the analysis be modified to take this aspect into account.

The two types of analyses are discussed in turn: First an analysis based upon time-based transitions is presented, and then analytic procedures for behavior-based transition frequency tables are outlined.

Time-Based Transition Frequency Analysis

The analyses outlined here are those that focus upon the degree of dependency among the behaviors. Because part of the subsequent discussion requires it, let f_{ijk} be the frequency of double transitions i to j to k—that is, f_{ijk} is the frequency of transitions from behaviors $A_i(t)$ to $A_j(t + 1)$ to $A_k(t + 2)$ for all time periods t. If we assume that the observed behavior sequence has stabilized—that is, that transitions between states or behaviors are not a function of time—then the methods to be outlined are appropriate. (The stability of the sequence of behavior can be assessed by the methods outlined earlier.) There are several hypotheses of common interest. These are hypotheses about the "order" of the matrix.

By order we mean the extent of sequential dependencies in the data. If the behavior at time t is well predicted by the behaviors at time $t - 1$ and $t - 2$, then the transition matrix is said to be of *order 2*. That is, if

$$P[\ldots A_iA_jA_k \ldots] = P[A_iA_j]\ P[A_k|A_iA_j]$$

for all states i, then the sequence is of order 2. That is, the behavior at any time is dependent on the behaviors that occurred during the previous two time periods. If the dependency extends only to the previous time period, then the sequence is of *order 1*. For sequences of order 1,

$$P[A_k|A_iA_j] = P[A_k|A_j],$$

or

$$P[\ldots A_iA_j \ldots] = P[A_i]P[A_j|A_i].$$

The analysis for order proceeds in a stepwise fashion. The first hypothesis to be considered tests for dependency of order 2 (or greater) against an hypothesis of order 1 (or less)—that is,

H'_2: The sequence is of order ≤ 1.
H_2: The sequence is of order ≥ 2.

The test of H'_2 is given by

$$X^2 = \sum_{i,j,k} = \frac{[f_{ijk} - f_{ij}(f_{jk}/f_j)]^2}{f_{ij}(f_{jk}/f_j)}, \tag{9}$$

which is asymptotically distributed as chi-square with $I(I-1)^2$ degrees of freedom. The quantity f_{ij} is the frequency of (ij) transitions, f_{jk} is the frequency of (jk) transitions, and f_j is the frequency of occurrence of behavior J. Then under hypothesis H'_2, the estimate of the expected transition probability is $\hat{p}_{k,j} = f_{jk}/f_j$, and the expected frequency of the (ijk) triple is $f_{ij}(f_{jk}/f_j)$, and the test in Eq. (9) follows. If hypothesis H'_2 is rejected, then the sequence is of order 2 (or greater).

Suppose that H'_2 is not rejected. Then it is appropriate to test whether the sequence is of order 0 or 1. A sequence of order 0 implies that the observed behavior is not dependent on any previous behaviors, whereas a sequence of order 1 implies that the observed sequence is dependent on the last occurring behavior. The hypotheses in this case are:

H_0: The sequence is of order 0.
H_1: The sequence is of order 1.

If the hypothesis H_0 is true, the estimate of p_j is $\hat{p}_j = f_j/(T-1)$. The test of H_0 is then

$$X^2 = \sum_{i,j} \frac{\{f_{ij} - f_i[f_j/(T-1)]\}^2}{f_i[f_j/(T-1)]}, \tag{10}$$

which is asymptotically distributed as chi-square with $(I-1)^2$ degrees of freedom. If H_0 is rejected, then the sequence is of order 1 (or greater). If the test for order 2 was done earlier, rejection of H_0 implies only that the sequence is of order 1. In situations in which only dependency or no dependency is to be tested, then only the test of order 0 versus 1 is required.

A word of caution about sequential analysis is appropriate. It is often thought that certain patterned sequences defy analysis by the methods described here. However, the pair of tests [Eqs. (9) and (10)] can reveal that patterning is present. Consider first a sequence of single alternations (...121212...). Such a sequence results in the 1st-order and 2nd-order transition frequency tables in the upper portion of Table 4.6. Note that because of the transition patterns, there are empty cells in the frequency

TABLE 4.6
Transition Frequency Matrices for Certain Patterned Sequences

Single Alternation (... 121212 ...)

	Time $t+1$				1 Time $t+1$		2 Time $t+1$	
						Time $t+2$		
Time t	1	2		Time t	1	2	1	2
1	0	X		1	0	X	0	0
2	X	0		2	0	0	X	0

1st-order frequencies · 2nd-order frequencies

Double Alternation (... 1122112211 ...)

	Time $t+1$				1 Time $t+1$		2 Time $t+1$	
						Time $t+2$		
Time t	1	2		Time t	1	2	1	2
1	Y	Y		1	0	0	Y	Y
2	Y	Y		2	Y	Y	0	0

1st-order frequencies · 2nd-order frequencies

Note: The frequencies in the upper matrices are $X = (T-1)/2$.
The frequencies in the lower matrices are $Y = (T-1)/4$.

tables, and note that the nonzero cells have equal frequencies. The test for a 2nd-order table yields $X^2 = 0$, and the hypothesis of a sequence of order 0 *or* 1 is not rejected. The test for order 0 yields $X^2 = T - 1$, where T is the number of time periods. Clearly, if T is even moderately large, the hypothesis of independence is rejected in favor of the hypothesis of a sequence of order 1. These tests are in accord with what one would expect. Next, consider a sequence of double alternations (...1122112211...). The transition frequency tables are summarized in the lower portion of Table 4.6. In this case, the cell entries for the 1st-order transition frequency matrix are all equal. The 2nd-order transition frequency matrix contains four empty cells, and the four nonzero cells contain equal frequencies. If the order tests are done in the appropriate sequence—the test for order 2 versus order 1, followed by the test for order 1 versus order 0—then the results are clear. The test for order 2 yields $X^2 = (T - 1)/2$, which is signficiant for moderate T. Thus the proper inference that the sequence is of order 2 will be drawn, and no further testing is necessary. However, if the test of order 0 versus order 1 were done first, a serious error would result, because that test would yield $X^2 = 0$, which is not significant. Because the tests are hierarchical, the knowledgeable researcher would stop testing for order with the first significant test statistic; thus the test for order 0 would not be done.

Tests similar to those presented here may be used to test for any order of dependency. However, most needs are met by the tests for order 0, 1, and 2. Should extended tests be necessary, references should be consulted, especially Anderson and Goodman (1957) and Kullback et al. (1962).

Behavior-Based Transition Frequency Analysis

When the transition frequencies are behavior-based, only transitions from one behavior to another are observed and coded. Consequently, the behavior transition matrix has entries of zero on the diagonal, because $f_{ii} = 0$ for all behaviors A_i. Thus the behavior transition matrix looks like that summarized in Table 4.7. In this situation, the frequencies of zero *on the diagonal* are called *structural* zeros to differentiate them from observed frequencies of zero. A structural zero is one constrained by the experimental design to be zero. An observed frequency of zero represents the transition frequency between two behaviors (states) that, although *experimentally* possible, is not observed.

The technique of the previous section must be modified to take into account the constraints imposed by structural zeros in determining the expected values and the degrees of freedom for the test of independence. Unfortunately, the expected values cannot be computed in closed form (i.e., by a simple formula). However, an iterative procedure may be used to determine the expected values in which they are estimated by a series of successive approximations until the values converge and become stable. The

TABLE 4.7
Behavior-Based Transition Matrix

Behavior	Behavior at Time t					
at Time $t - 1$	A_1	A_2	...	A_j	...	A_I
A_1	0	f_{12}	...	f_{1j}	...	f_{1I}
A_2	f_{21}	0	...	f_{2j}	...	f_{2I}
$\vdots$	$\vdots$	$\vdots$		$\vdots$		$\vdots$
A_i	f_{i1}	f_{i2}	...	f_{ij}	...	f_{iI}
$\vdots$	$\vdots$	$\vdots$		$\vdots$		$\vdots$
A_I	f_{I1}	f_{I2}	...	f_{Ij}	...	0

Note: Behavior $A_j(t)$ is the tth behavior observed in the sequence. Coded frequencies are the *transitions* between behaviors, $A_i(t - 1)$ to $A_j(t)$.

procedure, although straightforward, is rather cumbersome, and only the necessary formulas and procedures are given here. To clarify the technique, a worked example is given in Appendix A of this chapter.

The hypothesis that the observed behavior $A_i(t)$ is independent of the observed behavior $A_j(t - 1)$ given that the behavior transitions $A_i(t - 1) \rightarrow A_i(t)$ are not possible is usually called an hypothesis of *quasi-independence*, because "true" independence is not possible. True independence would be stated as:

$H: \quad p_{ij} = p_i^A p_j^B.$

The hypothesis of quasi-independence states that there exist some numbers g_i^A for each row i and g_j^B for each column j such that $p_{ij} = g_i^A g_j^B$, for all $i \neq j$. That is, the hypothesis to be tested is:

$H: \quad p_{ij} = g_i^A g_j^B \quad$ for all $i \neq j.$

Note that the hypothesis states that the probability that an observation falls in the (ij)th cell is determined completely by some *row* index (g_i^A) and some *column* index (g_j^B). The test for this hypothesis is:

$$X^2 = \sum_{i,j} \frac{[f_{ij} - \hat{F}_{ij}^{(u)}]^2}{\hat{F}_{ij}^{(u)}}, \quad i \neq j. \tag{11}$$

which is asymptotically distributed as chi-square with $(I - 1)^2 - I = I^2 - 3I + 1$ degrees of freedom. If the hypothesis H is rejected, then we conclude that the behaviors are sequentially dependent. As for the tests for time-based transition frequency tables, it is assumed that the sequence of behaviors is stable—that is, the transitions are not a function of time. We now describe the method for determining the expected values $\hat{F}_{ij}^{(u)}$.

Iteration Procedure for Expected Values. Where there are diagonal cells missing, the expected values must be found for $I(I-1)$ cells. The estimation of the expected values proceeds in a series of steps, and at each step the estimated expected values are refined. The expected values at iteration u are labeled $\hat{F}_{ij}^{(u)}$.

Step a. Set $u = 0$, and set

$$\hat{F}_{ij}^{(o)} = 1 \quad \text{if } i \neq j, \text{ and}$$

$$\hat{F}_{ij}^{(o)} = 0 \quad \text{if } i = j.$$

That is, the expected values off the diagonal are set initially to 1, and those on the diagonal are set to 0.

Step b. Set $u = u + 1$.

Step c. Calculate new estimates of expected values by means of the formula:

$$\hat{F}_{ij}^{(2u-1)} = \frac{\hat{F}_{ij}^{(2u-2)} f_i^A}{\sum_k \hat{F}_{ik}^{(2u-2)}}$$

$$= \frac{\hat{F}_{ij}^{(2u-2)} f_i^A}{\hat{F}_i^{A(2u-2)}}, \tag{12}$$

where $\hat{F}_i^{A(2u-2)}$ is the sum of the estimated expected values in the ith row that were determined at step $2u - 2$ (the previous step).

Step d. Calculate new estimates of expected values by means of the formula:

$$\hat{F}_{ij}^{(2u)} = \frac{\hat{F}_{ij}^{(2u-1)} f_j^B}{\sum_k \hat{F}_{kj}^{(2u-1)}}$$

$$= \frac{\hat{F}_{ij}^{(2u-1)} f_j^B}{\hat{F}_j^{B(2u-1)}}, \tag{13}$$

where $\hat{F}_j^{B(2u-1)}$ is the sum of the estimated expected values in the jth column that were determined at step $2u - 1$ (the previous step).

Step e. Are *all* estimated expected values essentially unchanged from those determined on the previous step? If so, then use these estimates as the expected values in Eq. (11). If they are not the same, go to Step *b* and continue through the sequence again.

At each step the expected values on the diagonal are equal to zero; thus actual computation of them by the iterative procedure is not necessary. Also, it should be clear that the test is appropriate only when more than two different behaviors are observed in the sequence ($I > 2$), because if there are only two behaviors, the sequence necessarily consists only of alternations. The two equations [(12) and (13)] are necessary because they adjust the expected values as a function of the row sums (f_i^A) and the column sums (f_j^B), respectively. Thus on each "pass" through the iteration procedure, there are two different adjustments to the expected values.

These methods may be extended to situations in which there are structural zeros off the diagonal as well, which would occur when certain behavioral transitions are not possible. In such cases, the estimated expected frequency for each cell in which there is a structural zero is indicated at Step *a* by setting the corresponding $\hat{F}_{ij}^{(o)} = 0$ and by reducing the degrees of freedom for the test by 1 for each additional constraint imposed. More extended discussion of these procedures may be found in Bishop et al. (1975, chap. 5), Goodman (1968), and Smith (1973).

MEASURES OF ASSOCIATION
IN BEHAVIOR SEQUENCES

The methods described earlier for the analysis of interaction sequences dealt primarily with the testing of hypotheses of various types of independence of Antecedent–Consequent transitions for dyads and behavior transitions in general. Given dependency in the transition table, it would be useful to determine the *degree* of dependence or relation between the variables A and B. In this section, we describe two approaches to the analysis of the degree of relation. We begin by describing a general measure of association and proceed to techniques based upon the asymmetrical or sequential nature of antecedent–consequent behavior sequences and behavior sequences in general. As in the earlier discussion of contingency tables, we make no assumption about any ordering of the variables (A or B).

The Cramér Statistic, *V*

The first index to be described is a measure of the degree of relation between the two variables A and B. The parameter ϕ_c for measuring the relation was proposed by Cramer and is defined by the expression

$$\phi_c^2 = \left(\sum_{i,j} \frac{p_{ij}^2}{p_i^A p_j^B} - 1 \right) \Big/ [\min(I,J) - 1], \tag{14}$$

where $\min(I,J)$ is the smaller of I and J, the number of rows and columns, respectively. If the variables are independent, then $\phi_c = 0$. The parameter is estimated by:

$$V^2 = \left(\sum_{i,j} \frac{f_{ij}^2}{f_i^A f_j^B} - 1 \right) \Big/ [\min(I,J) - 1]. \tag{15}$$

This statistic is related to the chi-square statistic for testing the independence of the two variables [see Hypothesis 4, Eq. (4)]. The relation is:

$$X^2 = V^2 n [\min(I,J) - 1].$$

The Cramér statistic V varies from 0 to 1, and as an index of dependence, its significance may be tested by means of the chi-square statistic to which it is related [Eq. (4)]. The quantity V^2 can be interpreted as an index of the squared discrepancy of observed and expected frequencies. The statistic is especially useful in comparing several tables that differ both in sample size and the degree of fit to independence. Other properties of the statistic are that its value is unchanged by interchanging rows or columns, and its value is identical (except for sign) to the Pearson product-moment correlation if the contingency table is 2 × 2. More extended discussion of the Cramér statistic may be found in Hammond, Householder, and Castellan (1970) and Hays (1973).

Asymmetrical Association and the Lambda Statistic, L_B

In the analyses of sequences of Antecedent–Consequent pairs, it is not always satisfactory to analyze and test for independence (that $p_{ij} = p_i^A p_j^B$). The Antecedent–Consequent ordering in the behavior sequence leads to the need for a measure based upon the "asymmetry" of the situation—that is, we often are interested in how well the Antecedents "predict" the Consequents, but the converse relation between Consequents and Antecedents is of less (or no) interest. Many indices have been proposed, perhaps the most useful of which is the *lambda statistic* of Goodman and Kruskal (1954).[2] Like the Cramér

---

[2]Although Goodman and Kruskal traced the index back to work of Guttman in 1941, the index is usually associated with them because of their series of papers containing extensive discussions of the index λ—among others—beginning in 1954.

statistic, V, it makes few assumptions about the categories. The index is designed to assess the relative decrease in the unpredictability of consequent behavior B (variable B) when the Antecedent behavior A (variable A) is known—that is, it is a measure of the proportional reduction in error in predicting B when A is known.

If we let $P[\text{Error}]$ be the probability of an error in predicting B and let $P[\text{Error}|A]$ be the probability of an error when the Antecedent behavior A is *known*, the general form of the index may be written as:

$$\lambda_B = \frac{P[\text{Error}] - P[\text{Error}|A]}{P[\text{Error}]}.$$

In order to calculate λ_B, we need to find the two probabilities, $P[\text{Error}]$ and $P[\text{Error}|A]$. Intuitively, the best guess of B when the Antecedent is unknown is to choose that B_j with the largest probability of occurrence, p_j^B. Similarly, if one knows the antecedent A_i, one would choose that Consequent behavior B with the largest probability of occurrence given A_i. Accordingly, let

$$p_m^B = \max_j p_j^B$$

denote the *largest* of the marginal probabilities p_j^B, $j = 1, 2, \ldots, J$, and let

$$p_{im} = \max_j p_{ij}$$

be the *largest* joint probability in the ith row (for Antecedent A_i); then $1 - p_m^B$ is the probability of an error in prediction of B when A is unknown, and $1 - \Sigma_i p_{im}$ is the probability of an error in the prediction of B when the Antecedent is known. The measure of association would be:

$$\lambda_B = \frac{\Sigma_i p_{im} - p_m^B}{1 - p_m^B}. \tag{16}$$

The index λ_B has several properties that are especially important to its proper interpretation:

1. It may vary from 0 to 1.
2. It is 0 if and only if A is of no help in predicting B.
3. It is 1 only if there is complete predictability.
4. If A and B are independent, then $\lambda_B = 0$. However, $\lambda_B = 0$ does not imply independence.
5. The value of λ_B is not affected by permutations of rows (or columns) of the frequency table.

If we knew the probabilities in Eq. (16), our task would be simple. However, because the probabilities are usually unknown, the probabilities and hence λ_B must be estimated. The appropriate estimate is:

$$L_B = \frac{\Sigma_i f_{im} - f_m^B}{n - f_m^B},$$ (17)

where f_{im} is the largest frequency in the ith row and f_m^B is the largest column marginal frequency f_j^B. The statistic L_B thus measures the relative decrease in the error of prediction of behavior B when one knows the Antecedent behavior A_i.

In order to illustrate the computation of L_B, a set of artificial data are summarized in Table 4.8. The data consist of 60 Antecedent–Consequent pairs. The computed value of L_B is .30, which indicates that there is a 30% decrease in the error of prediction of the behavior B when the Antecedent behavior A_i is known. The reader can verify that the probability of an error decreases from .717 to .5.

TABLE 4.8
Artificial Data for Computation of L_B

Antecedent	Consequent				Total
	B_1	B_2	B_3	B_4	
A_1	10	5	3	3	21
A_2	1	3	12	3	19
A_3	4	6	2	8	20
Total	15	14	17	14	60

$\Sigma_i f_{im} = 10 + 12 + 8 = 30, \quad f_m^B = 17$

$$L_B = \frac{30 - 17}{60 - 17} = \frac{13}{43} = .30$$

$$S(L_B) = \sqrt{\frac{(n - \Sigma_i f_{im})(\Sigma_i f_{im} + f_m^B - 2 \Sigma' f_{im})}{(n - f_m^B)^3}}$$

$$= \sqrt{\frac{(60 - 30)[30 + 17 - (2 \cdot 12)]}{(60 - 17)^3}}$$

$$= .115$$

Hypothesis Testing and Confidence Intervals. The statistic L_B has a complicated sampling distribution. However, for large cell frequencies f_{ij}, the asymptotic distribution is approximately normal. Thus it is possible to test various hypotheses about λ_B. Suppose that we wish to test the hypothesis:

$$H_o: \quad \lambda_B = \lambda_{Bo},$$

that is, we wish to test the hypothesis that λ_B has a particular value other than 0 or 1. We make use of the following result due to Goodman and Kruskal (1963, 1972). The statistic,

$$z = \frac{L_B - \lambda_{Bo}}{\sqrt{\dfrac{(n - \Sigma_i f_{im}) (\Sigma_i f_{im} + f_m{}^B - 2 \Sigma' f_{im})}{(n - f_m{}^B)^3}}}, \tag{18}$$

has an asymptotically unit normal distribution (i.e., a normal distribution with mean 0 and standard deviation 1). The summation $\Sigma' f_{im}$ is the sum of all of the *maximum* frequencies in the *column* associated with $f_m{}^B$. If there is only one maximum in that column, then $\Sigma' f_{im} = f_{im}$. As an example, for the hypothesis, $H_o: \lambda_B = .10$, significance level $\alpha = .05$, and the data in Table 4.8, $z = (.30 - .10)/.115 = 1.74$, and we can reject the hypothesis H_o that the value of λ_B is .10; that is, we may conclude that the decrease in error in predictability of B when A is known exceeds 10%. [It should be noted that the test, $H_o: \lambda_B = 0$, is not possible because Eq. (18) is not correct in that case.] Tests for hypotheses that λ_B has a particular value other than 0 can be one-tailed or two-tailed.

The denominator of Eq. (18) is the asymptotic standard error of L_B. In the subsequent discussion, it will be convenient to denote the asymptotic standard error as $S(L_B)$:

$$S(L_B) = \sqrt{\dfrac{(n - \Sigma_i f_{im}) (\Sigma_i f_{im} + f_m{}^B - 2 \Sigma' f_{im})}{(n - f_m{}^B)^3}} \tag{19}$$

It should be noted that this standard error depends on the pattern of frequencies within the table and not only the total number of observations. The computation for the asymptotic standard error for the data in Table 4.8 is outlined in that table, and the value .115 was obtained.

An approximate confidence interval for λ_B can be found. Suppose that we want the $100(1 - \alpha)\%$ confidence interval. Then if we let $z_{\alpha/2}$ be the abscissa of the unit normal distribution, where $(\alpha/2)$ of the distribution is above $z_{\alpha/2}$, the confidence interval[3] is:

$$L_B - z_{\alpha/2}S(L_B) \le \lambda_B \le L_B + z_{\alpha/2}S(L_B). \tag{20}$$

The 95% confidence interval for λ_B for the data in Table 4.8 is given by:

$$.30 - 1.96\,(.115) \le \lambda_B \le .30 + 1.96\,(.115)$$
$$.07 \le \lambda_B \le .53.$$

Comparison of Two or More λ_B's.   Using the asymptotic standard error $S(L_B)$, it is possible to test differences between the values of λ_B for two frequency tables (sets of data). Let $L_B^{(k)}$, $\lambda_B^{(k)}$, and $S(L_B)^{(k)}$ be the estimate L_B, parameter λ_B, and asymptotic standard error $S(L_B)$, respectively, for frequency table k. Then the statistic

$$z = \frac{[L_B^{(1)} - L_B^{(2)}] - [\lambda_B^{(1)} - \lambda_B^{(2)}]}{\sqrt{[S(L_B)^{(1)}]^2 + [S(L_B)^{(2)}]^2}} \tag{21}$$

is distributed as a unit-normal variate and provides a test for the difference between two λ_B's. The hypothesis tested is:

$$H:\quad \lambda_B^{(1)} - \lambda_B^{(2)} = \delta.$$

The common form of the test is that two parameters are equal ($\delta = 0$).

From the preceding argument, it can be shown that the $100(1 - \alpha)\%$ confidence interval for the difference $\lambda_B^{(1)} - \lambda_B^{(2)}$ is given by:

$$L_B^{(1)} - L_B^{(2)} \pm z_{\alpha/2} \sqrt{[S(L_B)^{(1)}]^2 + [S(L_B)^{(2)}]^2}. \tag{22}$$

Suppose that we have a set of M frequency tables, one for each of M dyads (or M different behavior sequences), have the computed statistic $L_B^{(m)}$ for each table, and wish to test the hypothesis:

$$H:\quad \lambda_B^{(1)} = \lambda_B^{(2)} = \ldots = \lambda_B^{(M)}.$$

If the hypothesis is true, and if the number of observations in each table is large, the statistic

---

[3]If the confidence limits obtained by use of the equation extend below 0 or above 1, they should be reduced so that the lower limit is not below 0 or does not extend above 1.

$$\sum_{m=1}^{M} \frac{(L_B^{(m)} - \bar{L}_B)^2}{[S(L_B)^{(m)}]^2} \tag{23}$$

is approximately distributed as chi-square with $M - 1$ degrees of freedom and is a test of the hypothesis. The term $\bar{L}_B$ is a weighted average of the separate $L_B^{(m)}$'s—viz.,

$$\bar{L}_B = \frac{\sum_{m=1}^{M} \{L_B^{(m)} / [S(L_B)^{(m)}]^2\}}{\sum_{m=1}^{M} [S(L_B)^{(m)}]^{-2}}. \tag{24}$$

The Measure of Association, λ_A. Thus far the discussion of the measures of asymmetric association has focused on the prediction of Consequents (Variable B) from Antecedents (Variable A). There is also a complementary measure of association, λ_A, which is a measure of the relative decrease in error of prediction of Antecedents from Consequents. The earlier discussion applies to the measure, λ_A, and the formulas may be used with a suitable change in subscripts:

$$\lambda_A = \frac{\sum_j p_{mj} - p_m^A}{1 - p_m^A}. \tag{25}$$

The estimator of λ_A is:

$$L_A = \frac{\sum_j f_{mj} - f_m^A}{n - f_m^A}, \tag{26}$$

and the asymptotic standard error of L_A is:

$$S(L_A) = \sqrt{\frac{(n - \sum_j f_{mj})(\sum_j f_{mj} + f_m^A - 2 \sum^c f_{mj})}{(n - f_m^A)^3}}, \tag{27}$$

where $\sum^c f_{mj}$ is the sum of all of the *maximum* frequencies in the *row* associated with f_m^A. For the data in Table 4.8, $L_A = .38$, and $S(L_A) = .122$. Thus, for these data, knowledge of the Consequent behavior at a particular time enables one to significantly reduce the error of prediction of the Antecedent behavior that occurred at that time.

It should be noted that L_B could be large while L_A would be quite small (and vice versa). For example, consider the data in Table 4.9. Computation of L_A and L_B by means of Eqs. (26) and (17), respectively, yields $L_A = 1.0$ and $L_B = .7$. Thus, although there is a 70% reduction in the error of prediction of Consequent B when the Antecedent A is known, there is a complete

TABLE 4.9
Artificial Data for Computation of L_A and L_B

Antecedent	Consequent					Total
	B_1	B_2	B_3	B_4	B_5	
A_1	5	0	15	0	0	20
A_2	0	10	0	0	25	35
A_3	0	0	0	20	0	20
Total	5	10	15	20	25	75

$L_A = 1$, $L_B = .7$, and $L_{AB} = .833$

elimination of error in the prediction of Antecedents from Consequents. Examination of Table 4.9 reveals the reason: Whereas knowledge of the Antecedent reduces the number of possible Consequent behaviors from five to either one or two, each of the Consequent behaviors is preceded by only *one* Antecedent. For example, either B_1 or B_2 follows A_1, but A_1 always precedes B_3. The following general rule can be stated: *If each column (row) of the frequency table contains only one nonzero cell, then L_A (or L_B) will be equal to 1.*

The Symmetrical Index, λ_{AB}. Suppose that for a given dyad or sequence of behaviors, one wished to achieve a *general* sense of predictability. The measures λ_A and λ_B each give an asymmetrical index of the predictability. For example, suppose that we have a situation in which at some times, we are concerned with the predictability of B from A, and at other times with the predictability of A from B. That is, we might choose a *single* behavior and want to know how well it can be predicted—in the case of a dyad, on the basis of the behavior of the other individual, or in the case of a single behavior seuqence, the behavior occurring either prior to or after the behavior in question. That is, we need an index of general predictability. Such an index is λ_{AB}:

$$\lambda_{AB} = \frac{\Sigma_i \, p_{im} + \Sigma_j \, p_{mj} - p_m^B - p_m^A}{2 - p_m^B - p_m^A}. \tag{28}$$

The index λ_{AB} is the average reduction in error of prediction when the prediction categories (A or B) are chosen at random. It is always between λ_A and λ_B but, in general, is *not* the average of the two indices. The estimate of λ_{AB} is:

$$L_{AB} = \frac{\Sigma_i \, f_{im} + \Sigma_j \, f_{mj} - f_m^B - f_m^A}{2n - f_m^B - f_m^A}. \tag{29}$$

For the data of Table 4.8, $L_{AB} = .34$; for the data of Table 4.9, $L_{AB} = .83$. The asymptotic standard error of L_{AB}, denoted as $S(L_{AB})$, can be used to test hypotheses about, and obtain confidence intervals for, the parameter λ_{AB}. Its form is rather complicated and cumbersome. Rather than present it here, its formula and an illustration of its computation using the data of Table 4.8 are given in Appendix B of this chapter.

Summary. The asymmetrical indices λ_B and λ_A provide information about the nature of dependency and relation in behavior sequences that complements the chi-square contingency analyses discussed earlier. Just as there are various types of independence that may be considered, the degree of predictability (or error reduction) of one variable given another depends on what sort of predictability is to be considered.

The aforementioned lambda measures assume only that the data are categorical. The sampling theory makes additional assumptions—that the various cell and marginal maximums (in the population) are unique; that no marginal probability is 1; and that the population lambda being considered (λ_A, λ_B, and λ_{AB}) is not 0 or 1. Although the assumption that the parameter is not equal to 0 limits the usefulness of the application of the asymptotic theory in hypothesis testing, the limitation is not serious if the researcher is cautious in the interpretation of the test.

When the categories in the frequency table are ordered, the ordering adds information to the table. Although not common, such orderings can occur in many ways in behavioral analysis—for example, if the possible behaviors consisted of a series of graded response categories. A useful measure for such ordered groupings was proposed by Somers (1962). The reader is referred to that reference and Goodman and Kruskal (1972) for details of its computation and use.

CONCLUSION

Throughout this chapter, many procedures for analyzing sequences have been presented. It was noted that in the analysis of sequences it is important to recognize that many hypotheses are relevant and should be tested. The Pearson chi-square statistics and the lambda coefficients provide complementary information about the structure of the sequences.

As the various techniques were presented, some cautionary comments were made. It is worthwhile to restate and summarize some of those again. In analyzing a contingency table, the underlying models assume that the categories are mutually exclusive and exhaustive and that sampling from the population is random. However, we found that for certain tests dealing with hypotheses of homogeneity of conditional distributions (Hypotheses Type

4A and 4B) the sampling of the row (or column) variable need not be random or exhaustive; however, in such cases, care must be taken in drawing the proper inference. The specific hypothesis tested in such cases is one of homogeneity of the column (or row) variable for the selected row (or column) variates—it is not a test of independence of the variables. These differences in hypotheses are important even though the computational formulas for the tests are the same.

Another caution was that extreme care must be used in pooling tables across subjects (or across a third variable). This is because it is possible to obtain inversions of conditional probability orderings when nonhomogeneous tables based on different frequencies are pooled. Therefore, the careful researcher will test the hypothesis of homogeneity of subjects prior to pooling data. It might be noted that this is somewhat akin to the problem in the analysis of variance that arises when data are collapsed across factors that occur in significant two- and three-way interactions.

The cautions reiterated above do not weaken the tests. If one is cognizant of the assumptions involved in the various models used in analyzing sequences—or any data for that matter—one is on much firmer ground for drawing proper inferences.

It should be noted that the procedures presented for the analysis of dyadic sequences can be applied to any behavior sequence. The primary distinguishing characteristic of antecedent–consequent sequences is that the antecedent and consequent variables may be different in type and number of levels. Consequently, the tests for stability of sequences of events and for the comparison of frequency tables can be applied equally well to either dyadic sequences or single behavior sequences.

Finally, the reader should note that the discussion of techniques is not exhaustive and is only suggestive of the many possibilities. One should consult the rferences, especially the book by Bishop et al. (1975) and the paper by Kullback et al. (1962) to gain a more complete understanding of the methods and techniques available for analyzing sequences.

APPENDIX A:
THE ITERATIVE COMPUTATION OF
THE CHI-SQUARE STATISTIC FOR
BEHAVIOR-BASED TRANSITION MATRICES

In the test for quasi-independence [Eq. (11)], the expected values must be estimated by an iterative procedure. The procedure and formulas for the technique were described earlier [Eqs. (12) and (13)]. In this section, the test for quasi-independence is carried out for a sequence of behaviors. The reader should refer to the earlier discussion for a general outline of the method.

In an observational study, three behaviors were observed. The observational period consisted of 60 behaviors, and the sequence of transitions is summarized as follows:

Behavior at $t-1$	Behavior at t			
	A_1	A_2	A_3	f_i^A
A_1	—	12	8	20
A_2	13	—	9	22
A_3	6	11	—	17
f_j^B	19	23	17	59

In the following, computation of the expected value for one transition is illustrated at each iteration, and the table of estimated expected value at that iteration is given.

$\hat{F}_{12}^{(0)} = 1$

$\hat{F}_{ij}^{(0)}$:

0	1	1	2
1	0	1	2
1	1	0	2

$\hat{F}_{12}^{(1)} = \dfrac{1 \times 20}{2} = 10$

$\hat{F}_{ij}^{(1)}$:

0	10	10
11	0	11
8.5	8.5	0
19.5	18.5	21

$\hat{F}_{12}^{(2)} = \dfrac{10 \times 23}{18.5} = 12.4$

$\hat{F}_{ij}^{(2)}$:

0	12.4	8.1	20.5
10.7	0	8.9	19.6
8.3	10.6	0	18.8

$\hat{F}_{12}^{(3)} = \dfrac{12.4 \times 20}{20.5} = 12.1$

$\hat{F}_{ij}^{(3)}$:

0	12.1	7.9
12.0	0	9.9
7.5	9.5	0
19.5	21.6	17.9

After going through the iterations until $u = 5$, the expected values stabilize. The final estimated expected values are

$\hat{F}_{ij}^{(10)}$:

0	12.9	7.1
12.1	0	9.9
6.9	10.1	0

Using these expected values in Eq. (11), the value $X^2 = .50$ was obtained. Because this is distributed as chi-square with 1 degree of freedom, we cannot reject the hypothesis that the sequence of behaviors are sequentially independent.

APPENDIX B:
THE ASYMPTOTIC STANDARD ERROR OF L_{AB}

The asymptotic standard error of L_{AB} is needed to test hypotheses about λ_{AB} and in order to determine confidence intervals for λ_{AB}. The asymptotic standard error $S(L_{AB})$ is cumbersome to write down formally, although its computation is straightforward even if it appears formidable:

$$S(L_{AB}) = \frac{\sqrt{(2n - U_m)(2n - U_s)(U_m + U_s + 4n - 2U_\cdot) - 2(2n - U_m)^2(n - \Sigma^* f_{im}) - 2(2n - U_s)^2(n - f_{\cdot\cdot})}}{(2n - U_m)^2},$$

where

$U_m = f_m{}^A + f_m{}^B$,   which is the sum of the row marginal maximum and the column marginal maximum.

$U_s = \Sigma_i f_{im} + \Sigma_j f_{mj}$,   which is the sum of the maximums in each row and the maximums in each column.

$U_\cdot = \Sigma^r f_{im} + \Sigma^c f_{mj} + f_{\cdot m} + f_{m \cdot}$,

with the variables with the asterisked subscripts defined as the following:

$\Sigma^* f_{im}$ = the sum of those f_{im}'s that are also f_{mj}'s—that is, the sum of those f_{ij}'s that are *both* row and column maximums.

$f_{\cdot\cdot}$ = the f_{ij} that is in both the row in which $f_m{}^A$ is found *and* the column in which $f_m{}^B$ is found.

$f_{\cdot m}$ = the f_{im} that is in the same row in which $f_m{}^A$ is found.

$f_{m \cdot}$ = the f_{mj} that is in the same column in which $f_m{}^B$ is found.

The sums $\Sigma^r f_{im}$ and $\Sigma^c f_{mj}$ were defined earlier in the text.

As an illustration of the computation of $S(L_{AB})$, the data in Table 4.8 will be used. For those data,

$\Sigma_i f_{im} = 10 + 12 + 8 = 30$
$\Sigma_j f_{mj} = 10 + 6 + 12 + 8 = 36$
$f_{\cdot m} = 10$
$f_{m \cdot} = 12$
$f_{\cdot\cdot} = 3$

$$\Sigma^* f_{im} = 10 + 12 + 8 = 30$$
$$U_m = 21 + 17 = 38$$
$$U_s = 30 + 36 = 66$$
$$U\cdot = 12 + 10 + 10 + 12 = 44$$

$$S(L_{AB}) = \frac{\sqrt{(120 - 38)(120 - 66)(38 + 66 + 240 - 88) - 2(120 - 38)^2(60 - 30) - 2(120 - 66)^2(60 - 3)}}{(120 - 38)^2}$$

$$= \frac{\sqrt{397704}}{6724}$$

$$= .094.$$

ACKNOWLEDGMENTS

Preparation of this paper was supported in part by National Institute of Mental Health Grant MH-23563. The author would like to thank John Bates, Peter Brower, Robert Cairns, Robyn Dawes, and William Timberlake for their helpful comments on an early draft of the manuscript.

REFERENCES

Anderson, T. W., & Goodman, L. A. Statistical inference about Markov chains. *Annals of Mathematical Statistics,* 1957, *28,* 89–110.

Bishop, Y. M. M., Fienberg, S. E., & Holland, P. W. *Discrete multivariate analysis.* Cambridge, Mass.: MIT Press, 1975.

Bobbitt, R. A., Gourevitch, V. P., Miller, L. E., & Jensen, G. D. Dynamics of social interactive behavior: A computerized procedure for analyzing trends, patterns, and sequences. *Psychological Bulletin,* 1969, *71,* 110–121.

Castellan, N. J., Jr. On the partitioning of contingency tables. *Psychological Bulletin,* 1965, *64,* 330–338.

Chatfield, C. Statistical inference regarding Markov chain models. *Applied Statistics,* 1973, *22,* 7–20.

Delius, J. D. A stochastic analysis of the maintenance behaviour of skylarks. *Behaviour,* 1969, *33,* 137–178.

Fentress, J. C. Development and patterning of movement sequences in inbred mice. In J. A. Kiger (Ed.), *The biology of behavior.* Corvallis, Ore.: Oregon State University Press, 1972.

Gardner, M. On the fabric of inductive logic, and some probability paradoxes. *Scientific American,* 1976, *234*(3), 119–124.

Goodman, L. A. An analysis of cross-classified data: Independence, quasi-independence, and interaction in contingency tables with or without missing entries. *Journal of the American Statistical Association,* 1968, *63,* 1091–1131.

Goodman, L. A. The multivariate analysis of qualitative data: Interactions among multiple classifications. *Journal of the American Statistical Association,* 1970, *65,* 226–256.

Goodman, L. A., & Kruskal, W. H. Measures of association for cross classifications. *Journal of the American Statistical Association,* 1954, *49,* 732–764.

Goodman, L. A., & Kruskal, W. H. Measures of association for cross classifications. III: Approximate sampling theory. *Journal of the American Statistical Association,* 1963, *58,* 310–364.

Goodman, L. A., & Kruskal, W. H. Measures of association for cross classifications. IV: Simplification of asymptotic variances. *Journal of the American Statistical Association,* 1972, *67,* 415–421.

Hammond, K. R., Householder, J. E., & Castellan, N. J., Jr. *Introduction to the statistical method* (2nd ed.). New York: Knopf, 1970.

Hays, W. L. *Statistics for the social sciences* (2nd ed.). New York: Holt, Rinehart & Winston, 1973.

Hazlett, B. A., & Bossert, W. H. A statistical analysis of the aggressive communications systems of some hermit crabs. *Animal Behaviour,* 1965, *13,* 357–373.

Hinde, R. A., & Stevenson, J. G. Sequences of behavior. *Advances in the Study of Behavior,* 1969, *2,* 267–296.

Hintzman, D. L. On testing the independence of associations. *Psychological Review,* 1972, *79,* 261–264.

Kullback, S., Kupperman, M., & Ku, H. H. Tests for contingency tables and Markov chains. *Technometrics,* 1962, *4,* 573–608.

Larntz, K. Small-sample comparisons of exact levels for chi-squared goodness-of-fit statistics. *Journal of the American Statistical Association,* 1978, *73,* 253–263.

Lewis, G. H. The assumption of stationary parameters in theories of group discussion. *Behavioral Science,* 1970, *15,* 269–273.

Lytton, H., & Zwirner, W. Compliance and its controlling stimuli observed in a natural setting. *Developmental Psychology,* 1975, *11,* 769–779.

Maxwell, A. E. *Analysing qualitative data.* London: Methuen, 1961.

Raush, H. L. Interaction sequences. *Journal of Personality and Social Psychology,* 1965, *2,* 487–499.

Slater, P. J. B. Describing sequences of behavior. In P. P. G. Bateson & P. H. Klopfer (Eds.), *Perspectives in ethology.* New York: Plenum, 1973.

Smith, J. E. K. On tests of quasi-independence in psychological research. *Psychological Bulletin,* 1973, *80,* 329–333.

Somers, R. H. A new asymmetric measure of association for ordinal variables. *American Sociological Review,* 1962, *27,* 799–811.

Steinberg, J. B., & Conant, R. C. An informational analysis of the inter-male behaviour of the grasshopper *Chortophaga Viridifasciata. Animal Behaviour,* 1974, *22,* 617–627.

II ILLUSTRATIONS

The main justification for our concern with interactional methods is the promise that these procedures will help to yield answers to the essential issues of social development. How well do they live up to their promise? And how do investigators in fact cope with the several problems that have been identified?

The questions are best answered by the investigators themselves. Accordingly, the next three chapters are concerned with the results of the application of interactional methods. The areas selected for discussion—coercion in the family, social development in infancy, and play in kittens—underscore the flexibility of the procedures. Particular attention should be given to the several ways that these investigators have solved the problems raised in the earlier chapters of this volume. One sees vast differences among investigators in how they choose to dissect, clump, and analyze their data. Where G. R. Patterson finds computer analyses to be indispensable, M. West and C. Eckerman prefer to remain "close" to the natural phenomena and their functions. The reports differ as well in terms of the stage at which the work is reported. Patterson's chapter summarizes more than a decade of study of coercive families, and West's chapter is one of the first attempts to employ interactional methods in the study of play in young mammals.

All of the investigators seem willing to employ whatever techniques—at any stage of the investigation—that may enhance their understanding of the interchange. One other bond that ties the investigators together is the common process that they follow in reaching decisions about categories, codes, timing, and the like: In all cases, the decisions are made only following intensive and extended observations of the interactions-to-be-explained.

It is regrettable that this part must be so brief, due to space limitations. One of the major discoveries yielded by the procedures—the early development of high levels of social reciprocity—deserves more attention than it was given. This phenomenon may well be the key to solving one central issue of social development—namely, the continuity and change of individual differences in social behavior.

5 A Performance Theory for Coercive Family Interaction

Gerald R. Patterson
Oregon Research Institute

INTRODUCTION

Ethologists (Eibl-Eibesfeldt, 1970; Hinde, 1974) and ecological psychologists (Barker, 1963) emphasize the contribution of field observation data as a necessary first step in constructing socially relevant theories about social interaction.

Although some earlier writers (Barker, 1963) judged field studies and experimental manipulations to be antithetical modes of investigation, this is not in keeping with the modern ethological spirit. Currently, both field study and experimental manipulations are viewed as necessary but not sufficient procedures in building a social interaction theory. Presumably, both methods would be employed at all stages of investigating a problem. This is in contrast to the traditional study of children's aggressive behavior in which the bulk of the work has been carried out in the laboratory but the relevance of the findings remains to be established. Given the current commitment to laboratory analogue studies of aggression, it is entirely possible that field studies will show that the findings are irrelevant for many settings (e.g., in some settings, positive reinforcers are simply not dispensed contingent upon children's aggressive behaviors, or aggressive behaviors modeled in complex social situations may not be attended to and therefore have little impact). That being the case, even the most compelling laboratory evidence attesting to the significance of this or that variable is of little moment. For final status within a theory, a variable, like a successful debutante, must put in an appearance in the real world of social interaction.

need more field studies

The present report summarizes preliminary studies designed to describe determinants for children's aggressive behaviors performed in one setting. Aggression was defined as an *aversive* event dispensed *contingent* upon the behaviors of another person. A child who performs these at high rates and/or intensities is likely to be labeled as *aggressive*. Coercion is the label for the process by which these aversive events control dyadic interchanges. Coercion refers to only a limited subset of the broad spectrum of phenomena usually subsumed under the term *aggression*. Many aversive stimuli intrude upon the individual but are not necessarily contingent upon behavior (i.e., street noise, the dentist's drill). In that coercion emphasizes contingent arrangements, it is also differentiated from the traditional use to which the term *aversive* is put.

As a first step in developing a coercion theory, it was necessary to develop an observation code system (Jones, Reid, & Patterson, 1975; Patterson, Ray, Shaw, & Cobb, 1969; Reid, 1978). The code was used to collect sequential data in the homes of children referred for treatment as out of control and in the homes of matched normal children. These data were analyzed to determine whether there were reliable relationships between aversive behaviors of the problem child and those provided by members of the family. These analyses led to the development of a set of hypotheses that constitute the coercion theory. The hypotheses in turn generated a set of experimental studies to test some additional implications of these ideas. The fact that both kinds of analyses are still going on emphasizes the preliminary status of the theory.

It was assumed that the function of the variables defining coercion theory was to make predictions about ongoing social behaviors. The emphasis upon accounting for changes in performance differentiates it from earlier studies of aggression that focused upon the question of how the behavior was learned. To test this function, the coercion variables were analyzed to determine the extent to which they accounted for intra- and interindividual, as well as inter-response, variations in performance rates. The more variance accounted for, the greater the utility of such a theory.

The following sections summarize the main findings relating to the development of such a theory.

SOME CHARACTERISTICS OF
A PERFORMANCE THEORY

Repeated observations of the same child interacting with family members over a period of weeks could be used to delineate his behavioral repertoire. Each response in the code system could be described by its base rate of occurrence. Further examination of such data shows day-by-day variations in these base rate values. It is assumed that these day-by-day fluctuations are *not* due entirely to error of measurement but rather represent a summary of the thousands of social interchanges in which the child engages on any given day. Presumably, these probability values are changing continuously.[1] Although some merely fluctuate about a mean value, others describe systematic changes across time. A proper theory about performance in social setting should account for both types of changes.

If one accepts the basic premises of modeling theorists such as Bandura (1973), then it is reasonable to assume that in our society the average 3- or 4-year-old has already *learned* most, or all, of the garden-variety coercive behaviors. Presumably in our culture, this early acquisition is facilitated by the ubiquitous presence of coercive peer and adult models in the home, nursery school, literature, and TV. Observations in the homes of normal families and in nursery schools reveal rich opportunities for viewing not only the aggressive responses but also their relative payoffs. In three different studies, interactions in the homes of normal families showed consistently high rates of noxious behaviors (Fawl, 1963; Reid, 1978; Wahl, Johnson, Johanssen, & Martin, 1974). Thus most parents and children can be assumed to have acquired a varied repertoire of aggressive behaviors. However, there are large interindividual differences in performance rates for coercive behaviors. As shown by many investigators, there are also large day-by-day variations in the rate of performance for the individual child. Furthermore, there are large differences in the rates with which various coercive responses are performed (e.g., hitting occurs about once every 100 minutes in families of normal children, whereas whining occurs about once every 25 minutes). As viewed by the writer, the function of a coercion theory is to account for the variance generated by these different sources.

When analyzing the data for a single individual, it becomes apparent that many or most of the responses are autocorrelated. Given that a child is playing at t_1, the probability increases (over the base rate for play) that he will be playing at t_2. These serial dependencies seem to obtain whether the time intervals are seconds, minutes, or hours (Patterson, 1977b). One might think of social behavior as being run off in "chunks." Given this perspective, one would expect that the usual measure of base rates for coercive behaviors are highly correlated with the frequency and duration with which these chunks occur. The details of these relationships are considered in a later section. For the present, it is sufficient to place this chunking phenomenon in center stage as the focal concern for a theory about performance. At the present time, we

---

[1]Data reviewed in Jones et al. (1975) showed that the resulting hierarchies were relatively stable over a 2-week interval. The mean intraindividual correlation was .42 for the clinical sample and .37 for the matched normal sample. In these analyses, the distributions for each of the 29 code categories were converted to two scores. The correlations test for the stability of the ordinal rankings of these two scores.

are only beginning to understand the complexities associated with this problem.

As a working base, it is assumed that performance variations are controlled by *immediately impinging environmental events.* Certainly any theory of social behavior must eventually contain more than just information about the immediate antecedents for a response. However, it is a reasonable place from which to *begin.* For example, Altmann (1965) observed the social interactions of rhesus monkeys. Given information about the immediately prior behavior of other rhesus monkeys, he found a reduction of 2.9 bits in uncertainty when predicting ongoing interaction. This reduction was by way of contrast to knowing just the base rate values for the individual response categories. As shown in Fig. 5.1, further reductions were provided by information about second- and third-order antecedents. Similarly, for disturbed boys, observation data from Raush (1965) showed that immediately prior social behavior accounted for 30% of the variance in the performance of ongoing social behavior. Karpowitz (1971) showed that roughly half of the social events of

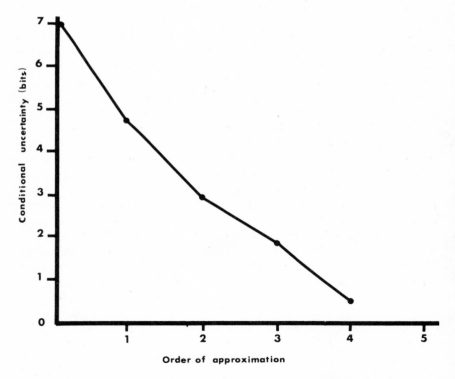

FIG. 5.1.   Relation between the order of approximation and the conditional uncertainty of any behavioral event. (From Altman, 1965.)

significance in controlling the child's behavior were to be found in the immediately preceding event. The general focus upon analyzing stimuli that control behavior is in keeping with the programmatic studies of both Berkowitz (1973) and Ulrich (1966).

If one views behavior as being typically "embedded" in ongoing dyadic or triadic process, then a focus upon immediacy and external control makes sense. The behavior of Person A has an impact on what the other person is *doing*, which in turn alters what Person A will do next. Bell (1968) and others have emphasized the need to study these bilateral effects. However, these interdependencies become the bane of existence for the scientist weaned upon the traditional modes of analyses. Sequential dyadic interactions have a number of complex dimensions, of which the bilateral effect is only one example. If one alternately arranges the coded behaviors for a mother and child on a time line, then by definition each event serves a dual role. It precedes an event on the time line, and it follows some other event. Thus it may both control that which follows and be controlled by that which precedes it.

In the current analyses, conditional probabilities describe a functional relation between a target event and a controlling stimulus. A controlling stimulus is one whose occurrence is associated with significant changes in the probability of events that precede or follow it on the time line. The conditional probability of event A, given event $B [p(A/B)]$ is compared to the base rate for event A [i.e., $p(A)$]. The analyses carried out thus far usually produce modest conditional probability values; they certainly do not suggest reflexive, or "wired in" relationships (Altmann, 1965; Kopfstein, 1972; Patterson, 1974; Raush, 1965). Rather, they are probabilistic statements that describe the subtlety and complexity of ongoing social behaviors.

At any given time, multiple stimuli impinge upon the organism; each may control different responses. Each event may control several behaviors. Several events may control the same response. In the following example, 15 hours of observations from a study by Patterson and Maerov (1976) were reanalyzed. The sequential interaction of a 6-year-old boy and his mother were described by 29 coded categories to identify networks controlling the occurrence of the boy's coercive whine and argue behaviors (R_j). This analysis focused only upon controlling events that immediately (6 seconds) preceded the responses.

Mother	Was Followed by Child	$p(R_j/A_i)$
Command	Argue	(.185)
	Whine	(.048)
Disapprove	Argue	(.115)
	Whine	(.153)

TABLE 5.1
Definitions of Terms for Stimulus Control and
Negative Reinforcement Arrangements

Events on the Time Line

1. A_i An antecedent event $\bar{A}_i$ would be an aversive antecedent event.
2. R_j A response following an event on the time line; $\bar{R}_j$ would be an aversive response.
3. $\bar{C}_i$ An aversive consequence that follows a response.
4. $\sim\bar{C}_i$ A nonaversive consequence could be *either* positive (C^+) or neutral (C).

Stimulus Control Arrangements

5. Acc   An acceleration consequence is associated with an increase in probability for the recurrence or persistence of R_2; i.e., $[p(R_2|R_1 - C_i) > p(R_2|R_1)]$.
6. Dc   A decelerating consequence is associated with a reduced probability for the occurrence of R_2; i.e., $p(R_2|R_1 - C) < p(R_2|R_1)$.
7. F^s A facilitating stimulus is an antecedent event associated with significant increase in the probability of R_1; i.e., $p(R_1|A_i) > p(R_j)$.
8. I^s An inhibiting stimulus is an antecedent event associated with a decrease in the probability of R_1; i.e., $p(R_1|A_i) < p(R_j)$.
9. $p(\bar{R}_2|\bar{R}_1 - \bar{C})$ The punishment acceleration index is the probability of a coercive response persisting, given the first was punished.

Arrangements Relating to Negative Reinforcement

10. NR   A negative reinforcement arrangement is defined by $\bar{A}_{11} - \bar{R}_{12} \sim \bar{C}_{21}$ in which an aversive antecedent is followed by an R_j, followed by removal of the aversive stimuli. The first subscript refers to the series (e.g., the first, or second, etc.). The second subscript identifies the person.
11. $p(\bar{A}|\bar{R})$ The probability of an aversive antecedent, given an aversive response.
12. $p(\bar{C}|\bar{R})$ The probability of an aversive consequence, given an aversive response.
13. $p(\sim\bar{C}|\bar{A} - \bar{R})$ The utility index for coercive response is defined by the probability that a coercive response will be effective in removing aversive antecedent stimuli.
14. $p(\bar{A} \rightarrow \sim\bar{C}|\bar{R})$ The NR schedule for a coercive response is defined by the proportion of coercive behaviors for which NR arrangements occur.

The base rate values for both coercive behaviors were about .01. Given that the mother's antecedent behaviors (A_i) provided a conditional probability of at least a fourfold increase over the base rate values, both antecedents would be thought of as facilitating events (F^s, see Table 5.1) for the two coercive responses. It is clear from these data that the boy's whine and argue behaviors could be activated by either the mother's asking him to do something or by her disapproving of something he has done. On days that the mother provided either or both of these at a high rate, then there should be concomitant increases in the rate of the boy's argue and whine. Both antecedents are functionally related to the same child behaviors; one might, therefore, think of responses as constituting a functionally defined class. By the same token, a class of antecedent events might be defined by their shared elicited responses. This kind of functional analysis was used by Patterson and Cobb (1973) to form two classes of coercive child behaviors that held across a sample of families. Members of the classes shared common networks of controlling antecedents.

The second kind of controlling events follow the response. For example, it is assumed that the reaction of the mother to the child's arguing and whining may alter the probability that whine or argue will persist into the next time frame. If she reiterates the command or disapproval, the coercive behaviors may be more likely to continue [i.e., her behavior is an accelerator (Acc) (see Table 5.1)].[2] If she changes the subject and speaks of something pleasant, the behaviors may be likely to stop [i.e., her behavior is a decelerator (Dc)]. Persistent use of accelerating consequences would be accompanied by extended coercive interchanges. Under certain conditions discussed in a later section, members of a dyad might very likely become trapped into repeated use of Acc and thus inadvertently produce more extended coercive interchanges.

There may also be concomitant increases in the *intensity* of the aversive events employed by one or both members. It is hypothesized that systematic increases in the probability of extended and/or high-amplitude interchanges are a prelude to development of a child who will eventually be labeled as *aggressive* or a parent labeled as *abusive*. An understanding of these extended coercive interchanges becomes the *sine qua non* for the development of a performance theory.

One descriptive study of these extended interchanges showed that each consecutive event within the episode seemed to set constraints upon the event that followed. In the report by Patterson (1974), more than 50 hours of observation were used to construct such a tree. The dependent variable was a class of child behaviors, Hostile; each member of the class was controlled by shared antecedents. Those consequences were identified that were accompanied by increases in the probability of the Hostile behaviors recurring (Accs, see Table 5.1). In Fig. 5.2, the data describe a series of reactions of a mother or father and their problem child. The probability of a Hostile initiation by the boy was .120. The probability that the mother or father

---

[2]An accelerator is not necessarily a reinforcer; conversely, a decelerator is not necessarily a punisher (e.g., the mand "Please close the door" followed by the C_i "Thank you"). In terms of its *immediate effect*, the latter would be coded as a decelerating consequence. The simultaneous long-term effect could be to increase the probability of compliance given the recurrence of the mand (e.g., the long-term effect is reinforcing). Similarly, in negative reinforcement arrangements, neutral and positive C_i serve as decelerators. In the same NR arrangements, aversive C_is are usually accelerators. Conditional probabilities as used here refer to immediate short-term effects. The reinforcement paradigm becomes an awkward perspective from which to view such relations.

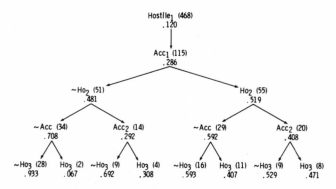

FIG. 5.2.   Probability tree: Given Denny's $Ho_1 \rightarrow Acc_i$. (From Patterson, 1974.)

would provide an accelerator following such an initiation was .286. The number below each symbol is the conditional probability for that event, given all the prior events in that sequence. For example, in row three, given Ho_1 followed by Acc, then the $p(Ho_2)$ is .519. Data from an accompanying probability tree showed that parents providing a nonaccelerating consequence (~Acc) was associated with lower p values for Hostile responding.

Given that the parents provided the first accelerating consequence (Acc), the data in Fig. 5.2 showed that this extended interaction seemed to set some unusual constraints upon the parents in that they were *increasingly likely* to *provide* a second Acc. The conditional probability of the first Acc was .286, and for the second, .408. These preliminary analyses suggest that investigation of extended coercive interchanges may well disclose additional findings that are counterintuitive. It is obviously of importance to intensively examine this process further—this type of analysis will probably contribute the most to our understanding of serial dependencies in behavior.

PERFORMANCE AND REINFORCEMENT MECHANISMS

It is assumed that events that control performance acquire this status because of their relation to both positive and negative reinforcement mechanisms. The possible relation between positive reinforcement and controlling stimuli is relatively straightforward. Some antecedent behaviors set the occasion for positive reinforcement (e.g., if the child brings a game to play when the mother is sitting and drinking her coffee, she may readily agree to play with the child). Given repeated trials, "mother sitting drinking coffee" could become a controlling event (a discriminative stimulus) for child approach behaviors. Repeated observations would show those periods in the day to be associated with high rates of child approach. In that sense, performance would vary as a function of the density of these antecedent events. The covariation could be expressed in correlational terms. Long-term, dramatic changes in positive or aversive reinforcing contingencies associated with the controlling stimulus would alter the status of the controlling events (Patterson, 1973; Patterson & Woo, 1976). The fact is, however, that parental reinforcement for coercive behavior seems relatively stable over time. Although not cited, over a 2-week interval Taplin and Reid (1977) found significant positive correlations for these parental schedules.

For a time this investigator believed the positive reinforcement arrangement to be crucial in determining children's coercive behaviors (Patterson & Gullion, 1968; Patterson, Littman, & Bricker, 1967). One study showed a high frequency of positive *consequences* by peer victims (cry, give up toy) for aggressive attacks in two nursery-school settings (Patterson et al., 1967). Studies of bullies by Olweus (1974) suggested that the stimulus for attack on the playground was *not* some aversive behavior provided by the hapless victim. Rather, the attack seemed provoked by the mere presence of the victim *in a setting unmonitored by adults*. From his clinical descriptions, the support mechanism seemed to be positive reinforcers supplied by the victim (cries, flinching, running) and peer-group-dispensed praise and approval. In those settings, one would expect coercive performance to covary with the level of adult supervision, which in turn determines the availability of victims. These descriptive studies do not, of course, establish the causal status of these peer- and victim-dispensed consequences as positive reinforcers for coercion in the schools. The findings, however, are consonant with the pattern, and they fit the early social-learning speculations about the support mechanism for deviant child behavior.

Similarly rich schedules of positive consequences have also been found by observation studies carried out in the home (Martin, Johnson, Johanssen, & Wahl, 1976; Sallows, 1972). The latter also showed these positive schedules to be significantly higher for coercive child behaviors in a sample of problem families than in matched nonproblem families. It was conceivable, then, that these consequences classified a priori as positive did indeed function as reinforcers. However, data from two studies have showed low-level nonsignificant correlation (across subjects) between schedules of positive consequences on the one hand, and the rates of coercive behaviors on the other (Johnson & Bolstad, 1973; Taplin & Reid, 1977). In addition, the latter showed that for a sample of treated cases the children's mean rate of deviant behavior *decreased* over a time period when parental schedules of positive consequences for the behaviors tended to *increase*! Forehand (1977) reviewed a number of studies that demonstrated that parent attempts to alter coercive child behaviors by nonreinforcement or positive reinforcement of competing prosocial behaviors were not successful. More studies are required, but the preliminary findings are very suggestive. It seems that for family interaction, the conceptualization of child coercive behaviors as being an operant controlled primarily by positive consequences dispensed by parents and siblings may be of limited value.

As an alternative, it is hypothesized that in the home, children's coercive behaviors serve the function of coping with the aversive inputs of others. The reinforcer involves termination of a noxious intrusion. This arrangement constitutes an operational definition of negative reinforcement [i.e., an aversive antecedent ($\bar{A}$) followed by the child's response, followed in turn by a nonaversive consequence ($\sim \bar{C_i}$)]. If this were indeed the key mechanism for coercion in the home, then the antecedent stimuli controlling performance of children's coercive behavior in that setting would tend to be aversive events provided by siblings and parents.

It is hypothesized that in the family during early stages of socialization, the 3- and 4-year-old child may be provided positive reinforcers for attacks upon young siblings (e.g., the victim cries, withdraws, and gives up the contested possession). However, the result of these interchanges is to produce changes in the probability of the victim's *initiating* his own coercive behaviors. This was shown in the observation study by Patterson et al. (1967). It is hypothesized that stage two may be followed by a stage three. Given that the parents do not interfere, then there will be increases in performance rates for both children. This escalation in rate eventually produces a stage four in which the mother is drawn into the fray as she attempts to control the process. At this point, the entire system is disrupted. The details of this formulation about changes in the system and the loose network of supporting data are summarized in Patterson (1976a). In keeping this formulation, the data show that indeed the coercive child resides in a coercive system. This being the case, then it follows that given the high coercive performance rates among family members, then the primary mechanism for the child's coercive behavior may be negative reinforcement (NR).

The implications that NR arrangements have for controlling stimuli are complex. First, it would predict that many of the controlling antecedents (F^s, see Table 5.1) would tend to be aversive. Thus the individual child's coercive performance would covary with the density with which these events are presented. Furthermore, the power [$p(R_j/\bar{A}$] of such an F^s would be partially determined by the NR schedules with which it is associated. Richer NR schedules should produce higher conditional probability values. This correspondence has in fact been demonstrated in an experimental study by Patterson and Woo (1976).

Given an NR arrangement with its aversive antecedent, then an aversive consequence should be associated with high probability that the child's coercive behavior will recur (e.g., if reinforcement has not occurred, the aversive stimulus persists). As yet no test has been made of this hypothesis.

Two studies have analyzed what happens when coercive behaviors are
punished (Kopfstein, 1972; Patterson, 1976). In both studies, using samples of
deviant children, punishment for coercive behaviors *increased* the probability
for the recurrence of persistence of the coercive behaviors. Neither study
analyzed the relation of aversive antecedents to the punishment acceleration
phenomenon. Whereas additional data is reviewed in a later section, these
findings suggest that some extended chunks of coercive behavior may relate
to unsuccessful attempts to punish coercive behaviors that are under NR
control.

What is Aversive? The foregoing discussion underlined the key role
played by aversive events. The next obvious question concerns the means by
which one defines aversive.

The code system was designed to sample 14 events thought a priori to be
aversive (Jones et al., 1975; Reid, (1978). The 14 categories described
relatively innocuous, even banal, events such as whine, cry, yell, tease,
sarcasm, hit, and so forth. Traditionally aversive stimuli have been defined in
one of two ways: (1) as those events that will lead the organism to learn means
of escape or avoidance; or (2) when arranged as a punishment, the events
suppress ongoing behavior (Campbell & Church, 1969; Nevin & Reynolds,
1973). Ordinarily one does not think of the ubiquitous irritants found in social
interactions as having either of these characteristics. However, the writer
assumes that they do in fact function in this manner. Furthermore, learning to
cope with these events is viewed as a primary social skill.

Two types of investigations have been carried out to test the merits of the a
priori classifications of aversiveness built into the original code system. In one
study, each of the code categories was rated by mothers of preschool children
on a nine-point scale for "aversive-pleasant" (Jones et al., 1975).[3] Events
perceived as extremely aversive were given low ratings. The 14 child behaviors
rated as most aversive corresponded to those code categories that had been
classed a priori as "coercive." Table 5.2 summarizes these ratings.

The second study (Patterson & Cobb, 1971) analyzed the impact of 12 of
the 14 aversive events found at a reasonable frequency as consequences for
ongoing prosocial behavior. In such an arrangement, if the consequences
were aversive, it should serve as punishment and thus suppress the response
for which it was made contingent. The data showed that when Talk was
followed by any of these events (Talk $\rightarrow \bar{C}_i$), there was a reduction in the
conditional probability that Talk would persist into the next time frame.
Table 5.2 summarizes these data. The two modes for testing aversiveness as

---

[3]Data providing children's ratings of aversiveness would be invaluable. Indeed, for many of
the analyses described in the report, such data would be far more appropriate than mother's
ratings.

TABLE 5.2
Two Tests of Status as Aversive Events

Consequences	Response Suppression $P(\text{Talk}_2|\text{Talk}_1 - C)^a$	Rating of Aversiveness
Command negative	.015	2.8
Hit	.089	2.3
Dependency	.158	2.8
High rate	.280	2.5
Non-comply	.222	1.9
Tease	.306	2.1
Yell	.321	2.1
Disapproval	.341	4.2
Ignore	.332	1.7
No response	.343	3.8
Whine	.411	2.2
Negativism	.385	2.8
Cry	Insufficient Data	4.2
Humiliate	Insufficient Data	2.0
Destructive	Insufficient Data	1.5

$^a p(\text{Talk}_2|\text{Talk}_1) = .519$. (It is the same person talking in both instances.)

aversive tend to converge. When ordered for magnitude, the two definitions correlated   +.48 (df = 10; n.s.).

NR Arrangements in Families.   At this point, it would be helpful to know if NR arrangements occur with any regularity in family interaction. Given that they do in fact exist, then it is also necessary to demonstrate that these arrangements actually control behavior.

The first question concerns the overall coerciveness of the family members. The study by Patterson (1976) showed that in the clinical sample the summary score for the 14 coercive behaviors (Total Deviant Score) was significantly higher for the problem child, the mother, and the older sibling, than was the case for his counterpart in the normal family. The means for younger siblings and fathers were also higher in the clincial sample but nonsignificant. These findings attest to the likelihood that children labeled as *aggressive* encounter higher rates of aversive behaviors from other family members. What are needed, however, are data demonstrating that these aversive intrusions are contigent upon the child's coercive behavior.

It becomes apparent that one peculiar characteristic of NR arrangements is that they produce both short-term *and* long-term payoffs, which are in fact antithetical, at least from the viewpoint of the victim. For the moment, however, the focus will be upon the short-term payoff that may result when the aversive intrusion terminates following the skillful use of an aversive counterattack. It is hypothesized that for most persons, coercive responses provide higher short-term payoffs than do prosocial behaviors in terminating noxious intrusions. In this sense, then, coercive responses are highly functional. First it would be expected that coercive responses would have a higher proportion of aversive antecedents than would prosocial behaviors. Incidentally, this assumption relates to an alternative mode for conceptualizing the whole problem. It is reasonable to assume that aversive behaviors elicit aversive behaviors; and no NR schedules need be involved (Ulrich, 1966; Ulrich, Dulaney, Arnett, & Muller, 1973). In either case, the prediction for high proportions of aversive antecedents for coercive behaviors would be the same.

To test this assumption, data were collected in the homes of 32 aggressive and 26 nonaggressive boys (Patterson & Cobb, 1973). The data showed that the probability of an aversive antecedent, given a coercive initiation by the child, was .227 for the nonproblem sample. The probability value for prosocial initiations was .063. The comparable values for the problem sample were .223 and .086. The findings from both samples support the notion that coercive child behaviors are more functionally related to noxious intrusions than are prosocial behaviors. However, the analyses were based on a population of events rather than subjects. Furthermore, the event population was pooled for all coercive responses. In Table 5.3, each of the coercive

TABLE 5.3
Antecedents, Utility Functions, and NR Schedules for 14 Coercive Responses:
Clinical Sample

Child's Coercive Response	N^*	Proportion of Aversive Antecedents $p(\bar{A} \mid \bar{R}_j)$	Mean Utility Function $p(\sim\bar{C} \mid \bar{A} - \bar{R}_j)$	Negative Reinforcement $p(\bar{A}\ \&\ \sim\bar{C} \mid \bar{R}_j)$
Disapproval	33	.321	.552	.189
Whine	22	.294	.430	.158
Non-comply	32	.234	.419	.130
Yell	18	.332	.450	.174
Destructive	11	.201	.284	.084
Physical				
negative	24	.327	.404	.191
Negativism	26	.187	.338	.078
Ignore	17	.579	.624	.400
Humiliate	19	.258	.156	.065
High rate	15	.304	.194	.098
Tease	26	.350	.382	.219
Command				
negative	17	.288	.304	.160
Cry	8	.334	.295	.112
Dependency	7	.129	.357	.081
Mean	14	.296	.371	.153

behaviors are analyzed separately for each subject. The across-subjects mean for members of the clinical sample were calculated; the N refers to the number of subjects in the sample who performed one or more target responses. The data, across subjects and responses, showed that about one out of three As were aversive. Both analyses agree in identifying a substantial number of aversive antecedents for children's coercive behaviors.

If children's coercive behaviors are functional in "turning off" attacks of family members, then one would expect to find a substantial proportion of occasions in which the coercive terminates aversive intrusions. This has been labeled the *utility value;* see Table 5.1 for a detailed definition. The data summarized in Table 5.3 showed some of the coercive responses to be surprisingly effective (e.g., Disapproval worked 56% of the time, and Ignore, 68%). Presumably, what one does to turn off an attack should vary as a function of who the other person and what that person was doing. As yet, such detailed analyses have not been carried out.

On the average, there are two chances out of three that the child's coercive response *does not* have an aversive antecedent. The calculation of the NR proportion (see Table 5.1) takes this into account as well as the information from the utility value. As shown in Table 5.3, NR schedules seem rather lean (i.e., on the average a coercive response might be involved in an NR arrangement about one time in six). Further analysis showed many of these schedules to be significantly higher in families of aggressive than nonaggressive children (Patterson, in preparation). Do these NR arrangements in fact determine these behaviors? There is, of course, no way of knowing this from the descriptive data now available. Thus far, two experiments have been carried out to test this hypothesis (Devine, 1971; Patterson & Woo, 1976).

In real life, the reinforcing arrangements for coercive behaviors in family interaction often provide dual reinforcement: (1) the removal of the aversive antecedent; *and* (2) a positive consequence such as "attend," "talk," "laugh," etc. This dual arrangement may relate to the rapid increases for coercive behaviors reported by parents of normal children. Atkinson (1971) showed that for preschool children, the ABABA reversal design showed that mother-ignore provided very tight control over a number of coercive child behaviors. The evidence showed that mother-ignore is probably an aversive event for most preschool children. Devine (1971) then designed a laboratory study to test the power of this type of positive plus negative reinforcement. Twenty-two mother/child pairs participated. After a baseline period, the mother was instructed to work on a task and ignore the child's overtures. For one group, the mothers' availability was made contingent upon the child's presenting a prosocial behavior, i.e., if the child played, the mother immediately attended to the child $[p(A \rightarrow \text{Play} \rightarrow \text{Mother Attend}]$. This arrangement provided both positive *and* negative reinforcement for that behavior. For the second group, the arrangement was contingent upon the child's performing a

TABLE 5.4
Changes in Latency and Duration for Two Groups[a]

Group Reinforced For:	Mean Duration Seconds			Mean Latency Seconds		
	Pre	Post	F	Pre	Post	F
Prosocial behaviors	29.9	64.2	6.12[b]	46.0	15.4	5.81[b]
Coercive behaviors	12.9	40.0	21.79[c]	60.3	16.6	9.75[b]

[a]From Devine (1971).
[b]$p < .05$.
[c]$p < .01$.

coercive response. Each trial was followed in turn by baseline free-play periods. There were four training trials. Table 5.4 summarizes the data for the two groups comparing the baseline and post-test trials for two measures of response strength. It was assumed that reinforcement would increase the duration for a response and decrease latency of its occurrence given the antecedent stimulus. These data showed that as few as four pairings were sufficient to produce significant changes in both measures of the response strength. The dual reinforcements seemed equally effective for prosocial and coercive responses.

Presumably, children interacting with family members soon learn that one of the more effective means for removing an aversive stimulus is to counterattack. For example, for one group in a nursery-school study, when the victims counterattacked, the aggression terminated his attack 69% of the time (Patterson et al., 1967). Over time, these NR arrangements produced increases in counterattacks and eventually to the former victim *initiating* his own attacks. It is assumed that in this manner the coercive child inadvertently trains his siblings to be coercive in their own right. However, as yet there are no comparable data showing the NR schedules by which sibling victims learn to become skilled coercers in their own right.

A Reinforcement Trap. During NR arrangements in natural settings, there can be two *simultaneous* effects that taken together constitute a reinforcement trap. On the one hand, when the mother "gives in," there is an immediate cessation of the child's coercive behavior. This reinforces the mother for submissive behaviors. On the other hand, it *increases* the likelihood that on future trials the coercive child behavior will occur and show increased duration of nonreinforcement. One is a short-term effect, the other a long-term effect. The fact that they arise from the same arrangement makes it difficult for the participants to track and label it.

To test this, Patterson and Woo (1976) carried out a series of three N_1 studies in the home. Over a series of trials, termination of mother-ignore strengthened the coercive child behaviors for which the arrangements were contingent. The training produced an increase in $p(\bar{R}_j/\text{Mother-Ignore})$; thus the long-term effect was achieved. The trials were accompanied by dramatic decreases in the within-trial duration measure (e.g., the child tended to whine for shorter periods of time.) The findings supported the notion of simultaneous long-term and short-term effects for all three families.

These studies only demonstrate the *possibility* that NR arrangements control *some* coercive child behaviors in *some* settings. They do *not* demonstrate that the schedules summarized in Table 5.3 were the prime determinants maintaining the performance of those coercive repsonses. Additional studies are necessary before such an assertion can be made.

Given that one accepts the notion of NR arrangements as constituting a primary support mechanism for some R_js in the family, then the implications for treatment are straightforward:

1. It is clearly necessary to treat the social system in which the child interacts (i.e., to reduce the rates of aversive behavior with which the child must cope).
2. Given this reduction, the child must also be taught that in the future there will be lower payoffs for coercive behaviors.

The details for a set of clinical procedures that fulfill these requirements are described by Patterson, Reid, Jones, and Conger (1975).

Intra-Individual Variance. Given that a child's aggressive behavior "works" [i.e., terminates the aversive inputs $(\sim C_i)$], then that $\bar{A}_i$ will become a discriminative stimulus for future attacks. The presence of these stimuli will be associated with an increased probability for those responses. Days characterized by high densities of these controlling stimuli will also show high rates of aggressive responses. Similarly, on days characterized by high densities of Accelerators, one would also expect to find high rates of aggressive behavior.

Observation data generally showed decreasing rates of coercive behaviors from the preschool to the school-age years at school (Green, 1933; Hartup, 1973) and at home (Fawl, 1963; Patterson, 1976). Such changes over time in mean level could be produced in several ways:

1. It is most likely that these decreases are accompanied by decreases in reinforcement and increases in punishment.
2. As shown in one study (Patterson, 1973), treatment can reduce the frequency with which controlling stimuli (F^S or Acc) are presented to the child.

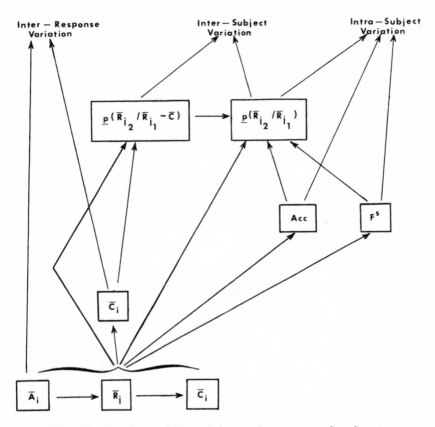

FIG. 5.3.   Coercion variables relating to three sources of performance variance.

There may well be comparable changes in frequency of controlling stimuli in normal families as the children mature or as members leave.

As shown in Fig. 5.3, the day-by-day shifts in rate of performance are thought to be a function of corresponding shifts in density for the two types of controlling stimuli. Thus far, only one attempt has been made to determine how much short-term intra-individual variance in performance can be accounted for by concomitant variations in frequency of controlling stimuli (Patterson, 1977b). The dependent variable was a class (Hostile) of one child's noxious behavior. The responses constituting the class had previously been shown to be under the control of overlapping networks of initiating stimuli. The dependent variable was used in a series of multiple regression analyses; four events served as the independent variables. The analysis was carried out

TABLE 5.5
Multiple Regression Analyses of Variations
in Performance of Hostile Behavior for Two Samples of Behavior[a]

Time Interval	Derivation Sample				Replication Sample			
	R	F	df	p	R	F	df	p
5 minutes	.259	2.01	6:127	< .08	.359	1.98	6:80	< .10
10 minutes	.393	1.83	6:60	< .20	.382	1.02	6:36	n.s.
20 minutes	.606	2.51	6:26	< .05	.461	.63	6:14	n.s.

[a]From Patterson (1977b).

separately for the baseline (50 sessions) and replication data collected during treatment (22 sessions). Only those data were used in which both parents were present. The results for the analysis of the three different time intervals for baseline and treatment are summarized in Table 5.5.

Jones et al. (1975) suggested that 30 to 50 minutes of sampling provided a minimally reliable estimate for any given code category. Given this finding, then the magnitude of the multiple correlations should increase as a function of increases in the time interval. The data in Table 5.5 are generally in keeping with this hypothesis. For the largest time interval, the data showed that stimulus control variables accounted for 20% to 36% of the variance. Additional analyses in that study showed that several of the variables were described by significant serial correlations. This in turn raised questions about the level of significance to be ascribed to the R values. Presumably, the magnitude of the correlation is a reasonable summary of the covariation even though the level of significance is in doubt.

For the present, these preliminary findings are promising. A functional analysis did identify controlling events that tended to covary with rates of the child's aggressive behavior. Obviously, many additional studies of this kind must be done before we have some idea of how much intra-individual variance is accounted for by stimulus control variables.

Inter-Individual Variance. Given the preceding formulation about the coercion process, it would seem that differences in negative reinforcement schedules should be the primary determinant for differences between individuals in their mean performance levels. For example, a score summarizing the proportions of reinforced aggressive responses would take into account individual differences both in the occurrence of the discriminative stimuli and in the frequency with which the response was provided a reinforcing consequence. One might also expect significant differences between aggressive and nonaggressive samples of children in the NR schedules for their coercive interactions with family members. In keeping with this formulation, data currently being analyzed (Patterson, in preparation) showed significantly higher negative reinforcement schedules for the aggressive than for the nonaggressive sample.

Given these findings, one might also expect that individual differences in rate of coercive behavior among aggressive children would correlate with differences in their NR schedules. However, as shown in Fig. 5.3, this is not the case. The problem lies in the fact that to account for performance one must first account for duration of responding (e.g., bursts). Children with high performance levels for coercion responses are more likely to engage in extended interchange once they initiate a coercive response. For example, in Patterson (1976a), the probability (based upon a sample of events) that any coercive response would persist into the next 6-second time frame was .30 for a nonproblem sample and .39 for a sample of aggressive boys. As shown in Fig. 5.3, performance differences relate to *duration*, which in turn relates to punishment acceleration and only indirectly to NR variables.

The variable that is the primary determinant for the duration of coercive responses is the punishment acceleration index, which describes the child's reaction to punishment. The coercive child, in contrast to the normal child, tends to *accelerate* ongoing aggression when punished (Kopfstein, 1972; Patterson, 1976b; Sallows, 1972). This sounds like a contradiction in terms until one learns that in the same families these same consequences were effective in suppressing prosocial behaviors (Patterson & Cobb, 1971).

The comparison of children referred for treatment as out-of-control with a matched nonproblem sample is summarized in Table 5.6 for two classes of coercive child behaviors. The data shows that parental punishment of nonproblem children suppresses both classes of coercive behavior. However, when the same kind of parental consequences were employed with the clinical

TABLE 5.6
Children's Reactions to Parental Punishment
for Two Classes of Coercive Behaviors[a]

Parental Consequence	Nonproblem Families	Clinical Families
Hostile		
Aversive	.23	.41
Base rate[b]	.29	.31
Socially aggressive		
Aversive	.12	.29
Base rate	.20	.29

[a]From Patterson (1976).
[b]Refers to the probability of the child's deviant behavior persisting given that the parents provided *any* type of consequence for the first deviant response.

sample, they had either no effect or actually accelerated ongoing coercive behaviors.

These findings led to the development of a score labeled as the *punishment acceleration index*. For each child, it consisted of the probability that his coercive behavior will persist into the next time frame, given that his first coercive response was followed by punishment $[p(\bar{R}_{j2}/\bar{R}_{j1} \rightarrow \bar{C}_i)]$. As shown in Fig. 5.3, this score relates both to average duration and the overall coercion performance scores. The latter (Total Deviant score) consists of the sum of the rates of all 14 coercive responses. It is expressed as rate per minute.

Two correlational studies were carried out to determine how much variance in coercion performance could be accounted for by the NR and burst-related variables. Data were obtained from observations of 33 families of boys referred as severe conduct problems. They were observed in their homes for a minimum of six sessions. Clinically, this was a mixed sample comprised of problem children, some of whom displayed low base-rate problems (i.e., stealing, truant, fire setting) *and* those who were socially aggressive. The observation code system and coercion theory were specifically tailored for socially aggessive boys. For this reason, two correlational analyses were carried out, one for the total sample of conduct problems and another for a subsample of 17 socially aggressive boys. The latter had Total Deviant scores $\geq .450$ responses per minute.

The dependent variable, the Total Deviant score, had a test/retest correlation over a 1-week interval of .78 ($df = 26$; $p < .01$). Four variables relating to negative reinforcement arrangements and two stimulus control variables constituted the independent variables. Pearson product moment correlations were calculated between each of the variables and the criterion measure. Correlations for the subsample are above the diagonal and below for the total sample. Table 5.7 present the data.

There was significant correlational support for the hypothesis that high performance levels are characterized by responses of long duration. Duration was defined by $p(R_2/R_1)$, the probability that a coercive response would persist or recur in the adjacent time frame. Children with higher performance rates were more likely to engage in coercive behaviors of longer duration. For the general sample, the correlation was +.45 ($p < .01$) and for the more homogeneous subsample, +.76 ($p < .001$).

In both samples, the duration measures were highly correlated with the tendency to accelerate when punished. The more likely a child was to accelerate when punished, the more likely his coercive behaviors were of longer duration. The duration measure correlated at low levels with several of the NR variables. The more likely aversive antecedents and rich NR schedules, the more likely the child's coercive responses would be of longer duration. The relationships are summarized in Fig. 5.3.

TABLE 5.7
Intercorrelations Among Variables for Two Samples

Variables	Criterion Coercive Performance Level TD Rate/Min	Negative Reinforcement Variables Aversive Antecedents $p(\bar{A}|TD)$	Probability Punishment $p(\bar{C}|TD)$	Utility Proportion $p(C^{\dagger}|\bar{A} - TD)$	NR Proportion $p(\bar{A} - C^{\dagger}|TD)$	Punishment Acceleration Score $p(TD_2|TD - \bar{C})$	Duration Score $p(TD_2|TD_1)$
Criterion							
Coercive performance							
TD rate per minute							
Negative Reinforcement Variables		*Socially Aggressive Boys N = 17*					
Aversive antecedents $p(\bar{A}|TD)$	-.03	.22	.09	-.03	.08	.58[a]	.76[c]
Probability of punishment $P(\bar{C}|TD)$	-.10	.67[c]	.84[c]	-.47[a]	.67[b]	.52[a]	Not analyzed
Utility function $P(\bar{C}|\bar{A} - TD)$	.11	-.35[b]	-.62[c]	-.54[a]	.47[a]	.24	Not analyzed
Negative reinforcement $p(\bar{A} - C^{\dagger}|TD)$	-.02	.75[c]	.18	.29	.29	-.30	Not analyzed
Burst Variables							
Punishment acceleration Score $p(TD_2|TD_1 - \bar{C})$	.34	.51[b]	.26	-.15	.48[b]	.24	
Duration score $p(TD_2|TD_1)$	.45[b]	.41[a]	.18	-.24	.32		+.56[a]

[a] $p < .05$.
[b] $p < .01$.
[c] $p < .001$.

Total Sample Out-of-Control Boys N = 32

139

The four variables from negative reinforcement arrangements and the two performance variables were used in a multiple regression analysis against the Total Deviant score as criterion variable. The R of .625 was significant; the F was 2.56 (df = 6:24; $p < .05$). The combined set of variables accounted for 39% of the variance. It was also of some interest to determine how well the variables accounted for variance in the subsample for which the coercion variables would be most relevant. Because of the better fit between sample and theory, the multiple correlation might be expected to be larger. This in turn could be offset by the more restricted range in the distribution of scores for all variables, which would lead to the prediction of lower correlations. The data in Table 5.7 showed that the mean duration measure accounted for almost all variance associated with the criterion (.76; df = 16; $p < .001$). To bring the relative contributions of the other variables into clearer focus, the duration variable was not included in the multiple correlational analysis. For the remaining five variables, the multiple R was .683; however, it was not significant (df = 5:11; $p < .10$). The analysis is currently being extended to a larger sample of socially aggressive boys.

VARIANCE AMONG COERCIVE RESPONSES

The variable observation data (Jones et al., 1975) showed that some coercive child responses occur at very high rates (i.e., Disapproval .134 responses per minute) whereas others occur at very low rates (i.e., Humiliate at .020). The question is: Are there any variables in coercion theory that relate to these differences?

It is assumed that the higher-rate coercive behaviors will be characterized by: (1) lower probabilities of being punished; and (2) higher probabilities of being negatively reinforced.[4] These statements, in turn, imply several assumptions. First, to take this position requires that in the subculture being analyzed there is consistency, *across* families, to the extent to which they punish or reinforce each coercive behavior. Second, it must be assumed that all the responses in the analyses are controlled by the same *kind* of contingencies. If, for example, one-half of the 14 coercive responses were maintained by NR arrangements and the other one-half by positive or mixed arrangements, then the correlational analyses would be doomed to failure.

---

[4]Certainly one could hypothesize that higher-rate R_fs were also accompanied by higher densities of facilitating and accelerating events. However, for the present, the writer assumes that information from these variables are contained within scores describing NR schedules. The mean NR index sums across time and subjects; this should reflect level differences in *mean* rates on densities of controlling stimuli.

One analysis showed across-sample consistency in the rankings for the kind of parental punishment used for deviant child behaviors (Patterson, 1976a). The rank ordering of 14 aversive consequences correlated .85 ($df = 9$; $p < .01$). Observation data provided the basis for comparing parents of problem and nonproblem children in terms of which punishments they used.

Patterson and Dawes (1975) used a Guttman scalogram analysis to identify a progression for a subset of coercive responses. Their analysis showed an across-subjects transitivity in progression for the following responses: Disapproval, Noncomply, Negativism, Tease, Physical Negative, Command Negative, and Humiliate. The reproducibility coefficient was +.92 in two different samples. The findings suggest the presence of a unidimensional construct such as negative reinforcement. Such an analysis is, of course, only suggestive, but it does imply that some process such as NR *may* accurately describe all of the seven responses involved in the analyses.

These seven responses were used in the present report to test for variables relating to differences in base rates among coercive responses. In the first analyses, data from three different samples were available from the Patterson and Dawes (1975) report. Rank order correlations were calculated between the mean base-rate values for the seven coercive responses and the mean probability of punishment for each. The correlations for the first two samples were $-.60$ and $-.72$; whereas, in the expected direction, the rank order correlations were not significant ($df = 6$). However, the data from a third sample (Johnson & Bolstad, 1973) produced a rho of $-.94$ ($df = 5$; $p < .05$). All three studies concurred in demonstrating that high-rate coercive behaviors received lower *proportions* of punishment. The three studies also provided low-order positive correlations between the parent ratings for aversiveness and the proportion of occasions in which they actually punished coercive child behavior.

For the current report, data were used from those subjects who actually performed the coercive response to estimate its base rate and the p value for the utility function. Using only the seven responses from the scalogram analyses provided a rank order correlation of +.59 ($df = 6$; n.s.) for the nonproblem sample. The comparable correlation was +.93 ($df = 6$; $p < .051$) for the clinical sample. Those coercive responses that were more effective in turning off aversive intrusions tended to occur at the highest rates (i.e., Disapproval, Noncomply, Hit).[5]

The base-rate values for this particular subset of coercive responses seem to covary with two variables: (1) proportion of responses receiving parental

---

[5]The variables $p(\bar{A}/\bar{R}_j)$ and NR schedules did not produce significant correlations with base rates of occurrence for either of the samples.

punishment; and (2) its utility in removing aversive intrusions from other family members. The same two variables would not covary with base-rate values for coercive responses determined by other than NR arrangements. However, given such a subset, the two variables account for a substantial amount of inter-response variance.

SOME ADDITIONAL FACETS
OF COERCION PROCESSES

There are other aspects of the relation between NR arrangements and performance that constitute phenomena in their own right. These processes include escalation and reciprocity. Each of these are considered in the following sections.

Escalation. Thus far, the entire discussion has focused upon a single dimension of aggression—changes in *rate* of performance. It is obvious, however, that changes in intensity may be of equal, or even greater, clinical importance. The reason for the apparent oversight lies in the difficulty of defining intensity changes when using a code system to view social interaction.

Over an extended series of aversive interchanges, there may be a gradual escalation in the *intensities* of the behaviors employed to both members of a dyad. Some writers such as Kempe and Helfer (1972) and Gil (1970) believe that such escalation may relate to child abuse into physical assault and homicides (Toch, 1969). Given unskilled parents, the child may be allowed to increase the intensity of his provocative-irritating behaviors. This in turn is likely to be matched by escalations in the intensity and rate of pain control techniques used by the parents.

The escalation process must begin by one person increasing the intensity of coercive behavior. The research literature suggests a number of variables relating to this initial increase. Cairns (1973) and his associates have carried out careful analyses of this aspect of the process. Cairns and Nakelski (1971) showed that animals reared in isolation were overly reactive to the ordinary grooming and greeting overtures of the other member. These high-rate, high-intensity reactions were reciprocated by the other member of the dyad. The interchanges then quickly escalated to attack behaviors. Knutson (1973), in his review, showed that similar dyadic processes characterized interchange even in the pain-elicitation laboratory studies. For example, in a shock-elicited aggression arrangement, if one subject were drugged, the aggression was effectively eliminated!

The study by Hall (1973) showed that films portraying dyadic aggression elicited higher rates of interpersonal aggression that did films of aggression against inanimate objects. Even if only one boy observed the dyadic film, then in the post-test trial, his higher rates of aggression tended to elicit similar reactions from the other child. This suggests to the writer that perhaps modeling of more intense coercive behaviors may facilitate one or more member's escalation in intensity. In some instances, trial-and-error learning may be involved. In this situation, a fortuitous increase in intensity effectively turns off the aversive behaviors of the other person.

Some illustrative data for within trial escalation are available from 12 of the mother–child pairs studied by Devine (1971). The preschool children and their mothers participated in the previously described laboratory study in which trials of mother–child interactions were alternated with brief trials in which the mother was present but not available. The interactions were coded every 6 seconds; in addition, the decibel levels for the child behaviors were recorded continuously. This subset of 12 subjects had performed at least one sequence consisting of nine or more coercive behaviors. Figure 5.4 summarizes the changes in intensity for the first extended series performed by the children. The data from play behaviors were from the free-play situation. They showed that escalation in intensity did not necessarily accompany extended chains of prosocial behavior. The *median* decibel level was used because of the extreme across-subject heterogeneity for the sequence of reactions. For example, three children never employed high-intensity behaviors. Two other children *began* at maximum intensity and then de-escalated. Seven children showed clear within-trial escalation in intensity.

Patterson (1976b) analyzed the extended chains of coercive child behavior from the clinical sample of problem children. For each dyad, each response within a chain was scored for its aversiveness. The score was based upon the mean ratings of aversiveness provided by mothers of preschool children in the study by Jones et al. (1975). Within-trial analyses of these aversiveness scores

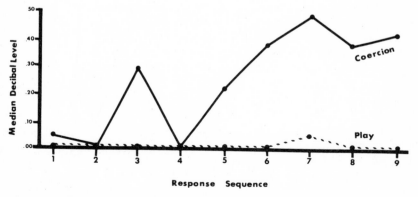

FIG. 5.4.   Within-trial escalation in intensity of child's coercive behavior.

showed that in extended coercive interchanges the problem child quickly escalated to maximum intensity. He remained at that level until the other person withdrew. Mothers, on the other hand, tended to introduce aversive responses late in the interchange and then quickly to terminate their aversive involvement. Evidently there are rules for within-trials escalation, well understood by both the victim and the winner. It would be interesting to know if the members of the dyad could verbalize the rules.

Given that one member does in fact escalate in intensity, the empirical findings show that the other member is likely to follow suit during that same trial. O'Leary and Dengerink (1973) noted such within-trial increases in intensities for dyads participating in shock experiments (i.e., if S_1 increased the shock intensity for S_2, then S_2 was likely to respond in kind). Self-report data from adolescents also suggest a perceived monotonic relation between the intensity of attacks and intensity of counterattacks (Graham, Charwat, Honig, & Wiltz, 1951).

There are no data that demonstrate the relation between reinforcement mechanisms such as NR and across-trial escalation in intensity. This, of course, is a crucial omission. This is a pivotal point necessary to our understanding of the process by which the practiced coercer gains skills. Presumably, the practiced coercer will be characterized by: (1) more extended durations; and (2) a tendency to escalate intensities within the chain. Ulrich, Dulaney, Arnett, and Muller, (1973) have commented upon this as a characteristic of trained fighting rats. Toch (1969) has also described this as a characteristic of assaultive male adults. However, empirical findings for animals or for human subjects are in short supply.

The status of winner and loser may be crucial to this dyadic process. Given relatively equal status, both persons would probably escalate the intensity and/or duration of their interchanges to the point that high-amplitude behavior may be employed often and that one or both may inflict serious injury. However, if one member accepts the role of loser, this may ensure against an endless spiral of increases in rate and intensity.

Reciprocity.

> He who would do good to another must do it in minute particulars. General good is the plea of the scoundrel, hypocrite, flatterer. —William Blake

The notion of reciprocity was implicit within the escalation hypothesis (e.g., if within a trial one member increases the intensity of aggression, the other would be likely to respond in kind). Among sociologists, the notion of equity, reciprocity, and exchange theories have the status of descriptive laws (Burgess & Nielsen, 1974; Gouldner, 1960). In applying this type of analysis to social interactions, one might summarize the concept as: "You pretty much get what you give." The equity in social exchange applies to both positive and aversive behaviors and is found in both correlational and experimental studies.

This writer assumes that for many social behaviors, equity obtains at the molecular level of dyadic interchange.[6] For example, in the classic observation study by Raush (1965), the probability of a friendly act for S_1 following a friendly behavior presented by S_2 was .92 for a normal sample and .55 for a clinical sample. In the same study, when S_1 provided an aversive event, the probability that S_2 would respond in kind was around .8 for both samples. As a general case, it seems that the performance of an event by S_1 is associated with an increased probability that S_2 will respond in kind. Perhaps this is an example of modeling effects at the molecular level (i.e., S_1 models for S_2, who then imitates, and an observer summarizes the exchange as being reciprocal).

Equity at the molecular level of interaction seems to hold for an amazing range of social behaviors. For example, observation data from the laboratory studies by Bales (1953) showed that when S_1 was antagonistic, the probability was .36 that S_2 would react in kind. Similarly, given the use of humor by S_1, the probability was .68 that S_2 would respond in kind. As Rosenfeld (1967) demonstrated, the level at which both members of the dyad function can be altered by manipulating the behavior of one person. In that study, increases in the interviewer's rate of smiles or approvals were reciprocated by the children being interviewed.

These descriptive findings do not in any way clarify *why* it is that such equities exist. Burgess and Nielsen (1974) showed that inequitable exchanges would be maintained if the amount of reinforcement was large relative to other alternatives. Parametric studies are only beginning to get under way. Specifically, one needs to identify the determinants for punishing or reinforcing another person (e.g., why does S_1 initiate approval?). Why does S_2 respond in kind? Kendon (1967) has made impressive strides in this direction by identifying gaze as a covariant for initiating an utterance.

If one summarizes data for positive consequences from extended dyadic interchanges, it is almost always the case that the resulting across-subjects correlations are positive and significant. Given the equity holding at the

---

[6]This is in contrast to some of the traditional exchange theories, which are cast along either cognitive or economic lines [i.e., Thibaut & Kelley (1959) and Homans (1961)]. The review of these theories by Nord (1969) highlights the differences between these theories and the relatively atheoretic, molecular stance taken in the present report. As those studies show in a zero sum game situation it is seldom that one obtains either cooperation or reciprocity. The writer assumes that in families social interaction is usually not analogous to the competition game theory models reviewed by Nemeth (1970). This writer assumes that there is *not* a *fixed* and therefore limited supply of positive and aversive events (e.g., my receiving six reinforcers in no way limits the number you may receive).

molecular level for most types of exchanges, then such correlations are not surprising. For example, in three studies reviewed by Patterson, Weiss, and Hops (1976), the median across-subject correlation was + .97 between spouses' daily reports of exchanges of pleasant events. Reid's (1967) analysis of family interaction showed an average correlation of + .55 among family members in their exchange of positive behaviors. In this latter analysis, rates of interaction were partialed out.

Patterson and Reid (1970) hypothesized that friendship, or mutual satisfaction, with a relationship would relate to both the level or amount *and* the equity of positive and aversive exchanges. The network of empirical studies provide general support for these notions. For example, the study by Ray (1970) showed that during the acquaintance process, a person's liking for other group members covaried with the amount of positive consequences given. In that study, persons who were attracted to each other also tended to be more reciprocal in their exchanges. Similarly, the laboratory study by Rosenfeld (1966) showed a correlation of .70 between frequency of positive nods of the head and ratings of attraction.

Patterson and Reid (1970) also hypothesized that families of aggressive children would be characterized by higher coercive rates for all family members and more frequent asymmetries in the exchange of aversive events. Following across-trials escalation in rate and intensity among family members, it was assumed that one or more would adapt the role of loser. This would imply an asymmetry in exchange, in that the winner would tend to give more pain than was received. The hypothesis was supported by observation data collected by Longabaugh, Eldred, Bell, and Sherman (1966). This data showed marked asymmetries in the exchanges of schizophrenic patients with staff and other patients. Patterson's data (1976b) showed that in families the mother fulfills the role of the loser/victim. At this molecular level during extended interchanges, the winner performs one or more coercive responses than does the victim. We suspect that the winner also interjects more $\overline{A}$, which produce high rates of compliance from the victim (i.e., from the victim's standpoint, "Why start a fight?"). This, in turn, should lead to lower reciprocity correlations for aversive exchanges particularly when examining data from families in conflict. In the studies of married couples reviewed by Patterson et al. (1976), the reciprocity correlations for positive exchanges consistently accounted for twice as much variance as did the correlations for aversive exchanges. The findings did *not*, however, support the notion that distressed couples had lower correlations for aversive exchanges than did nondistressed couples.

There are a number of studies reviewed in Wills, Weiss, and Patterson (1974) that showed that the *aversive* components of marital interaction are major determinants of marital interaction. In that study, a multiple-regression analysis showed that aversive events accounted for significantly

TABLE 5.8
Mean Rate of Approval for Family Members of Two Samples

Family Member	N	Mean Rate Per Minute Clinical Sample	N	Nonproblem Sample	t (one-tailed)
Mothers	27	.050	27	.096	2.42[b]
Fathers	18	.039	18	.108	1.97[a]
Problem child	27	.017	27	.028	1.72[a]
Boys ≤ 6	10	.031	15	.031	—
Boys ≥ 7	37	.011	37	.030	3.28[c]
Girls ≤ 6	12	.010	7	.021	1.62
Girls ≥ 7	22	.010	22	.031	2.94[c]

[a] $p < .05$.
[b] $p < .01$.
[c] $p < .001$.

more variance in the measure of couple satisfaction than did the occurrence of positive events.

The System Is Disrupted.   As asymmetries occur among one or more dyads, then other changes follow. One outcome is a lower rate of positive consequences for members of a coercive system. It is also reasonable to assume that these low levels of positive consequences may have been the aversive stimuli that led to the childrens' acquisition of coercive behaviors in the first place. However, for the moment, it is hypothesized that reduced positive consequences is an outcome rather than a cause, and it is assumed that within disrupted families, the exchange of positive consequences will be equitable albeit at lower levels.[7]

Regarding the level hypothesis about positive exchange, the data in Table 5.8 summarize the findings for rates of Approval provided by various family members. Six to 10 hours of baseline observations in the homes of 27 families of aggressive boys and 27 nonproblem boys provided the data (from Reid, 1978). The findings are expressed as rate per minute. For five of the six comparisons, the results were significant and in the predicted direction. Members of coercive systems provide less approval than do members of

---

[7]No hypothesis about equities in the exchange of positive behavior is offered. It is the writer's clinical impression that such exchanges will be equitable in all families (i.e., the reciprocity correlations will be positive and of high magnitude). The exchanges between the mother and preschool chid might constitute an exception. The observation study by Charlesworth & Hartup (1966) showed that younger children tend not to reinforce other persons at very high rates.

relatively noncoercive families. It is of interest to note that parents in both samples provided at least three times as much approval as did the children.

The writer assumes that if one person is permitted to significantly escalate his rate and/or intensity of coercive behavior, then a process is set in motion that will very likely result in the disruption of the entire system. At first, two children, for example, may escalate their rates of coercive behavior until both are being controlled by NR arrangements. Eventually one will assume the role of victim and withdraw from a disproportionate number of coercive chains. If these interchanges occur at a high rate, then, at *some* point, one or more parents will attempt to intervene. Unless adept in the use of child management skills, the parent is trained by the children to escalate in the same process. Eventually all or most of the family are performing coercive behaviors at high rates with the accompanying: (1) disruption in communications; and (2) problem-solving skills. Most will also describe: (3) feelings of anger; and (4) loss of self-esteem. By and large, the family members will: (5) tend to have limited amounts of social interaction; and (6) perhaps engage in few recreational activities together.

Thus far, there are only a limited set of findings directly relating coercion processes to family disruption. Laboratory observations and self-report data were collected for distressed and nondistressed couples by Birchler, Weiss, and Vincent (1975). The data showed that married couples in general seem to drift into an aversive mode of communication. But both sets of couples were more aversive to spouses than they were to strangers! This was particularly true of distressed couples. When placed in a situation where they were requested to solve social problems, the distressed couples continued to employ significantly more aversive behavior. The effect of this was that the other person reciprocated, and thus problem solving was effectively sidetracked. It is the writer's impression that the similar disruptions in communication and problem solving occurs in families of socially aggressive children.

Given high rates of aversive interaction, it is reasonable to assume that members will eventually withdraw and thus avoid such encounters. The Birchler et al. (1975) study collected data over a 30-day period on recreational activities. As expected, the nondistressed couples engaged in significantly more such activities together. These findings are in agreement with our clinical impression of families of aggressive children in that they share very few recreational activities. Attempts to do so often result in continuous strife and bedlam.

The hypothesis is about lowered self-esteem and feelings of anger for all members has been partially tested. The self-report data for mothers of aggressive children showed elevated scores on the MMPI (Minnesota Multiphasic Personality Inventory) scales relating to anger (Pd), depression (D), and a general elevation on all clinical scales (Patterson, 1976b). After training in child management skills, there were signficant decreases for most of these scales.

EXPERIMENTAL MANIPULATIONS

The earlier discussion emphasized the covariations between child behavior and environmental events. This integral feature of coercion process implies a causal status for the term, *controlling*. Given such an emphasis, it is necessary to carry out experimental manipulations to demonstrate this status in other than correlational terms.

It was also hypothesized that settings differed in the kinds of controlling stimuli available for coercive child behaviors. Finally, there was the assumption that there are continuous shifts in the probability values for these controlling events. This in turn emphasized the need to understand the process that produces these shifts. The experimental studies in the following sections examine these underpinnings for the coercion theory.

Testing the Causal Status of Controlling Stimuli

Ethologists such as Eibl-Eibesfeldt (1970) and Hinde (1974) emphasize the necessity of subjecting functional relations identified from field observations to experimental manipulations. However, the translation of the idea into action proved a difficult task. Efforts within the Social Learning Project to design procedures appropriate to complex social behaviors emerged only gradually over a period of years. The initial designs were for the laboratory setting and only gradually were manipulations introduced in field settings.

The first study examined the general question of whether some aspect of a mother's behavior could be demonstrated to function as a stimulus in controlling coercive child behaviors. Atkinson (1971) investigated "mother present but not available" as a stimulus for the coercive behaviors of nine preschool boys. The behaviors were expected to occur when the stimulus was presented. However, it was not at all clear that they would terminate when the stimulus was removed. It seemed entirely possible that they would continue as a function of some internal stimuli. Although control has been obtained in laboratory discrimination training, the stimuli were simple and the reinforcement history entirely unknown. It seemed unlikely that such clear-cut discrimination could be demonstrated when using complex social stimuli and entirely unknown reinforcement histories. To provide some modicum of control in the midst of all these uncertainties, the study was conducted in a laboratory setting. In the reversal design (ABAB), the first phase was a baseline period during which the mother was available to the child. During the experimental session, she made no response to his initiations. This was followed by a second baseline period and another experimental period. Seven child behaviors were demonstrated to be under stimulus control (e.g., they showed the expected increases when the "stimulus" was present and decreases when the stimulus was absent). The ANOVA for repeated measures showed the control to be significant for four coercive behaviors. The study by Devine (1971) replicated and extended the effect.

The results from these analogue studies were encouraging. They suggested the following:

1. Presenting a "powerful" stimulus could produce a wide range of coercive initiations from a young child. This finding was not, of course, a surprise (e.g., most parents could list a variety of social stimuli that will "make" a child whine, cry, or yell).

2. The fact that removing the stimulus produced abrupt cessation of the coercive behaviors did, however, come as a surprise even to some of the mothers involved. Neither they, nor we, had thought that the child's behavior would be under such tight stimulus control. It seemed possible that the social environment did indeed provide for rigorous discrimination training, at least for some coercive behaviors for this one stimulus event.

The first two studies left unanswered the question of critical concern to the present discussion: Can one identify controlling events from sequential observation data and demonstrate that these more subtle events also have causal status? This question would require that one first observe and then manipulate. An unpublished study by K. Whalen and W. Ishaq investigated this question. In the first session, preschool children interacted freely with their mothers in a laboratory setting. Analyses of sequential interaction data indentified those behaviors of the mother that seemed to control the child's initiating a Whine (WH). A few days later they returned for a second interaction session. Trial 2 followed an ABA design. Each condition lasted for 10 minutes. After the first baseline, the controlling event that was identified in the prior session was introduced. The second baseline followed. The mean results for the 10 subjects are summarized in Fig. 5.5. The p(WH) was calculated by dividing the number of Whines by the total number of child behaviors.

This second study seemed to show that in a highly structured laboratory situation, one could use observation data first to identify a controlling stimulus and then to demonstrate its causal status experimentally. The manipulation was successful for every one of the subjects. However, during Trial 1, the majority of the Whines were controlled by the same controlling event. For nine of the 10 subjects, the controlling event was mother-tease; for one it was mother-ignore. Given this limitation, then Session 1 contributed little unique information. However, the fact that tight stimulus control had

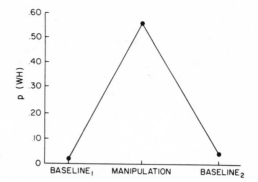

FIG. 5.5. Changes in $p(WH)$ during trial two.

now been replicated 10 times provided the team with some new-found confidence in the approach.

The next study by Patterson and Whalen (1976) was the first attempt to study both stages in a field setting—the home. Several observations sessions in the home of a preschool child and mother provided the data for the functional analysis. The event mother-ignore was identified as a controlling even for WH. The decision rules and method of data analysis were similar to those described in Patterson (1974). The F^s was employed in an ABA design on 2 successive days to manipulate WH. The results are shown in Fig. 5.6.

When the event was introduced, the behavior increased; when it was withdrawn, the behavior returned approximately to baseline. This is the first study that clearly illustrates the two-stage approach. Field observation data did in fact provide a controlling event that survived experimental manipulation.

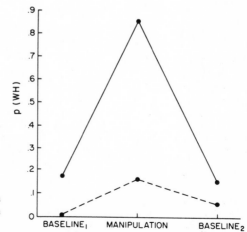

FIG. 5.6. Effect of mothers' F^s on two different days. (From Patterson & Whalen, 1976.)

At this point, the entire focus has been upon a single response—Whine. It was assumed, however, that the simple but surprisingly powerful experimental procedures could be applied to investigating a wide range of coercive responses. As noted earlier, a complex network of events may control the occurrence of a single response. In the same vein, a single antecedent may elicit several responses. In fact, one might think of these responses with shared antecedents as constituting a class. The procedures and decision rules for the construction of such functional classes have been described in Patterson and Cobb (1973) and Patterson (1974, 1977a). Sequential analyses of baseline data would identify the class. During the ABA manipulation, one would expect the members of the entire class of responses to be affected by the introduction of a single controlling event. Data from a study by Patterson and Maerov (1976) were reanalyzed to test this hypothesis.

In that study, 15 hours of observation data were used to obtain a sample of mother–child interactions sufficient to identify a class of child behaviors controlled by a single mother behavior. Table 5.9 summarizes the results for this analysis.

The analysis showed that each of these responses was likely to follow the mother giving a command; $p(A_i)$ was .0138. If one adds to this the A_i, mother-command/disapprove (a double-coded A_i), then one accounts for 75% of p(noncomply) and 42% of p(Argue). The remaining responses were largely controlled by other antecedents.

What constitutes an adequate definition of "class"? Should it be required only that each R_j be controlled by an A_i common to all responses? Or should it be required that the shared A_i account for some large proportion of $p(R_j)$ [e.g., $\geq$ 40% overlap, as was the case for the classes constructed by Patterson and Cobb (1973)]? Such matters cannot, of course, be established by fiat but rather by empirical means. In Table 5.9, the fourth column contains the compound probability $p(A_i)p(A_i/R_j)$. It can be thought of as an estimate of how much of $p(R_j)$ is accounted for by that single A_i[e.g., the compound value .005 for $p(R_2/$ mother-command) is 51% of p(Noncomply)]. Summing all the

TABLE 5.9
A Functional Analysis of Coercive Child Behaviors

Child Response	$p(\bar{R}_j)$	$p(\bar{R}_j\|M\text{-}Command)$	$p(A_i)p(\bar{R}_j\|A_i)$	Proportion of $p(R_j)$ Accounted for by M-Command as A_i
Noncomply	.0098	.363	.0050	51%
Argue	.0096	.185	.0026	27%
Disapproval	.0105	.032	.0004	4%
Tease	.0055	.032	.0004	7%
Whine	.0115	.048	.0007	6%

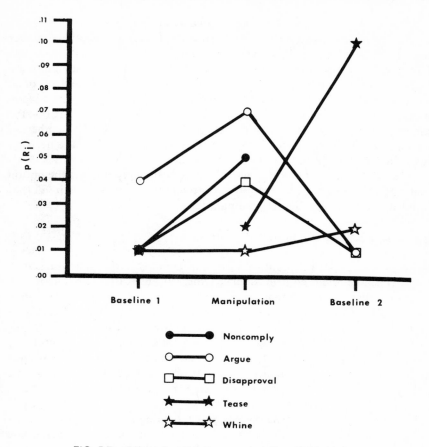

FIG. 5.7.   Effect of mother/command on five child behaviors.

compound probabilities for all the A_is for Noncomply would, of course, equal 1.00

If percent of $p(R_j)$ is crucial, then the experimental manipulation should show a clear effect for Noncomply a borderline effect for Argue, but no precise control for the other three responses. On the other hand, if all that is required is a shared significant A_i, then all five responses should reflect the impact of the F^s introduced following an ABA design. In this design, each condition lasted 10 minutes. The base-rate probabilities were calculated for each condition for each of the five responses. The results are summarized in Fig. 5.7.

The data showed that Noncomply, Argue, and Disapproval were well controlled by the manipulation; the remaining two were not. For example, Whine showed no increase when mother-command was introduced but did increase during the second baseline. Similarly, Tease continued to accelerate during the second baseline period. Obviously, these responses were under control of stimuli other than that which was being manipulated in the study. The findings suggest that forming a class based upon responses sharing a single A_i will lead to some false positive errors in predicting the effects of an experimental manipulation such as the one described here. It would seem, then, that the more powerful means of defining a class would require that the shared network of As account for at least 40% of the $p(R_j)$ for all members of the class. It should be noted that the latter is entirely arbitrary as a decision rule. This, too, must be examined empirically.

These are only pilot studies, but the findings strongly support the notion that one can use field observation data to identify controlling stimuli that stand up under experimental manipulation.

Some Alterations in Controlling Status

Perhaps one *can* identify controlling events, demonstrate their causal status, and determine their contributions to the variance associated with performance changes. Given that *it is so* raises the more interesting question of "Why?" What determines this status in the first place and what maintains it as such? There is, of course, a massive literature from experimental psychology and social learning theory that relates to these questions in a general way (Bandura, 1973). Thus far, only two studies from the Social Learning Project have been completed that focus specifically upon this question. Both test the notion that altering negative reinforcement arrangements will alter the status of controlling events.

Assume that a mother-behavior has been identified which clearly controlled some specific coercive child behavior. If each time the pair occurred, the coercive behavior was punished, it should alter the status of the mother's behavior as a controlling stimuli (i.e., the mother A_i event becomes a discriminative stimulus for punishment instead of reinforcement). Repeated pairings would produce reductions in the probability of the discriminative stimulus eliciting the coercive response.

In the Patterson and Whalen (1978) Study, the p(child-Whine/ mother-Ignore) varied from .83 to .43 across observation sessions. Then for one trial, the child was involved in repeated pairings of mother-ignore → child-whine → child in Time Out. He was also given positive reinforcement (gold stars) contingent upon a competing prosocial response. Following that trial, the conditional probability p(Whine/mother-ignore) dropped to .00. The data demonstrated an altered status for the controlling event. However, the effects of reward and punishment were confounded. And the manipulation occurred for only a limited number of trials.

The second study by Patterson and Maerov (1976) employed only the punishment arrangement. This time the contingencies were used for a period of 5 days in the home. This was followed by two post-test observations. The conditional probability was .363 at baseline, .120 for the first post-test, and .071 for the second. This was a clear demonstration of altered status as a controlling stimulus. Another obvious arrangement for altering status would be to *increase* the schedule of negative reinforcement arrangements (i.e., mother-ignore → child-whine → mother-attend). The effect of such repeated pairings would be to *increase* the value p(Whine/mother-ignore). This effect was in fact obtained for three consecutive mother/child pairs in a study by Patterson and Woo (1976).

The three studies provide findings that suggest that the magnitude of control elicited by social events can be altered by changes in reinforcement and punishment arrangements.

It is assumed that the p values for many social controlling events are constantly shifting as the result of ongoing social interactions. For most instances, the values fluctuate within some broad bandwidth. However, given a massive intrusion such as that often found in modern social engineering procedures, there may well be profound shifts in the number of controlling stimuli and the magnitude of their control. One might in fact consider these shifts as a subtle measure of therapy process (e.g., compare networks of social events that control deviant child behaviors before and after treatment). Treatment consists of reducing reinforcement for the child's coercive behaviors. Time out or point losses are also made contingent upon their occurrence. The p values for the events controlling these behaviors should reflect these alterations. Such a baseline to termination comparison was in fact made in Patterson (1973) and showed the predicted shifts in controlling networks following intervention in the family of an extremely coercive child. The number of controlling events was reduced; for many, the p values were lowered as well.

Analyses of Settings

It has been noted by Cairns (1973) and his colleagues that "the problem for a systematic analysis of aggression is to specify the ground rules by which the behavior of the child in one setting is generalized and expressed in other settings" (Hall, 1973, p. 6). Three studies have shown no generalization of treatment effects for aggressive children from one setting to another (Johnson, Bolstad, & Lobitz, 1976; Wahler, 1969, 1975). Three different observation studies of problem children have shown zero-order correlations between rates of deviant behavior in the classroom and the home (Bernal, Delfini, North, & Kreutzer, 1976; Johnson et al., 1976; Patterson, Cobb, &

Ray, 1972). It should be noted, however, that in all three studies roughly 50% of the children referred to as deviant in one setting were shown to be deviant in the other setting as well. The across-setting status as a trait obtains only for the very general category of out-of-control. The correlational studies cited earlier showed that it does not apply to maintenance of ordinal ranking for overall performance; nor does it apply to the specific *kind* of coercive behaviors employed.

The writer assumes that the stimuli controlling aggression in the home and the classroom are almost *entirely different* (i.e., the agents *and/or* agent behaviors that set the occasion for reinforcement in one setting may not even occur in another setting). For example, teasing may occur in the home and classroom but in one instance it is provided by a younger sister and in the other by older peers. These are probably very different stimuli. It is also assumed that the reinforcement mechanisms are positive for most classroom coercive behaviors and negative for many topographically similar responses occurring in the home. If this were true, then the antecedents are likely to be neutral (positive in the one setting and aversive in the other).

It is assumed that the well-practiced coercer fresh from a victory in the home will attempt to enlarge and extend his theater of operations. In the Alderian sense, coercion is for him a lifestyle, a means for producing *immediate* changes in an otherwise slow-moving social environment. He can be observed applying his skills in stores, nursery schools, and classrooms alike. Similarly, children who acquire their skills in peer interactions at school may try them out at home. However, the new settings involve new controlling stimuli, as well as different reinforcement and punishment contingencies. If this were true, then generalization of treatment effects across settings would not be expected. Thus far, only one series of N_1 "studies" has been carried out to test these hypotheses.

The Patterson and Maerov (1976) study provided intensive observation data for two subjects in both the home and the classroom. Their data showed that, by and large, *different* deviant behaviors occurred in the two settings. When the same response category occurred in the two settings, it was generally controlled by *different* events dispensed by *different agents*. However, for both subjects there was one behavior category controlled in both settings by the same antecedent category. When either the teacher or the parent presented the subject with a command, there was a very good chance that the child would noncomply. That particular covariation is itself an artifact of the code system in that noncomply can *only* occur following a command or request. However, the fact of interest is that the conditional probabilities for p(Noncomply/Adult-Command) were very high in both settings. In fact, the magnitude was roughly the same. They differed only in that at home the command was dispensed by the mother and at school by a teacher (female). If across-setting generalization were ever to occur, it should have been in these circumstances. For both subjects, the pairing of mother-command → child-noncomply was paired with Time Out. Repeated trials produced dramatic reductions in the conditional probability of noncomply given mother-command. In neither case, however, did the effects generalize to the classroom.

The results support the general social learning formulation in demonstrating that behavior is under control of stimuli specific to the setting. This, of course, is a position strongly taken by Mischel (1968) and other social learning theorists. If children's aggression is to be controlled, then each setting seems to require its own reprogramming (i.e., its own therapy procedures).

DISCUSSION

The general notion is that there is much about deviant child behavior in general, and socially aggressive behavior in particular, that is under the control of negative reinforcement arrangements. For the moment, it is assumed that these NR relations apply more to high-rate coercive families than to nonproblem families, and more to the home as a setting than to the neighborhood or the playground and classroom. Certainly one could imagine a classroom in which the teacher was so dedicated to the laissez faire philosophy that NR arrangements were frequent occurrences. However, such a school is more likely the exception than the rule. It should be noted in passing that this issue has hardly been explored as yet, and systematic studies of stimulus control are badly needed, such as those currently underway by Alice Harris (in preparation).

Given negative reinforcement as the mechanism, means that for the most part *low-key aversive* events play a central role in this process. Is it possible that a wide range of coercive child behavior is really under control of such seemingly innocuous aversive events as "disapproval," "tease," or "whine"? The data summarized here were certainly not compelling; however, they are suggestive and generally support this assumption. It is interesting to note that few modern textbooks on psychopathology accord such events status as important determinants.

The utility of the variables introduced here were evaluated in two very different manners. First, it was assumed that theories should account for performance (i.e., variations in behavior). The coercion variables seemed to relate moderately well to variations in rates among coercive responses and to variations among individuals. The problem of accounting for intra-individual variations in rate over time posed several methodological problems. For this reason, it was difficult to assess the contribution of the variables to this problem. At a minimum, the studies showed that the variables accounted for 37% of the variance; and at a maximum, 86%.

The second consideration had to do with the utility of these variables as they contributed to an understanding of how families can get caught up in the process of producing a coercive child or assaultive parent. The introduction of the concepts of reciprocity escalation and the reinforcement trap gave such application of coercion theory a plausible aura. There is of course no ready means for quantifying this contribution. But the clinical phenomena to which they relate are readily recognizable by clinicians who work with such families.

In summary, a loosely structured network of variables has been described that provides a plausible account of how so-called aggressive child behaviors might be learned and maintained in some families. The variables have been defined sufficiently well to fullfill minimal psychometric requirements. The hypotheses about *how* these variables apply to family process are eminently testable. The preliminary checks suggest that the variables account for a modest amount of variance in several areas of coercion performance. Taken together, the findings show that the approach warrants further testing.

ACKNOWLEDGMENTS

The data analyses and preparation of the manuscript were funded by NIMH grant MH 25227. The data were originally collected as a result of an extended series of grants from the NIMH Section on Crime and Delinquency.

The formulation owes a great deal to the critical efforts of my colleagues R. Jones, J. B. Reid, and H. Dengerink. The writer also owes a debt to Lita Furby, Robyn Dawes, and Hal Dengerink's students for their critiques of an earlier draft of this paper.

REFERENCES

Altmann, S. Sociobiology of rhesus monkeys. II. Stochastics of social communication. *Journal of Theoretical Biology*, 1965, *8*, 490–522.

Atkinson, J. A. *Nonavailability of mother-attention as an antecedent event for coercive mands in the preschool child.* Unpublished master's thesis, University of Oregon, 1971.

Bales, R. F. The equilibrium problem in small groups. In T. Parsons, R. Bales, & E. Shilo (Eds.), *Working papers in the theory of action.* New York: Free Press, 1953.

Bandura, A. *Aggression.* New York: Holt, Rinehart & Winston, 1973.

Barker, R. G. The stream of behavior as an empirical problem. In R. Barker (Ed.), *The stream of behavior.* New York: Appleton-Century-Crofts, 1963.

Bell, R. A reinterpretation of the direction of effects in studies of socialization. *Psychological Review*, 1968, *75*, 81–94.

Berkowitz, L. Words and symbols as stimuli to aggressive responses. In J. F. Knutson (Ed.), *The control of aggression: Implications from basic research.* Chicago: Aldine, 1973.

Bernal, M. E., Delfini, L. F., North, J. A., & Kreutzer, S. L. Comparison of boys' behavior in homes and classrooms. In E. Mash, L. Hamerlynck, & L. Handy, (Eds.), *Behavior modification and families.* New York: Brunner/Mazell, 1976.

Birchler, G. R., Weiss, R. L., & Vincent, J. P. Multimethod analysis of social reinforcement, exchange between maritally distressed and nondistressed spouse and stranger dyads. *The Journal of Personality and Social Psychology,* 1975, *31,* 349–360.

Burgess, R. L., & Nielsen, J. M. An experimental analysis of some structural determinants of equitable and inequitable exchange relations. *American Sociological Review,* 1974, *39,* 427–443.

Cairns, R. B. Fighting and punishment from a developmental perspective. In J. K. Cole & D. D. Jensen (Eds.), *Nebraska Symposium on Motivation.* University of Nebraska Press, 1973.

Cairns, R. B., & Nakelski, J. S. On fighting mice: Ontogenetic and experimental determinants. *Journal of Comparative Physiology,* 1971, *74,* 354–364.

Campbell, B. A., & Church, R. M. *Punishment and aversive behavior.* New York: Appleton-Century-Crofts, 1969.

Charlesworth, R., & Hartup, W. W. *An observational study of positive social reinforcement in the nursery school peer group.* Princeton, N.J.: Research Bulletin, Educational Testing Service, 1966.

Devine, V. T. *The coercion process: A laboratory analogue.* Unpublished doctoral thesis, State University of New York at Stony Brook, 1971.

Eibl-Eibesfeldt, I. *Ethology, the biology of behavior.* New York: Holt, Rinehart & Winston, 1970.

Fawl, C. Disturbances experienced by children in their natural habitat. In R. Barker (Ed.), *The stream of behavior.* New York: Appleton-Century-Crofts, 1963.

Forehand, R. Child noncomplies to parent commands: Behavioral analysis in treatment. In M. Herser, R. M. Eisler, & P. M. Muller (Eds.), *Progress in behavior modification* (Vol. 4). New York: Academic Press, 1977.

Gil, D. G. *Violence against children.* Honolulu: Hawaii University Press, 1970.

Gouldner, A. W. The norm of reciprocity: A preliminary statement. *American Sociology Review,* 1960, *25,* 161–177.

Graham, F. K., Charwat, W. A., Honig, A. S., & Wiltz, P. C. Aggression as a function of the attack and the attacker. *Journal of Abnormal and Social Psychology,* 1951, *46,* 512–520.

Green, E. H. Group play and quarreling among preschool children. *Child Development,* 1933, *4,* 302–307.

Hall, W. M. *Observational and interactive determinants of aggressive behavior in boys.* Unpublished doctoral dissertation, Indiana University, 1973.

Hartup, W. W. *Violence in development: The functions of aggression in childhood.* Paper presented at the meeting of the American Psychological Association, Montreal, Quebec, Canada, September 1973.

Hinde, R. The study of aggression: Determinants, consequences, goals, and functions. In J. DeWit & W. Hartup (Eds.), *Determinants and origins of aggressive behavior.* The Hague: Mouton, 1974.

Homans, G. C. *Social behavior: Its elementary forms.* New York: Harcourt, Brace, 1961.

Johnson, S. M., & Bolstad, O. D. Methodological issues in naturalistic observations: Some problems and solutions for field research. In L. Hamerlynck, L. C. Handy, & E. J. Mash (Eds.), *Behavior change: Methodology, concepts, and practice.* Champaign, Ill.: Research Press, 1973.

Johnson, S. M., Bolstad, O. D., & Lobitz, G. Generalization and contrast phenomena in behavior modification with children. In E. Mash, L. Hamerlynck, & L. Handy (Eds.), *Behavior modification and families.* New York: Brunner/Mazell, 1976.

Jones, R. R., Reid, J. B., & Patterson, G. R. Naturalistic observations in clinical assessment. In P. McReynolds (Ed.), *Advances in psychological assessment* (Vol. 3). San Francisco: Jossey-Bass, 1975.

Karpowitz, D. H. *Stimulus control in family interaction sequences as observed in the naturalistic setting of the home.* Unpublished doctoral dissertation, University of Oregon, 1972.

Kempe, C. H., & Helfer, R. *Helping the battered child.* Philadelphia: Lippincott, 1972.

Kendon, A. Some functions of gaze direction in social interactions. *Acta Psychologica*, 1967, *26*, 22–63.

Knutson, J. F. Aggression as manipulatable behavior. In J. F. Knutson (Ed.), *The control of aggression: Implications from basic research.* Chicago: Aldine, 1973.

Kopfstein, D. The effects of accelerating and decelerating consequences on the social behavior of trainable retarded children. *Child Development*, 1972, *43*, 800–809.

Longabaugh, R., Eldred, S. H., Bell, N. W., & Sherman, L. J. The interactional world of the chronic schizophrenic patient. *Psychiatry*, 1966, *29*, 78–99.

Martin, S., Johnson, S., Johansson, S., & Wahl, G. The comparability of behavioral data in laboratory and natural settings. In E. Mash, L. Hamerlynck, & L. Handy (Eds.), *Behavior modification and families.* New York: Brunner/Mazell, 1976.

Mischel, W. *Personality and assessment.* New York: Wiley, 1968.

Nemeth, C. Bargaining and reciprocity. *Psychological Bulletin*, 1970, *74*, 297–308.

Nevin, J., & Reynolds, G. *The study of behavior.* Glenview, Ill.: Scott Foresman, 1973.

Nord, W. R. Social exchange theory: An integrative approach to social conformity. *Psychological Bulletin*, 1969, *71*, 174–208.

O'Leary, M. R., & Dengerink, H. A. Aggression as a function of the intensity and patterns of attack. *Journal of Research in Personality*, 1973, *7*, 482–492.

Olweus, D. Personality factors and aggression with special reference to violence within the peer group. In J. DeWit & W. Hartup (Eds.), *Determinants and origins of aggressive behavior.* The Hague: Mouton, 1974.

Patterson, G. R. Changes in status of family members as controlling stimuli: A basis for describing treatment process. In L. Hamerlynck, L. C. Handy, & E. J. Mash (Eds.), *Behavior change: Methodology, concepts, and practice.* Champaign, Ill.: Research Press, 1973.

Patterson, G. R. A basis for identifying stimuli which control behaviors in natural settings. *Child Development*, 1974, *45*, 900–911.

Patterson, G. R. The aggressive child: Victim and architect of a coercive system. In E. Mash, L. Hamerlynck, & L. Handy (Eds.), *Behavior modification and families.* New York: Brunner/Mazell, 1976. (a)

Patterson, G. R. *Mothers: The unacknowledged victims.* Paper presented at the meeting of the Western Regional SRCD, Oakland, California, April 1976. (b)

Patterson, G. R. Accelerating stimuli for two classes of coercive behaviors. *Journal of Abnormal Child Psychology*, 1977, *5*, 335–350. (a)

Patterson, G. R. A three-stage functional analysis for children's coercive behaviors: A tactic for developing a performance theory. In D. Baer, B. C. Etzel, J. M. LeBlanc (Eds.), *New developments in behavioral research: Theory, methods, and applications. In honor of Sidney W. Bijou.* Hillsdale, N.J.: Lawrence Erlbaum Associates, Inc. 1977. (b)

Patterson, G. R., & Cobb, J. A. A dyadic analysis of "aggressive" behaviors. In J. P. Hill (Ed.), *Minnesota Symposia on Child Psychology* (Vol. 5). Minneapolis: University of Minnesota Press, 1971.

Patterson, G. R., & Cobb, J. A. Stimulus control for classes of noxious responses. In J. F. Knutson (Ed.), *The control of aggression: Implications from basic research.* Chicago: Aldine, 1973.

Patterson, G. R., Cobb, J. A., & Ray, R. S. Direct intervention in the classroom: A set of procedures for the aggressive child. In F. W. Clark, D. R. Evans, & L. A. Hamerlynck (Eds.), *Implementing behavioral programs for schools and clinics.* Champaign, Ill.: Research Press, 1972.

Patterson, G. R., & Dawes, R. M. A Guttman scale of children's coercive behavior. *Journal of Consulting and Clinical Psychology,* 1975, *43*(4), 594. (See Document #02332 for 7 pp. of supplementary material. Order from Microfiche Publications, 440 Park Avenue South, New York, N.Y., 10016. Remit in advance $1.50 for microfiche or $5.00 for photocopies. Make checks payable to Microfiche Publications.)

Patterson, G. R., & Gullion, M. E. *Living with children: New methods for parents and teachers.* Champaign, Ill.: Research Press, 1968. (Rev. ed., Research Press, 1976.)

Patterson, G. R., Littman, R. A., & Bricker, W. Assertive behavior in children: A step toward a theory of aggression. *Monographs of the Society for Research in Child Development,* 1967, *32*(5), (Serial No. 113).

Patterson, G. R., & Maerov, S. *Functional analysis of stimuli controlling coercive behaviors in two settings.* Paper presented at the meeting of the Association for the Advancement of Behavior Therapy, New York, December 1976.

Patterson, G. R., Ray, R. S., Shaw, D. A., & Cobb, J. A. *Manual for coding of family interactions,* 1969 revision. (See NAPS Document #01234 for 33 pp. of material. Order from ASIS/NAPS, c/o Microfiche Publications, 440 Park Avenue South, New York, N.Y., 10016. Remit in advance $5.45 for photocopies or $1.50 for microfiche. Make checks payable to Microfiche Publications.)

Patterson, G. R., & Reid, J. B. Reciprocity and coercion: Two facets of social systems. In C. Neuringer & J. L. Michael (Eds.), *Behavior modification in clinical psychology.* New York: Appleton-Century-Crofts, 1970.

Patterson, G. R., Reid, J. B., Jones, R. R., & Conger, R. E. *A social learning approach to family intervention* (Vol. 1). *Families with aggressive children.* Eugene, Ore.: Castalia, 1975.

Patterson, G. R., Weiss, R. L., & Hops, H. Training of marital skills: Some problems and concepts. In H. Leitenberg (Ed.), *Handbook of operant techniques.* Englewood Cliffs, N.J.: Prentice-Hall, 1976.

Patterson, G. R., & Whalen, K. *Establishing causal status for controlling stimuli found in the natural environment.* Unpublished manuscript, 1978.

Patterson, G. R., & Woo, D. *The reinforcement trap.* Unpublished manuscript, 1976.

Raush, H. L. Interaction sequences. *Journal of Personality and Social Psychology,* 1965, *2,* 487–499.

Ray, R. S. *The relation of interaction, attitude similarity, and interpersonal attraction: A study of reciprocity in small groups.* Unpublished doctoral dissertation, University of Oregon, 1970.

Reid, J. B. *Reciprocity and family interaction.* Unpublished doctoral dissertation, University of Oregon, 1967.

Reid, J. B. *A social learning approach to family interaction* (Vol. II). *A manual for coding family interactions.* Eugene, Ore.: Castalia, 1978.

Rosenfeld, H. M. Approval-seeking and approval-inducing functions of verbal and nonverbal responses in the dyad. *Journal of Personality and Social Psychology,* 1966, *4,* 597–605.

Rosenfeld, H. M. Nonverbal reciprocation of approval: An experimental analysis. *Journal of Experimental Social Psychology,* 1967, *3,* 102–111.

Sallows, G. *Responsiveness of deviant and normal children to naturally occurring parental consequences.* Unpublished doctoral dissertation, University of Oregon, 1972.

Taplin, P. S., & Reid, J. B. Changes in parent consequation as a function of family intervention. *Journal of Clinical and Consulting Psychology,* 1977, *4,* 973–981.

Thibaut, J. W., & Kelley, H. H. *The social psychology of groups*. New York: Wiley, 1959.

Toch, H. *Violent men*. New York: Aldine, 1969.

Ulrich, R. E. Pain as a cause of aggression. *American Zoologist*, 1966, *6*, 643–662.

Ulrich, R. E., Dulaney, S., Arnett, M., & Muller, K. An experimental analysis of nonhuman and human aggression. In J. F. Knutson (Ed.), *The control of aggression: Implications from basic research*. Chicago: Aldine, 1973.

Wahl, G., Johnson, S. M., Johansson, S., & Martin, S. A operant analysis of child-family interaction. *Behavior Therapy*, 1974, *5*, 67–78.

Wahler, R. G. Setting generality, some specific and general effects of child behavior therapy. *Journal of Applied Behavior Analysis*, 1969, *2*, 239–246.

Wahler, R. G. Some structural aspects of deviant child behavior. *Journal of Applied Behavior Analysis*, 1975, *8*, 27–42.

Whalen, K., Ishaq, W., & Patterson, G. R. *Causal status of field identified controlling stimuli.* Unpublished manuscript, 1975.

Wills, T. A., Weiss, R. L., & Patterson, G. R. A behavioral analysis of the determinants of marital satisfaction. *Journal of Consulting and Clinical Psychology*, 1974, *42*(6), 802–811.

6 The Human Infant in Social Interaction

Carol O. Eckerman
Duke University

INTRODUCTION

This chapter recounts continuing attempts to achieve an understanding of the ways in which human infants interact with one another. Along the way, knowledge has been gained about: (1) how infants' reactions to one another change during the second year of life; (2) the role of toys in prompting or shaping the responses of infants to one another; and (3) the occurrence of various types of social influence between infant peers. But the original quarry—*social interaction* in all its richness and subtlety—remains elusive. This chapter thus describes the reasoning behind several attempts, the results of each, and the ideas and questions about social interaction generated in the process. First, however, the reasons for undertaking the study of infant peers require explication, because undoubtedly they have shaped the inquiry.

Prompting the study of social encounters between infant peers was the conviction that an understanding of infant sociability required study of the infant's encounters with the variety of individuals peopling his world. This conviction rests upon the growing realization that the infant's social behavior is sensitively tuned to the appearance and behavior of his social partner and to the broader setting, both animate and inanimate, for the social encounter (e.g., Lewis & Rosenblum, 1974; Rheingold & Eckerman, 1975). It follows, then, that the infant's behavior in a given social encounter (e.g., mother–infant) can no longer be assumed to index his general social development; rather, an important aspect of that development may be the diversity of ways in which he responds to different persons or to the same person in different settings. A promising strategy for understanding infant sociability, then, would be to observe the infant in diverse social encounters and to search for regularities amidst the expectation of diversity.

The suggested strategy throws our current knowledge of the infant's social encounters into sharp relief. Past research on infant sociability has centered upon but two types of encounters: those with the adults most familiar to the infant (mothers and now sometimes fathers), and those with adults completely unknown to him (strangers). Descriptions of encounters with the other adults peopling an infant's world (more familiar strangers, neighbors, relatives, doctors, etc.) are infrequent but provocative (e.g., Ross, 1975). Descriptions of encounters with other infants are rare and often limited to children reared together; in their place until recently have stood claims that infants fail to react in any social manner to one another prior to about 2 years of age. Descriptions of encounters with siblings are rarer still.

The study of infant peers in interaction is thus seen as one step in broadening our understanding of the infant's social encounters and hence his sociability. The infant's encounters with other infants were examined first because infant peers offer possibilities for social interaction markedly different from those of adults. It was thought that the study of infant–infant encounters might reinforce some of the conclusions about early sociability heretofore based on infant–adult encounters and might force a reexamination of others. The infant's attachment to adults, for example, has been explained variously as: (1) the result of being the recipient of caretaking and nurturance; or (2) an adaptive behavior serving the function of protecting the infant from predators; or (3) the consequence of prolonged reciprocal interactions. And fear of the stranger has been explained as a reaction to discrepancies from expected social stimulation. Yet these explanations would apply only with difficulty to any social attraction found between infant peers.

The study of peers also holds special promise for teasing out the skills that the infant brings to a social encounter from those that are brought by a more adept partner. What interaction we see between infant peers, and what social skills that interaction implies, can be attributed to the infants themselves. In infant–adult encounters, or infant–sibling encounters, there is more difficulty and less certainty in knowing what skills belong to the infant rather than his partner.

Our study of peer interaction began 5 years ago. At that time, the literature abounded with claims of the nonexistence of peer interaction during infancy. The claims were based upon a handful of studies, most over 4 decades old, and most with institutionalized children. Yet a reexamination of the early studies yielded evidence of many more seemingly social interactions between peers than the summary statements then and later acknowledged. Infants under 1 year of age were described as watching and contacting one another, smiling and vocalizing to one another, offering and taking toys, imitating each other, and making sounds for the sake of their social effect; infants during the second year were described as also laughing at one another, biting and hitting each other, showing toys and protecting toys from one another, engaging in friendly bouts of giving and taking toys, performing for one another, and engaging in the same activity in a cooperative manner (e.g., Bridges, 1933; Buhler, 1930; Maudry & Nekula, 1939). Still, the existing studies gave little information about how frequently or under what conditions the various types of interaction occurred, and nowhere was there a description of the interactions occurring among peers reared at home rather than in an institution. Thus the first step in studying peer interactions among infants seemed to involve simply observing home-reared infants together and describing the ways in which they react to and act upon one another.

CHANGES DURING THE SECOND YEAR
OF LIFE IN HOW INFANTS REACT
TO UNFAMILIAR PEERS

In beginning the task of describing how infants act upon and react to one another, numerous decisions of strategy were made. Perhaps the most far-reaching decision was to search for *commonalities* in infants' reactions to one another rather than for stable differences in how individual children reacted. The search for ways of behaving common to every infant at a given point in his development and in a given setting was predicated on the belief that such orderliness exists and that commonalities provide a useful backdrop against which to examine individual differences.

Further decisions were made: The infants observed were to be drawn from a population of normal, home-reared children on the basis of age alone; and they were to be observed in a naturally occurring setting for infant–infant encounters. Home-reared children were chosen, because most of our current theories about infant sociability are based upon this population. Age alone was the basis for grouping infants because the additional possibly relevant factors (e.g., sex, family composition, socioeconomic status, birth order, mother–infant interaction) were so numerous as to preclude selection on all bases and, more importantly, because the focus was upon discovering commonalities despite variations in life experiences and biological make-up. The choice of children completely unfamiliar with one another avoided the problems attendant upon quantifying or describing familiarity and allowed the inclusion of all children, many of whom had had little, if any, prior experience with peers.

A naturally occurring setting for infant encounters was desired to minimize the unknown effects of experimenter intervention, but the setting had to be controlled enough to allow the discovery of commonalities in reaction to the same setting. A compromise was reached: A controlled laboratory setting was structured to mimic the essential features of what transpires when two mothers with simliar-age children get together at one's home to visit and leave their children free to play. The two mothers sat together on the floor, talked with one another, and left their children free to do as they wished in a small room (2.8 × 2.9 meters) furnished only with several attractive toys on the floor and pictures on the wall. Each toy (a pulltoy, a dump truck, and a set of three large blocks) was present in duplicate. The mothers responded with a smile or a word or two to the children's social overtures but did not initiate interaction with them or direct their activities unless to prevent physical harm.

The youngest infants chosen for study were 10 months of age, an age by which infants can locomote proficiently enough to approach and/or withdraw from a peer at will and an age at which infants are widely considered "attached" to one or more adults. The oldest infants observed were 24 months of age, an age when prior investigators had concluded that truly social peer interactions had begun.

Four main concerns guided the construction of a system for recording the infants' behavior:

1. The behaviors that peers engaged in were not well known, hence the recording system should be open to the discovery of new behaviors.
2. The recording system should be applicable to infant–infant encounters in natural settings so that laboratory findings could later be checked in natural settings.
3. Wherever meaningful, the infant's reactions to his peer should be recorded in a manner similar to those reactions to his mother or others to allow comparison.
4. Above all, the behaviors recorded should be defined as much as possible in terms of overt motor actions, minimizing inferences by the observers, and thus minimizing the extent to which our understanding of peer interaction is prejudged.

To develop the recording system, two observers simultaneously and independently observed several pairs of infants in the study setting and wrote narrative descriptions of the ways in which one infant appeared to act upon or react to his peer. Study of the narrative descriptions led to the distinguishing and defining of 18 behaviors seemingly related to the peer; and with these definitions in hand, the study proper began.

The study was conducted and initially analyzed in two parts. First, 14 pairs of like-aged children, either 10 to 12, 16 to 18, or 22 to 24 months of age, were observed. The previously established definitions were refined on the basis of this experience, and predictions of changes in these behaviors with age were developed from analyses of variance performed on the observations. Then, 16 remaining pairs were observed with the definitions in final form to test the predictions concerning age changes. The second set of observations replicated the first, increasing confidence in both the system of recording behavior and the findings.

Because the procedures and findings of this initial study are now published (Eckerman, Whatley, & Kutz, 1975), they are recounted only briefly here. The pairs of unfamiliar peers met together for 20 minutes, and two independent observers behind one-way windows recorded their behavior toward one another, the mothers, and inanimate features of the setting. The two observers focused upon a single infant at a time and alternated 15-second periods of observing with 15-second periods of recording the behaviors on a checklist. Every 2 minutes their focus shifted from one child to another. The resulting record thus consisted of 40 observations, 20 of each child; and the data took the form of the total number of periods for a pair in which a behavior was observed.

The peer-related behaviors were defined in such language as "hold out a toy toward the peer within his reaching distance, while looking and/or vocalizing to the peer" (*offer a toy*) or "emit a vocal sound or series of sounds, that may or may not be distinguishable as words, while watching the peer" (*vocalize*). The 18 peer-related behaviors were grouped into five conceptually based categories for statistical analyses. After checking that interobserver agreement on these categories was adequate (generally above .90 when calculated by dividing the smaller of the two observers' scores by the larger), the data were submitted to a multivariate analysis of variance with the single factor of the infants' age. The finding of a reliable change in peer-related behaviors with age then prompted univariate analyses of variance of the component behavior categories.

Notable was the sheer extent and variety of behaviors observed that were seemingly related to the presence of an unfamiliar peer. One or more peer-related behaviors occurred in over 60% of the observations at each age. When watching was excluded, one or more of the other peer-related behaviors still occurred in over 30% of the periods at the youngest age and in over 55% of the periods at the oldest age. The behaviors customarily studied as social behaviors toward the mother (smiling, vocalizing, and touching) occurred with peers, but not as frequently as peer-related behaviors involving the play material. Vocalizing and smiling at the peer were more frequent at each age than touching the peer. The infant behaviors customarily studied with new adults (fussing and crying) occurred only once with the new peer. The most prominent peer-related behaviors were those that involved both the peer and a toy. At each age, the peers synchronously contacted the same play material, offered and accepted toys, took toys from the peer's hand or toys he had just put down, struggled over toys, and duplicated each other's actions with toys. At the oldest age, the peers also engaged in coordinated play with the toy materials. The behaviors that increased reliably with age were those involving the play materials.

The findings then: (1) suggested that the origins of a variety of forms of peer interaction were to be found in infancy; (2) emphasized the ways in which the actions of an infant seem to influence his peer's activities with toys, or the ways in which objects may be used by peers in social interaction; and (3) indicated that the unfamiliar peer was a salient feature of the novel play setting.

It remained to ask whether these findings were specific to the original study setting or whether they could characterize other, naturally occurring encounters between young children. Informal observations in parks, shopping malls, and at swimming pools suggested that the findings were generalizable, but a more formal assessment was made in a day-care center with a group of six 2-year-olds. The six children, four boys and two girls, were observed repeatedly over a period of 6 weeks in their usual school setting with no intervention by the observers. The children were observed between 9 and 10 a.m. in two moderate-sized adjoining rooms containing numerous toys, a child's table, and chairs. The adult female caretaker was present, but during that period of the day she directed the children's activities minimally, intervening only when a child was in danger or broke one of her "rules." Using a slightly expanded checklist, two independent observers observed each child for eight observation periods a day using the same time-sampling procedures as before.

The move to the day-care center meant a shift from observing pairs of unfamiliar children in a novel play setting with their mothers to observing a group of very familiar children in a familiar setting with a caretaker. Despite the many dimensions of change, the basic findings were the same. The somewhat older day-care group (average age = 31.0 months) was compared with the oldest group of the prior study (average age = 23.0 months). All the same behaviors occurred—and with comparable relative frequencies. The most prominent peer-related behaviors were those involving play materials; together they occurred during 60% of the observation periods in both settings. Again, contact of the same play material was more frequent than direct involvement in the peer's play; and duplicating the peer's action, struggling over a toy, and coordinating activities with a toy were the most frequent of the latter activities. Physical contact with peers was minimal for both groups; and distal social signals (smiles, vocalizations, gestures) were more frequent than physical contact, occurring in just 2% more of the observation periods in the day-care center.

The same observation system has been used for other purposes in two more groups of 2-year-olds in a day-care center and in two groups of young 3-year-olds meeting together 6 hours a week. Again, the same picture emerges, although such details as the absolute frequency of coordinate play or verbalization vary.

These assessments of generalizability led to greater confidence in the behavior categories devised and the controlled play setting and prompted a return to the laboratory for studies of the determinants of peer-related behaviors.

HOW "SOCIAL" ARE
THE PEER-RELATED BEHAVIORS?

So far our work had described and counted a variety of infant behaviors that appeared related to the presence and/or activity of a peer. Unexamined were those aspects of the peer or his behavior critical for their occurrence. It could be claimed that the peer-related behaviors were in no way "social," that the infant was not reacting to the peer per se but rather to the inanimate aspects of the setting. Our setting for observing peer interaction, as well as that of others, had a salient feature in addition to an unfamiliar peer—the presence of novel play materials—and the most prominent peer-related behaviors were those that involved both the peer and a toy. Such behaviors as contacting the same object as the peer, accepting a toy, taking a toy, taking over a toy, struggling over a toy, and duplicating a peer's action with a toy can be construed as reactions not to the peer but rather to the movements of the toys the peer produces. The infant may be interested in and responding solely to the inanimate spectacle a peer's actions create; the fact that this spectacle is created by a peer, or any social being, may be irrelevant. Furthermore, the physical contacting of the peer and the vocalizing and smiling seemingly directed toward him also may be byproducts of the infant's interest in toys. For example, when one infant moves toward or contacts a peer, he may be moving toward a toy and may simply find the peer in his path.

To evaluate whether in fact there are social components to the peer-related behaviors described in the original study, a subsequent study (Eckerman & Whatley, 1977) contrasted the behaviors seen when peers met in a setting devoid of toys (readily manipulable objects) with those seen in the customary play setting. It was reasoned that the behaviors directed toward the peer in the setting devoid of toys could more readily be attributed to the appearance and behavior of the peer per se. In this sense they would be social behaviors, although the question of whether an infant conceives of a peer more as a complex toy or as a person would remain unanswered and beyond the scope of our studies.

Forty-four pairs of unfamiliar infants, one-half 10 to 12 months and one-half 22 to 24 months of age, were observed with their mothers in a laboratory playroom. At each age, one-half the pairs met for 16 minutes in a spacious room devoid of furnishings except for a large circular children's table, pictures on the wall, and a carpet. The other one-half of the pairs met in the same room, but with the addition of four boxes that could be nested or stacked, a pull-toy with removable peg men, and a set of three large blocks. The two ages, representing the extremes of the age range of the initial study, were included to assess whether younger children might respond more to the inanimate aspects of the setting and older children more to its social features. The mothers sat on the floor along one end of the room and talked with one another, leaving their children free to do as they wished. They could respond with a smile or word or two to the children's overtures, but they did not initiate interaction or direct their activities except in the rare instance that a child appeared in danger.

The peer-related behaviors recorded included those of the original study with a few additions and revisions. *In proximity* (being within 2 feet of some part of the peer's body for at least 3 continuous seconds), *approach peer* (moving from out of proximity to peer to within proximity by a continuous movement through at least 2 feet, with attention to the peer), and *follow peer* (moving simultaneously with the peer and behind and in the same direction as the peer for at least 5 continuous seconds) were added to assess correspondence in the infants' location in space. *Resist* (protest or physically resist peer's taking of an object) and *relinquish* (release without protest toy that peer takes) were added to the exchange activities. *Alternate actions* subsumed most of the behavior categorized in the original study as *coordinate play*. *Alternate actions* was coded when the child being observed "took turns" with his peer in directing behaviors to one another at least twice within a span of a few seconds; whether his peer-directed behavior took the same form as the peer's or was a different but related action (e.g., offer toy—accept toy) was noted. In contrast to the time-sampling procedure of the original study, behaviors were now continuously recorded on a sheet marked off in 10-second intervals. Two independent observers focused upon one infant at a time, alternating the infant focused upon every minute. The pair was considered the unit of analysis, and the primary data consist of the frequencies of each of the peer-related behaviors summed over the two infants and the 16-minute session.

To contrast how the peers interacted in a setting devoid of toys versus the more customary play setting, six sets of behaviors were chosen that are customarily thought of as social and that can occur either in the presence or absence of toys. These behaviors are visual regard of the peer, distal social signaling to the peer (vocalize, smile, laugh, gesture, fuss, cry), proximity to peer, physical contact with peer (touch, strike), duplicating the peer's action, and alternating actions with the peer. Each occurred at least as frequently when no toys were present, and most occurred markedly more often in the absence of toys. A multivariate analysis of variance performed on the six sets of behaviors with the two factors of age and toy condition indicated that these behaviors were reliably more frequent both in the absence of toys and with increased age. There was no evidence, however, that the effect of the toy condition differed for the two ages studied.

Subsequent univariate analyses of variance indicated which of the component behaviors differed reliably in frequency for the two toy conditions and two ages. Without toys, the infants vocalized, smiled, and gestured more to one another, contacted one another more, and duplicated each other's actions more often. Although the difference was not reliable, at the older age they also alternated their actions almost five times more often. The older infants, as compared to the younger ones, more frequently smiled, vocalized, and gestured at one another and duplicated each other's actions. Again, no evidence was obtained for any of these behaviors that the effect of the toy condition differed for the two ages. Clearly, these peer-related behaviors that occurred more frequently in the absence of toys cannot be interpreted as reactions to the changing sights and sounds of toys incidentally produced by a peer. Rather, the behaviors appear directed toward the person and action of the peer himself; and in this sense, they are social.

Examining which activities of a peer were duplicated may provide further information about what aspects of a peer's behavior are of special import to the infant. Over one-half of the 113 separate instances of duplicated acts that were observed involved an infant engaging in a common play action (e.g., patting, fingering, climbing) with an inanimate fixture of the room (the radiator, table, wall, rug, mirror, or door). Also frequent were duplications involving the peer alone. The infants touched, patted, rubbed, or hit one another (23%); and they waved "bye-bye," pointed, clapped and shook their hands at each other, dangled their legs from the table, changed from walking to crawling, and raced across the room in duplication of one another (13%). Infrequent were duplications involving distinctive sounds (5%) or the novel toys (4%).

Thus the infants of both ages seemed to duplicate those actions of the peer that were very familiar to them, actions that probably characterized their own play activities; and many of the duplicated actions involved only the person of the peer. It is tempting to speculate that the appeal of these actions resides less in the actions themselves and more in the peer's performance of actions similar to those enjoyed by the observing infant.

ASSESSING SOCIAL INFLUENCE
BETWEEN INFANT PEERS

Much remains to be asked and captured about how each infant's actions influence the other's—about social interaction per se. The work so far has produced only counts of how often infants direct a variety of behaviors toward a peer and documentation that many of these behaviors are responses to the person and action of the peer himself rather than to inanimate spectacles created by the peer. But the peer-related behaviors so far isolated also imply several processes of social influence, each of which awaits study.

Consider how three peer-related behaviors carry different implications about social influence. An infant's accepting of a toy offered by his peer implies immediate social influence; furthermore, the specific form of one infant's act (an offer) appears to determine the different form of his peer's action (an acceptance). In *alternate same action*, each child repeatedly performs the same action in turn; that is, each pauses for the other to act and then duplicates his peer's act. Such a sequence again implies immediate social influence; each child's action seems to determine the other child's next action. Yet the specific content of the action seems secondary; it may be patting the table, twirling oneself about, or jumping into a mother's lap. What is critical is the match in the activity and the turn-taking, the timing of each's actions. Finally, the sheer frequency with which two infants touch the same toy at the same time (*same play*) suggests that each is influencing the other's choice of what toy to manipulate, but the amount of same play says little about whether any specific instance reflects social influence or how much of the same play results from social influence rather than from other factors such as a shared preference for toys. It is to the analysis of these processes of social influence that our efforts now have turned.

Isolating the ways in which one infant's behavior influences that of another infant is a difficult task. Mastering the task, however, is central to an understanding of early development, for the question of social influence incorporates questions about the development of social skills during infancy and the functions of social interaction for the child's development. Understanding what aspects of another person lead to differential responsiveness by the infant provides knowledge about both social perception and learning. Understanding how these aspects of a person alter the infant's behavior is basic to reasoning about how social interaction functions to alter the infant's experience and hence development.

Assessing social influence in the freely occurring interactions of infants has at least two essential components: (1) the establishing of an orderly relationship between the behavior of the two children; and (2) a determination of the factors responsible for that relationship. One of the most prominent relationships found between the behavior of young peers is that of a correspondence in the form of behavior shown by the two infants at similar points in time. The infants are found close together in space, touching the same objects in a room, doing the same things with objects, making the same sounds, moving in the same way, and engaging in the same actions in turn. The prominence of this correspondence in behavior was seen in the prior study comparing peer interaction with and without toys; some type of correspondence occurred over 30% of the time for both ages and both toy conditions. The frequent occurrence of this correspondence, together with its potential function of expanding the infants' opportunities to learn about their social and nonsocial world, make this relationship of correspondence the first target for analyzing social influence. Our task now is to establish how this correspondence in behavior comes about.

One approach might be to employ increasingly restrictive definitions to capture correspondences in behavior due to social influence. For example, one could code only those instances when one infant watches his peer initiate contact with a certain object and then within 5 seconds himself initiates contact with the same object. Such definitions may persuade oneself or one's audience, but the problem remains: How many of these instances could be expected from alternative explanations? Definitions based upon a complex of behaviors (e.g., watching first, then contacting) make the computation of "chance" probabilities of occurrence difficult, if not impossible. A more serious difficulty also exists; restrictive definitions prejudge the extent and form of social influence that can be discovered. You record only what has been defined. When studying a phenomenon not well-known, especially when studying the developmental origins of a phenomenon, restrictive definitions presume knowledge usually not available. For example, an infant's action upon a toy may cause a peer to act upon the same toy, but at 10 months of age there may be an average lag of 20 seconds between the two children's actions, and at 2 years the lag may be as short as 5 seconds. Defining imitation as one child duplicating another's actions within 5 seconds would lead to the erroneous conclusion that 10-month-olds rarely influence each other's actions. Restrictive definitions, then, close off the possibility of discovering salient variations in the phenomenon studied.

Ongoing work is exploring an alternative approach that allows for discovery about social influence while still taking as its primary datum the freely occurring interactions between the infant peers. The times of occurrence of relatively simple elements of behavior (e.g., location in space, object contacted, actions upon objects) are recorded for each infant individually. Then the temporal relationships existing between the two infants in these elements are established and assessed against the relationship generated by alternative models of what factors determine the infants' behavior.

The approach has necessitated a shift from reliance upon on-the-spot recording of behavior to multiple recordings from videotapes of the peer interaction. Videotapes are supplemented with on-the-spot recordings of behaviors difficult to judge from the tapes (e.g., facial expression, direction of vocalization). The camera person is instructed to keep both infants in view at all times and to zoom in for close-ups whenever possible—a task requiring both dexterity and the successful prediction of infant behavior!

The sample data presented come from two pairs of 18-month-olds that were observed in a laboratory playroom twice a week for 4 weeks. During the first week, each child came with his mother to the playroom once with his peer and once alone; the order of conditions was counterbalanced across pairs.

During the remaining 3 weeks, each pair met twice a week in the playroom. The mothers again sat on the floor and talked to one another; they responded with a word or smile to their children's overtures but did not initiate interaction or direct their activities except for the rare instances when a child was in danger. For the visits without a peer present, an unfamiliar female adult played the role of the second mother. The playroom was simply furnished with a children's table, a wall mirror, pictures, and several pairs of attractive toys. One toy and its duplicate, chosen according to a random order, were placed on the table at the start of each meeting and were used only for that meeting. Thus peers initially unfamiliar with one another met together for about 30 minutes on seven separate occasions. Their visit alone to the same playroom assessed their choice of activities in the absence of a peer.

The question of whether one infant's actions upon an object influence another infant to act upon the same object illustrates the approach. The time elapsing between one child's initiation of action upon an object and the other child's initiation of action upon the same object or its duplicate is recorded, and this *time* becomes the basic datum for assessing social influence. Nine objects were considered—each of the three sets of toys present during all play sessions, the toys introduced for that play session alone, the table, the radiator, the mirror, the walls and doors, and the mothers. Initiation of action upon an object was defined as the child either moving an object or moving his hands or feet upon the object; action upon an object was terminated when either the loss of contact with the object was accompanied by the initiation of manipulation of another object or when the loss of contact with the object lasted for at least 10 seconds, whichever occurred first. Viewing the videotape of a play session, a coder focused upon a single child and used an electronic digital recording device (Datamyte) to record the time of occurrence of each initiation and termination of action upon each of the nine objects. The sequential listings obtained for each child of a pair were later combined on the same time scale. From the combined record, coders determined each time one of the infants initiated action upon an object that the other infant was not already contacting; the coders then recorded the time elapsing before the other infant initiated action upon the same object or its duplicate.

The temporal relationships found between the peers' initiations of contact with objects are summarized in Fig. 6.1. The ordinate represents what proportion of the initiations were followed by the peer's initiation of contact with the same object within a set time interval (a match); the abscissa represents time intervals of increasing duration. The data plotted with closed symbols in the left-hand column are from sessions when both children were together in the playroom; those represented by open circles result from treating the data from sessions in which each child played alone in the playroom as if they came from a session with the two children together. The latter data, from individual sessions, thus estimate the temporal relationship

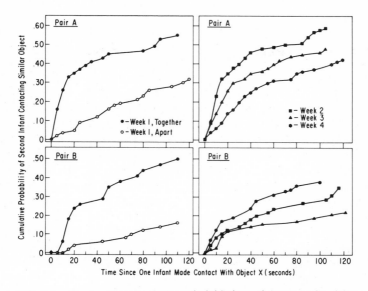

FIG. 6.1.   Temporal correspondence in initiations of contacts with objects between two infants coming to a playroom either together (closed symbols) or separately (open symbols). The data plotted are averages for the two infants of a pair.

between the two children's initiations of contact with objects to be expected from common toy preferences, common temporal trends in what objects are manipulated, and other such "chance" factors. The extent to which the solid curve deviates from the open curve reflects the amount of social influence occurring between the peers, and the form of the solid curve reflects temporal parameters of the social influence.

Social influence is clearly demonstrated for these two pairs of 18-month-olds. When the children met together in Week 1, they matched each other's initiations of contacts with objects often and rapidly. Of the initiations for Pair A, 36% were matched within 20 seconds; over 25% for Pair B were matched within 30 seconds. In contrast, the control data from the individual play session yielded many fewer matches. The linear form of the control function also indicates that matches of initiations occurred no more readily in the seconds immediately following a peer's initiations than in subsequent seconds—a criterion for the absence of social influence.

The rapidity with which the matching initiations occurred differed for the two pairs. Matches for Pair A were most frequent during the first 5 seconds after initiations; but the modal frequency for Pair B was between 10 and 15 seconds. For both pairs, however, most of the matches that appear to be the result of social influence occurred within 30 seconds of initiations.

The right-hand column of Fig. 6.1 shows the changes found in this form of social influence as the infants became more familiar with one another and the play setting. For Pair A, matches remained frequent and rapid during Week 2 and then decreased progressively during Weeks 3 and 4. For Pair B, a different picture emerged; matches decreased markedly and progressively during Weeks 2 and 3 and then became more frequent again during the final week. The curvilinear form of each function, however, attests to the continuing occurrence of social influence. Understanding how this process changes with familiarity requires more information, not yet available, about many other changes in the infants' interactions during these weeks. The data are presented here only to illustrate one potentially useful way of analyzing social influence. Providing that sufficient data are available, functions can be fit mathematically to such data points to provide estimates of the temporal parameters of social influence.

Approaches that rely upon the naturally occurring interactions of infants nevertheless remain limited by their correlational nature. To firmly establish causal relationships in social interaction and to assess the separate effects of aspects of a person's behavior that occur together, manipulative studies seem required. When one infant initiates contact with an object, he usually moves toward it and looks at it also, and the substance of his contact takes different forms upon different occasions. He may just touch the object, or he may move it in ways relatively simple or complex, relatively familiar or novel. The observing infant may respond differentially to all these aspects of a person's behavior, yet only with great difficulty can they be teased apart in the naturally occurring interactions. Studies systematically varying the behavior of one member of an interacting dyad are needed to further the attack upon the origins of social influence.

One such manipulative study has grown out of the correspondence found in the behavior of infant peers. The goal of engaging a 12- or 18-month-old as a collaborator in research has been abandoned temporarily, and adults are behaving with infants in ways thought important in peer interaction. The adults, and experimenters, are under no delusion that they appear to the infants as overgrown 1-year-olds. Rather, the process of social influence responsible for the correspondence between two infants' behaviors is thought to be a general one. Observing infant peers in interaction served to highlight the process, because each member of the dyad was similarly influenced; but the process is thought to occur with many, if not all, of the persons composing the infant's social world. An unfamiliar adult, then, becomes a convenient partner for beginning to assess relevant aspects of another's behavior.

A 1-year-old comes with his mother to a new room containing several simple toys and an unknown adult. The female adult and mother talk with one another, respond simply to the infant's overtures, and leave the child free to do as he chooses in the new setting. The adult is programmed to behave differently for different groups of infants. For one group, she simply continues to talk with the mother; but for other groups, she periodically makes something more happen in the room following a predetermined sequence of happenings. The happenings may simply be a change in her location relative to the toys, or they may involve her acting upon the toys. And her actions upon the toys may be relatively repetitive or variable. Comparing how the infants of the different groups explore this setting addresses several questions about social influence. Do these happenings, for instance, increase the time that infants spend manipulating the inanimate environment, or the diversity of objects they manipulate, or the diversity of ways in which they manipulate each object? Do the infants go to the toy that the adult manipulates, and does the form of her action upon the toy influence the form of the infant's action? Do these happenings increase the infants' social responsiveness to the adult? The study thus promises to establish causal relationships between another person's behavior and that of the infant and to begin the task of assessing the contributions of these relationships to the infant's functioning and development.

The re-examination of the possibilities for social interaction between young peers thus continues. Starting against the backdrop of claims that peers fail to interact during infancy, the examination began by describing what transpired when pairs of unfamiliar infants first met. Once a variety of behaviors seemingly directed toward the peer were documented, the question became whether these behaviors could be thought of as social behaviors or whether they were simply reactions to the inanimate spectacles that another infant creates. Finding that infants were socially responsive to one another then prompted the study of processes of social influence. The questions surrounding current work are far-reaching ones: To what aspects of social beings do infants respond, how does the behavior of other persons alter the infant's behavior, and how may social interaction contribute to the infant's current functioning and subsequent development? Answers to such questions promise enhanced understanding of infant sociability and of the origins of interpersonal influence.

ACKNOWLEDGMENTS

This research was supported in part by Duke University Research Council Grants. Dr. Judith L. Whatley has been a valued colleague in most of the work discussed, contributing greatly to both the conduct and analysis of the studies and the directions in which the reasoning about peer interaction has evolved. We thank too Mr. Stuart Kutz, Ms. Jayne McGehee, and Ms. Margaret Adams for their aid in individual studies.

REFERENCES

Bridges, K. M. B. A study of social development in early infancy. *Child Development*, 1933, *4*, 36–49.

Buhler, C. *The first year of life.* New York: John Day, 1930.

Eckerman, C. O., & Whatley, J. L. Toys and social interaction between infant peers. *Child Development*, 1977, *48*, 1645–1656.

Eckerman, C. O., Whatley, J. L., & Kutz, S. L. Growth of social play with peers during the second year of life. *Developmental Psychology*, 1975, *11*, 42–49.

Lewis, M., & Rosenblum, L. A. (Eds.). *The effect of the infant on its caregiver.* New York: Wiley, 1974.

Maudry, M., & Nekula, M. Social relations between children of the same age during the first two years of life. *Journal of Genetic Psychology*, 1939, *54*, 193–215.

Rheingold, H. L., & Eckerman, C. O. Some proposals for unifying the study of social development. In M. Lewis & L. A. Rosenblum (Eds.), *Friendship and peer relations.* New York: Wiley, 1975.

Ross, H. S. The effects of increasing familiarity on infants' reactions to adult strangers. *Journal of Experimental Child Psychology*, 1975, *20*, 226–239.

7 Play in Domestic Kittens

Meredith J. West
University of North Carolina at Chapel Hill

INTRODUCTION

Watching young animals play is a delightful pastime. Studying young animals at play is another matter. Beyond the fact that play is apparently easy to recognize (Loizos, 1967; Miller, 1973), there seems to be nothing else simple about it. The inescapable impressions of its spirited and enjoyable nature defy easy translation into objective terms. Statements about its goalless or purposeless character are semantically appealing but limited by our inability to define these terms in relation to behavior in general (Hinde, 1970). Theories of play remain untested partly because of the difficulties of studying a behavior we cannot define and partly because we do now know how to manipulate the presence of play while preserving intact the occurrence of related behaviors.

Despite these obstacles, play remains of interest to students of development because of the unavoidable fact that their subjects, whether they are kittens, monkeys, or children, devote so much time to it. In addition, theories of play tempt us to believe that play is of developmental significance. Play is often thought of as a preparatory mechanism allowing animals to "practice" species-typical behavior without a risk to their survival (Beach, 1945; Loizos, 1967). Aggressive, predatory, and sexual behaviors of adult animals are thought to be affected by early opportunities to execute their components during play. Studies relevant to this proposal have produced interesting results (Eibl-Eibesfeldt, 1970; Poole, 1966; Suomi & Harlow, 1975), but, in all cases, it has been impossible to determine that adult performance was affected only by youthful play experience.

179

More general proposals have focused upon play's role as a mechanism of socialization or learning. Play is thought to foster friendly relations among peers and allow them to learn to interact socially without impunity (Bekoff, 1972; Novak & Harlow, 1975; West, 1974a). Obviously, play signals friendly relations, but whether it produces them remains to be established. As a more general mechanism of learning, play seems a plausible candidate, but as yet we do not know how to demonstrate the specific nature of the presumed learning.

Many theories of play's function imply that it is of future benefit to the young animal. This is due partly to the resemblance of play activity to adult behavior and partly to the fact that observers can see little in the immediate context to explain its occurrence (Berlyne, 1969). We may also be biased in this respect by our knowledge that these animals will grow up into rather predictable adults in terms of how they find food, behave with mates, rear their young, and manage many aspects of their social lives. Thus, when we see youthful play activity of no known function, it is tempting to conclude that it has evolved to meet relevant future needs.

These theoretical difficulties illustrate that play is a troublesome construct—it seems to be an important behavior, and yet no one knows exactly how or why. Play's puzzling nature is also indicated by a look at the history of the "study" of play. It is hard to think of an area of behavior that over the last 100 years has so regularly attracted theoretical attention while at the same time has so completely escaped empirical study. In recent years, this lop-sided situation has developed a new twist—several of the major theoretical articles reviewing what we do and do not know about play have concluded by suggesting that it may not be possible to study play anyway (Berlyne, 1969; Welker, 1971). The paradox seems clear: Play should not be studied although it has not been studied. Happily, some recent investigators have proved themselves immune to such logic, and studies of the play of many species of mammals are underway (see *American Zoologist*, 1974, *15*). Investigators wishing to study play, however, face several difficulties. First, they cannot look to past studies for help in designing appropriate methodology. Few paradigms, good or bad, have been developed to work from. This is not a minor deficit when one thinks of the rich methodological history of many behaviors such as learning. Second, because of the overabundance of theories, investigators may be tempted to hurry through the initial descriptive stages in order to confront many of the theoretical contradictions. Premature attempts to manipulate the frequency of play or to alter its developmental course will only be of passing significance if 10 years from now we decide they are based on inadequate definitions of the concept itself. Woodworth (1940) once commented that:

> Psychology finds it convenient to transform its verbs into nouns. Then what happens? We forget that our nouns are merely substitutes for verbs, and start

hunting for the *things* [Woodworth's italics] denoted by the nouns—for substances, forces, faculties—but no such things exist; there is only the individual engaged in these different activities [p. 19].

With respect to the study of play, what this suggests is that we investigate thoroughly the nature and dynamics of the activities we term *play* before attempting to study its causation, function, or development. Looking at what animals actually do when we say they are playing seems logical as a first step, but it is one that has not been used extensively. Although the information gained will certainly not rid us of all the problems encountered when considering play, it may provide new directions in our management of this troublesome concept. The methods and concepts of interactional analysis hold promise in this respect, as they may aid us in detecting information about play that we previously ignored or were unable to realize in empirical terms.

The research described here focuses on several questions concerning the content of play in domestic kittens. Although kittens are often described as players par excellence, few systematic studies of their play exist (Barret & Bateson, in press; Egan, 1976; Leyhausen, 1956). The present investigation started with what seemed like the most basic question: What do kittens do when we say they are playing with inanimate objects or peers? Two "forms" of play were chosen because both are prevalent during youth and because it seemed reasonable to study play not only by comparing it to nonplayful activity but by looking for differences within forms of the activity as well (Berlyne, 1969; Bijou, 1976).

CONSTRUCTION OF THE PLAY CATEGORIES

Before turning to the studies themselves, a few words are in order about the procedure used to construct the categories of play. In retrospect, neither the word "procedure" nor "construct" seems appropriate, because the categories were not really constructed (i.e., they were there all the time); it was just a matter of learning to see them in the same way that a bird-watcher comes to identify different species or a wine taster "learns" how to differentiate and describe many wines.

The first and most essential step was to observe two litters of kittens daily for several hours from the time the kittens were born until they were 3 months old. Although many notes were taken during this period, none were used as data, and few would have qualified as good observations. These notes were amply supplemented by the experience of caring for and living with the kittens, an equally essential factor because there is no way to separate out what was gained through intentional observation or through incidental encounters. In addition, extensive still photography of the kittens' activities was carried out, not so much to have a permanent visual record but to try and duplicate with the camera what was being done with paper and pencil—to try and isolate visually the components of kitten play. Using a camera has an advantage because in order to get a picture of a specific behavior, one is forced to attend to minute behavioral detail in order to anticipate when it will occur. Such training is important because it teaches one to recognize what happens before, not after, an event.

From these written and photographic records, along with a liberal dose of insight gained from the "live-in" arrangements, the categories listed in Table 7.1 emerged. Many of the categories went through several stages of revision and could have undergone more, depending on the questions being asked. For the purposes of these studies, where the basic question was to determine what kittens do when we say they are playing, the catergories were sufficient to capture the major postural and motion components of kitten play. Essentially, they describe the bodily postures and accompanying limb, tail, or

TABLE 7.1
Definitions of Kitten Play Behaviors

Scoop: kitten picks up an object with one of the front paws by curving the paw under the object and grasping it with its claws (Object Play)

Toss: kitten releases an object from the mouth or paw with a sideways shake of the head or paw (Object Play)

Grasp: kitten holds an object between the front paws or in the mouth (Object Play)

Poke/bat: kitten contacts an object with either of the front paws from either a vertical (poke) or horizontal orientation (bat) (Object Play)

Bite/Mouth: kitten places an object in the mouth and closes and opens its mouth around the object (Object Play)

Belly-up: kitten lies on its back, its belly up, with all four limbs held in a semivertical position; the tail is straight back and may be moved back and forth; the hind limbs may move in treading movements and the forelimbs may be used to paw at an object or kitten; the mouth is typically open (Social and Object Play)

Stand-up: kitten stands near or over another kitten or object with its head oriented toward the head and neck region of the other kitten; the kitten's mouth is open and it may lunge toward the other with its mouth or raise a paw toward the other (Social and Object Play)

Face-off: kitten sits near another kitten and hunches its body forward, moving its tail back and forth, and lifts a paw toward the other often with swiping motions (Social Play)

Vertical stance: kitten extends its back legs so the kitten is in a bipedal position with the forelimbs outstretched and perpendicular to its body (Social and Object Play)

Horizontal leap: kitten arches its back, curves its tail upwards and toward its body, and leaps off the ground (Social Play)

Side-step: kitten arches its back, curls its tail upwards, and walks sideways (Social and Object Play)

Pounce: kitten crouches with its head held low or touching the ground, its back legs tucked in and tail straight back often moved back and forth; kitten then moves its hindquarters back and forth and moves forward and upward by extending its back legs (Social and Object Play)

Chase: a kitten runs after an object or kitten (Social and Object Play)

---

mouth movements used by kittens when they approach, contact, or manipulate another kitten or an inanimate object. When these activities were between two kittens, they were considered *social play*; when they were between a kitten and an object, they were termed *object play*. Some of the play categories occurred in both contexts, as indicated in Table 7.1.

Because it was not possible to have a second observer present during the daily observation periods, observer agreement was obtained only during the initial phase of the work after the categories had been defined. Recorded by two observers were 50 sequences of play with objects and 100 social play sequences. The subjects were kittens from the two litters used in the preliminary stages. Agreement on the play categories used in a given sequence was 86%, and agreement on the sequence of categories observed was 85%. Most disagreements concerned the number of categories appearing (e.g., two pounces in a row vs. one, and not whether a pounce occurred at all).

Play with inanimate objects would appear to be the simpler of the two behaviors to analyze due to the restricted role of the object. Object play can be loosely defined as repeated approach, contact, and manipulation of objects. In order to learn more about its content, 350 instances of object play were recorded, 14 each from 25 9-week-old kittens (West, 1974b). Eleven categories of behavior were identified and defined (Table 7.1). A sequence of object play was defined as all behaviors occurring after and including the first appearance of one of the 11 behaviors and continuing until the kitten ceased to look at or contact the object for 10 seconds or until both object and kitten were out of view. These sequences were then examined to detemine several properties of object play.

The first question asked concerned the initiation of object play. Although eight of the 11 behaviors were observed to begin object play, two were used most often: Vertical stances and poke/bat responses initiated 21% and 35% of all sequences respectively (Table 7.2).[1] These responses also occurred most often during a sequence, accounting respectively for 15% and 29% of all behavior seen during a sequence. Biting/mouthing and belly-up postures were next in order of frequency.

Several of these behaviors also occurred repetitively. Of all poke/bats, 42% were followed by poke/bats with as many as 11 repetitions (Table 7.2). Vertical stances, side-steps, belly-ups, and bite/mouth responses also occurred successively; however, the number of repetitions was typically two or three.

Thus, although object play can involve a number of behaviors, the same few behaviors, most notably vertical stances and poke-bats, appear to predominate the activity in terms of both initiation and maintenance of it.

---

[1]Looking at an object was presumed to also be occurring but by itself was not considered as a play.

TABLE 7.2
Proportion of Occurrence of Play Patterns
Within Object Play Sequences

	Proportion Occurrence as First Response	Proportion Occurrence in Any Position	Proportion Successive Occurrence
Belly-up	.07	.09	.09
Stand-up	.10	.05	.00
Vertical stance	.21	.15	.27
Pounce	.10	.03	.00
Side-step	.07	.04	.14
Chase	.00	.10	.00
Poke/bat	.35	.29	.42
Grasp	.00	.05	.00
Scoop	.05	.04	.00
Toss	.00	.04	.00
Bite/mouth	.05	.12	.08

It was difficult to determine the particular behaviors most likely to terminate an object play sequence because over one-half of the sequences ended when the object became lodged in an inaccessible location. Sometimes the kitten would poke at it several times and abandon it, or the kitten would disappear into the space housing the object, making observation impossible.

These data suggest an emphasis upon motion, repetition, and steretoyped bodily approaches as primary descriptive components of object play in kittens. The fact that it is a *sequence* of activity, that it is composed of *repeated* elements of approach and manipulation, and that the sequences may be partially or completely *duplicated* with the same or similar objects, provides bases for comparison to other behaviors seen with objects and possible grounds for functional interpretations.

COMPARISON TO OTHER
OBJECT-RELATED BEHAVIORS

A behavior that is often linked to play is exploration. Welker (1959) has stated that: "At a certain point in the sequence of investigation of a novel stimulus may come a stage at which the motor behaviors change subtly and the behavior takes on the characteristic appearance of play [p. 764]." It might then be argued that play is a more "vigorous" form of exploration. This is certainly the case if we loosely define exploration as, for example, any manipulation of an object. If we use the term to refer to behaviors such as looking, listening, sniffing, touching, etc., that are used to acquaint the animal with the properties of unfamiliar objects and events, we should predict a decline in exploration over time with the same object. If play is functionally linked to exploration, it too should decline. This result was not obtained in a study of kittens' exploratory and playful responses to unfamiliar and familiar objects (West, 1977). Across two test sessions separated by a 5-day familiarization period, play with the same objects increased in frequency, but exploration decreased. These results suggest that play can be differentiated from exploration, at least in kittens.

Another behavior frequently linked to object play is hunting. Here the linkage is to a behavior occurring in the future, an approach questioned earlier. These data provide empirical reasons as well for questioning this procedure. There is certainly a similarity between object play and hunting in that both stress approach and manipulation. If, however, we take the term "hunting" seriously, object play seems to be inefficient practice at best. Play with objects resembles activities with captured not uncaptured prey. The term hunting, however, implies lack of capture. The use of postures such as the vertical stance also hardly seems to be an appropriate initiation to an alert prey object. In fact, descriptions of feline hunting stress the use of "stealthy" approach through stalking and pouncing (Leyhausen, 1956), behaviors used infrequently in object play. The best practices for hunting is probably hunting, as others have suggested.

No one has ever adequately explained cats' tendencies to manipulate captured prey in a manner very similar to the way kittens play with objects. But it is this behavior that bears the strongest resemblance to object play; thus any functional relationships should be applied at this point. Few would want to suggest, however, that object play is "preparation" for the functionally ambiguous activity of posthunting manipulation of prey, as this would only further confuse matters.

As suggested earlier, a more fruitful area to examine for answers may be the immediate context of play itself. Before looking at this context, social play must also be considered because both of these activities occur in the same developmental period.

SOCIAL PLAY IN KITTENS

Social play also involves approach, contact, and manipulation. The fact, however, that here both participants are capable of contributing to the interaction would suggest that the actual content might differ. It also means that the methods of analysis must be sensitive to the dyadic nature of the interaction. In order to learn about this behavior, 1500 instances of social play, compiled from observations of 22 kittens, were recorded and analyzed (West, 1974a). These data were first examined in ways similar to object play.

The play of 6- and 12-week-old kittens was also compared to learn more about developmental changes in the activity. It was thought that the content of social play might change during this 6-week period as the kitten acquired experience in executing the various play responses and obtained social feedback as to their consequences.

Eight behaviors were identified as comprising social play (Table 7.1). Six of these also occurred during play with objects. The two seen only during social play were face-offs and horizontal leaps.

The behavior used most often to initiate social play at either 6 or 12 weeks was a pounce: 42% of all first responses at 6 weeks and 37% at 12 weeks were accounted for by this response (Table 7.3). Belly-up and stand-up responses accounted for 28% and 33% of all first responses at 6 and 12 weeks, respectively. Side-steps decreased in frequency from 20% at 6 weeks to 3% at 12 weeks; vertical stances increased from 8% to 24%.

The interactional consequences of these behaviors were then examined. How "successful" were these behaviors in eliciting a playful response from another kitten? Also, which playful behaviors did they elicit? Pounces were successful in eliciting play on 92% of the occasions they were used at 6 weeks, and 90% at 12 weeks (Table 7.4). At both ages, the response of the other kitten was most often a belly-up (52% and 51%, respectively). Belly-up postures, when used to initiate play, had success rates of 89% and 84%, respectively, at the two ages. For stand-up postures, the rates were 82% and 88% at each age. For both of these behaviors, the play response produced by the other kitten was the complement of the other—a belly-up in response to a stand-up initiation, and vice versa. All three of these initiating behaviors therefore had relatively high success rates and tended to elicit one of the two behaviors in return.

TABLE 7.3
Social Play Behaviors as a Function of Position
in a Play Sequence at 6 and 12 Weeks of Age

	6 Weeks			12 Weeks		
	First	Middle	Last	First	Middle	Last
Belly-up	.13	.36	.14	.16	.23	.09
Stand-up	.15	.21	.07	.17	.20	.10
Pounce	.42	.07	.00	.37	.07	.00
Side-step	.20	.11	.03	.03	.04	.00
Face-off	.00	.03	.00	.00	.20	.06
Vertical stance	.08	.08	.00	.24	.10	.00
Horizontal leap	.00	.03	.20	.00	.04	.25
Chase	.02	.00	.53	.03	.15	.50

TABLE 7.4
Proportion of Occurrence of Social Play Patterns
in Response to Play Initiation at 6 and 12 Weeks of Age

Play Pattern of Initiator	Play Pattern Used in Response								
	BU	SU	P	SS	FO	VS	HL	CH	Other[a]
6 Wks.									
Belly-up	.30	.40				.19			.11
Stand-up	.62	.20							.18
Pounce	.52	.05		.15		.20			.08
Side-step	.12			.50		.13			.25
Vertical stance	.43							.17	.40
Chase	.10			.30		.30			.30
12 Wks.									
Belly-up	.11	.38			.25	.10			.16
Stand-up	.55	.10			.11	.12			.12
Pounce	.51	.03		.05		.19		.12	.10
Side-step				.35			.45		.20
Vertical stance	.49	.05					.25		.21
Chase	.45					.25			.30

[a]The category "other" refers to any nonplayful response.

The decline in the use of side-steps might have been due to the combined effects of its lower success rate (75%) and the play response elicited by it. Side-steps were most often followed by side-steps. It was further observed that this duplication often led to a side-step response by the initiator, followed by the same response by the other kitten, and so forth. Why this form of repetition was not a preferred form of interaction is unclear but suggests that for play to ensue, the kittens' behaviors must complement but not duplicate each other's. The increase in the use of the vertical stance might then be accounted for by the fact that when it did occur at 6 weeks, it elicited a belly-up. Thus the type of response elicited may have led to its higher use at 12 weeks.

These results suggest that the content of play may be affected by kittens' previous experiences in playing. This observation emphasizes the need for more precise ways to probe the play interaction beyond the first two responses seen. This is, however, quite difficult, because the initiating kitten's response to its partner's first response (thus the third response seen) is a product not only of the other kitten's behavior but the first kitten's behavioral state as well. Thus, the first kitten may now be more or less excited than when it first initiated the play bout, depending on how exactly the other kitten responded. In addition, contextual factors may be important. For example, the fact that kittens use more than one type of initiation at 12 weeks and beyond may be affected by the play setting itself. Kittens may be at different distances from one another prior to play together. If two kittens happen to be close together, a belly-up or vertical stance may suffice to effect contact, but pounces may be more appropriate when kittens are initially farther apart. This problem could be studied by comparing play in different settings: Kittens confined to small cages, for example, may show a lowered frequency of pouncing.

Data concerning the content of ongoing play confirm the impression that the initiating behaviors serve to promote physical contact. The most frequent behaviors anywhere is an ongoing sequence of belly-up and stand-up postures at 6 weeks and belly-up, stand-up, and face-off postures at 12 weeks (Table 7.3). The belly-up and stand-up postures were also frequently alternated by the two kittens, so that these behaviors followed themselves on 67% of the occasions that any play response occurred. Face-offs also appeared in conjunction with these behaviors at 12 weeks, so that 42% of all face-offs are followed by one of these other two postures. The termination of a social-play sequence was most often marked by chases or horizontal leaps at either age. Both of these behaviors serve to increase distance between the kittens.

COMPARISON OF SOCIAL- AND OBJECT-PLAY BEHAVIORS

Social play in kittens involved initial approach and contact accomplished by one of several means, followed by alternation of several forms of physical contact and subsequent separation. How does this compare with play with objects? Although these two activities share at lease six behaviors and an overall structure in common, there are differences worth noting. First, repetitions of the same behavior occur frequently during object play and infrequently during the social play of older kittens. Although two behaviors may be alternated in social play, exact duplication is rare. Second, play with objects involves a series of approaches, contacts, or separations, whereas social play typically proceeds from approach to contact to separation. This may, in part, however, reflect the nature of the categories used and the fact that social and object play were analyzed in different ways.

Obviously, these differences reflect the fact that (1) objects don't move by themselves and kittens do, and (2) a moving object and moving kitten supply different forms of feedback. It is difficult to know how to proceed to study further the idea of differential feedback other than to look for other characteristics of these activities that may reflect these differences. The comparative frequency of social and object play in adults may be an example. Although both activities are quite frequent in kittens, juvenile and adult cats engage in much less social play than object play (West, 1974b). The decline in social play coincides with increasing sexual behavior, independence from maternal care, and greater dispersion among the littermates. Observations of male and female cats reared together from birth for 1 year in the laboratory revealed that the sexual behavior of the males was frequently rebuffed by the females except during their brief period of estrous. In general, females became less tolerant of any close contact with males, playful or otherwise. Observations on another group of cats reared together for several years has also indicated that on the rare occasions that adult cats play socially (male or female), the interactions are briefer and often end with one participant growling or hissing at the other. Two hundred and fifty sequences of adult play collected over a 2½-year period have been analyzed in the manner described for kitten social play. Most sequences (87%) consisted of only three moves, a pounce by the initiator, followed by a chase of the two participants. Sometimes only a chase occurred, sometimes only a pounce. What seemed to have happened is that the middle had dropped out of the play. Belly-up and stand-ups almost never occurred, in contrast to their high frequency in kitten social play. The females accounted for 85% of the social play observed, male–female encounters for 10%, and male–male interactions for only 5%. Thus, adult play not only is infrequent in contrast to kitten play; it is different in form. It is worth noting, however, that these changes in social play do not seem to reflect a unitary decrease in social interactions among adult cats. The adults frequently groomed one another, rubbed noses, and slept together— social behaviors of a clearly amicable nature. Other observers of free-ranging domestic cats have also reported the presence of these social behaviors among adults (Laundré, 1977; Leyhausen, 1956). It may be that the adult cats' decline in social play reflects a lessening tolerance of close physical contact except under very special circumstances. The internal and external feedback conditions necessary for social play may thus occur less frequently. Negative signals from unresponsive or intolerant companions combined with negative feedback experienced during close encounters may together account for adult cats' decline in interest in social play. Object play, on the other hand, may decline somewhat due to decreased opportunity as a result of conflicting responsibilities (finding food, rearing young, etc.), but (also due to the unchanging nature of the object's reactions), it may remain a preferred activity of adults as well as kittens.

Although social play can be differentiated from object play, it does share certain similarities. In fact, it resembles play with objects more than any other feline activity. Social play has, however, most often been likened to aggressive behavior and termed "play-fighting." Although both activities involve direct contact, the most identifiable signs of aggression—injury to an opponent and/or concomitant signs of fear or stress—are absent during play. This absence has been noted in several other animals as well [e.g., polecats (Poole, 1966) and rhesus monkeys (Symons, 1974)].

CONSEQUENCES OF PLAY

These data for object and social play represent a first step in answering the question: What do kittens do when they play with objects or peers? The next questions one could ask concern the consequences and functions of these activities for young kittens. One obvious feature of both of these activities is that kittens playing are kittens in motion. Thus a primary consequence of play is that kittens obtain exercise during the developmental period of rapid physical growth. The content of play can also be viewed in more specific exercise terms. During play, the kitten moves its body in relation to the movements of the object or other kitten and thus must be accumulating "correlated sensory-motor feedback resulting from self-initiated movement" (Gibson, 1969, p. 249). There have been numerous investigations demonstrating the importance of self-produced movement for perceptual-motor development (Dru, Walker, & Walker, 1975; Held & Hein, 1963). Thus a beneficial consequence of play may be the acquisition or refinement of perceptual-motor skills. It could be and has been argued that kittens need not play to acquire this experience (Loizos, 1967). Although this is certainly the case, the fact that kittens play as much as they do suggests that this counterargument may be hypothetically accurate but empirically misleading. Play may not be the exclusive source of perceptual-motor experience, but it is probably the most natural and most extensive source for normally reared, healthy kittens.

Social play may also have consequences related to the development of peer relations. The period of most social play coincides with the decline of the mother–kitten relationship in terms of her direct involvement in daily care (Haskins, 1975; Rosenblatt, Turkewitz, & Schneirla, 1961). It may be that the kittens' developing social capabilities both ease and promote the transition to independence from maternal care. Rosenblatt and others have suggested that mother cats become less tolerant of proximity to their kittens around the sixth week of life. As they have noted, part of the reason lies in changes in the mother and part in changes in the kittens. A large proportion of kittens' play initiations to peers are reciprocated, and in almost no case does the peer reject playful initiations with aggressive behavior. Mother cats, however, if disturbed too many times by their playful offspring, will swat or growl at them as well as attempt to leave. It may be, then, that the tendency of young kittens to behave playfully changes the mother's and kittens' mutual interest in one another and thus facilitates peer-directed activity.

The fact that social play in kittens is essentially a peer-directed activity may be revealing about the function of social play. Because social play stresses contact between the littermates, it helps to keep the kittens physically together. This may be an extremely important function in a species such as the domestic cat where the mother frequently has to leave the litter unattended.

Contrary to the popular stereotype in children's books and elsewhere, the mother cats observed in these studies almost never travelled with their kittens, even when the kittens were proficient locomotors (West, 1974b). This was especially striking in feral mother cats, who managed their kittens' lives with no human interference at all. These mothers typically left their litter without any of the kittens attempting to follow because they left when the kittens were asleep or playing together and thus preoccupied. Thus, the form of social play exhibited by kittens may have evolved because kittens who play together remain accessible to the returning mother but safe during the time that she cannot attend to them. That kittens need protection was made dramatically clear when on several occasions I observed that male cats killed young kittens or when a wandering kitten (from a singelton litter) was trampled by a horse. This suggests that different forms of social play may have evolved in species of mammals where the young travel with the mother. There are not enough data at this point to know, but in many ungulates, for example,their social play appears to involve much more extensive locomotion (Geist, 1971). In any case, these observations suggest that one way to begin to understand the function of play is to look at the developmental and socio-ecological requirements of the young rather than at the accomplishments of the adult. The observations discussed here all point to play as a set of behaviors eminently suited to the period of youth. The variability in the amount of play exhibited by adult cats might then be explained by how "adult-like" and individual cat's environment actually is. If cats are relieved of the necessity to find their own food or to rear young (i.e., if they are kept in a very kitten-like environment), more play may result.

There is another dimension of social play to be considered. If we forget for a moment about the "play" label and look at the kittens' activities as examples of social interchanges, there appear to be several characteristics of comparative interest. Recent studies of young children have described the development of turn-taking and reciprocal activity patterns as important components of social interaction (Cairns, 1979; Garvey, 1974; Mueller & Lucas, 1975; Sherman, 1975). Children at any early age demonstrate in their peer relations the ability to complement each others' behavior by reciprocating with similar but varied behavioral and verbal expansions, the capacity to pause and wait for a "turn" in a game or bout of play, and the ability to cooperate in developing the theme and content of lengthy interchanges. Some of these components also occur in rudimentary form in social interactions among kittens. For kittens to play socially, both kittens must contribute by performing similar but different forms of physical contact. The frequent alternations of belly-up and stand-up postures highlight this form of social interaction. The low frequency of exact duplications of each other's behavior also attests to the complementary rather than redundant nature of the activity. The increased use of the face-offs postures between bouts of contact may also reflect the kittens' developing abilities to vary the "roles" of initiator and respondent within the interaction as well as the capacity to pause and wait for the other's response. Although we still have much to learn about the organization of social interactions in kittens, children, and all the species in between, it may be that the simple social exchanges of kittens and those of children rest on similar principles of social dynamics.

SUMMARY AND CONCLUSIONS

The content of social and object play is a rich combination of behaviors affording kittens extensive opportunities for developmental progress. Although these data have been interpreted to suggest that play is of benefit to young kittens, they should not necessarily be viewed as arguments for the retention of the construct of play in its present form. The term *play* connotes behaviors performed when there is nothing else of biological importance to do (Berlyne, 1969; Huizinga, 1950). These data, however, attach developmental significance to the play activities themselves. Although the term *play* may remain useful as a signal to observers about what is *not* happening (i.e., the animals are not hungry, sleepy, frightened, etc.), only detailed descriptions and analysis of the behaviors we call *play* will be of long-standing use to students of development. The methods and concepts important to such studies are those of importance to the study of any interaction. Furthermore, our decisions or hesitations about the labeling of activities as play or nonplay should not delay our study of the behaviors themselves. To watch young animals play is to see in action many of the perceptual, cognitive, and social accomplishments we seek to explain. To ignore such activity until we find new labels or constructs would be to deprive ourselves of a wealth of opportunities to learn about behaviors that are at the very heart of the study of development.

REFERENCES

Barrett, P., & Bateson, P. The development of play in cats. *Behaviour*, in press.
Beach, F. A. Current concepts of play in animals. *American Naturalist*, 1945, *79*, 523–541.
Bekoff, M. The development of social interaction, play, and metacommunication in mammals: An ethological perspective. *Quarterly Review of Biology*, 1972, *47*, 412–434.
Berlyne, D. E. Laughter, humor, and play. In G. L. Lindzey & E. Aronson (Eds.), *Handbook of social psychology*. Reading, Mass.: Addison-Wesley, 1969.
Bijou, S. W. *Child development; The basic stage of early childhood*. Englewood Cliffs, N.J.: Prentice-Hall, 1976.
Cairns, R. B. *Social development: The origin and plasticity of social interchanges*. San Francisco: Freeman 1979.

Dru, D., Walker, J. P., & Walker, J. B. Self-produced locomotion restores visual capacity after striate lesions. *Science*, 1975, *187*, 265–266.

Egan, J. Object-play in cats. In J. S. Bruner, A. Jolly, & K. Sylva (Eds.), *Play*. New York: Basic Books, 1976.

Eibl-Eibesfeldt, I. *Ethology: The biology of behavior*. New York: Holt, Rinehart & Winston, 1970.

Garvey, C. Some properties of social play. *Merrill-Palmer Quarterly*, 1974, *20*, 163–180.

Geist, V. *Mountain sheep*. Chicago: University of Chicago Press, 1971.

Gibson, E. J. *Principles of perceptual learning and development*. New York: Appleton-Century-Crofts, 1969.

Haskins, R. *Eliciting conditions, form, and function of kitten vocalizations*. Unpublished doctoral dissertation, University of North Carolina, 1975.

Held, R., & Hein, A. Movement produced stimulation in the development of visually guided behavior. *Journal of Comparative and Physiological Psychology*, 1963, *56*, 872–876.

Hinde, R. A. *Animal behaviour: A synthesis of ethology and comparative psychology*. New York: McGraw-Hill, 1970.

Huizinga, J. *Homo ludens: A study of the play element in culture*. Boston: Beacon, 1950.

Laundré, J. The daytime behavior of domestic cats in a free-roaming population. *Animal Behaviour*, 1977, *25*, 990–998.

Leyhausen, P. Verhaltenstudien an katzen. *Zeitschrift für Tierpsychologie*, 1956, *Bieheft*, 2, 1–120.

Loizos, C. Play behavior in the higher primates. In D. Morris (Ed.), *Primate ethology*. Garden City: Anchor, 1967.

Miller, S. Ends, means, and galumphing: Some leimotifs of play. *American Anthropologist*, 1973, *75*, 87–98.

Mueller, E., & Lucas, T. A developmental analysis of peer interactions among toddlers. In M. Lewis & L. Rosenblum (Eds.), *Friendship and peer relations*. New York: Wiley, 1975.

Novack, M. A., & Harlow, H. F. Social recovery of monkeys isolated for the first year of life: L. rehabilitation and therapy. *Developmental Psychology*, 1975, *11*(2), 453–465.

Poole, T. B. Aggressive play in polecats. *Symposium of the Zoological Society, London*, 1966, *18*, 11–22.

Rosenblatt, J. S., Turkewitz, G., & Schneirla, T. C. Early socialization in the domestic cat based on feeding and other relationships between female and young. In B. M. Foss (Ed.), *Determinants of infant behavior*. London: Methuen, 1961.

Sherman, S. J. *Interchanges in children: Stability, formation, and contextual constraints*. Unpublished doctoral dissertation, University of North Carolina, 1975.

Suomi, S. J., & Harlow, H. F. The role and reason of peer relationships in rhesus monkeys. In M. Lewis & L. Rosenblum (Eds.), *Friendship and peer relations*. New York: Wiley, 1975.

Symons, D. Play and communication in rhesus monkeys. *American Zoologist*, 1974, *14*, 317–322.

Welker, W. I. Genesis of exploratory and play behavior in infant racoons. *Psychological Reports*, 1959, *5*, 764.

Welker, W. I. Ontogeny of play and exploratory behaviors: A definition of problems and a search for new conceptual relations. In H. Moltz (Ed.), *The ontogeny of vertebrate behavior*. New York: Academic Press, 1971.

West, M. J. Social play in the domestic cat. *American Zoologist*, 1974, *14*, 427–436. (a)

West, M. J. *Play in domestic kittens*. Unpublished doctoral dissertation, Cornell University, 1974. (b)

West, M. J. Exploration and play with objects in domestic kittens. *Developmental Psychobiology*, 1977, *10*, 53–57.

Woodworth, R. *Psychology* (4th ed.). New York: Henry Holt & Co., 1940.

III SUMMARY AND CONCLUSIONS

An overview of this volume can serve a double duty: to summarize the ideas found in the several chapters, and to provide guides for the conduct of interactional research. The contributors represent diverse academic backgrounds, theoretical interests, and research styles. Not surprisingly, they do not agree on all points. There is nonetheless a basic consensus on the broader issues of methodological and analytic strategy. The following statements are offered both as guidelines and as proposals to be evaluated, investigated, and extended.

8 Toward Guidelines for Interactional Research

Robert B. Cairns
University of North Carolina at Chapel Hill

INTRODUCTION

The aim of this chapter and, in a larger sense, the entire volume is to bring into focus the common themes and issues surrounding interactional research. The preceding chapters demonstrate that the art of interactional analysis is in a stage of rapid growth. Given the multiple areas of application, it may seem risky—even presumptuous—to abstract guidelines at this time. There is indeed a risk that some of the proposals may be irrelevant or even wrong. But we judge on these matters that the hazards of inaction are greater than those of action. Certain methodological and analytic pitfalls are recurrent, subtle, and capable of thrusting the field into needless disputes.

PROPOSED GUIDES

On Research Designs

Interactional methods are not limited to a particular application—whether field or laboratory research, whether manipulative or naturalistic study. Because the methods permit them to be used in "natural" settings, it has sometimes been assumed that they apply only to those settings. That assumption is in error. As Parke indicates in Chapter 1, the procedures are design-free in that they can be used with equal power in experimental laboratory work as well as in nonmanipulative laboratory studies. There is a continuum, not a dichotomy, in the laboratory–field interface. A singular advantage of the observational-interactional procedures is that they permit a sensitive and powerful assessment of experimental effects in diverse contexts.

As a safeguard against the pitfall of mistaking correlational effects for causative ones, it is imperative that investigators combine, at different stages of their research, manipulative procedures with nonmanipulative ones. The prior chapters cite several instances in which the strategies have been employed with success in disentangling interactional phenomena. This work constitutes a model for future research on social and cognitive processes.

On Knowing the Phenomena

The second guideline concerns the nature of the preparation necessary for successful interactional research, whatever the topic and whatever the species. The key is "Know the phenomenon." In that the formulation of codes, designs, and decisions about timing depends on the prior intimate knowledge of the nature of the interaction-to-be-explained, most successful investigators spend a great deal of time simply learning about the phenomena before making these decisions. It is at this phase of research—the initial phase—that it is not unusual for one's most compelling and significant insights to occur. The time-consuming and often tedious task cannot be assigned to one's research associates unless they are also assigned the responsibility for formulating the rest of the design. Indeed, this initial step is one of the most important ones in interactional research.

What are the pitfalls here? The major error is to think of the task of category development and decisions about timing to be independent of the discovery and hypothesis-testing process. In interactional designs, these "methodological decisions" are in fact an integral feature of the research task. They directly reflect the investigator's insights about the nature of interactional phenomena. The fundamental difference between "traditional" designs and interactional ones lies not on experimental/naturalistic or field/laboratory dimensions. The basic difference lies in the freedom that the investigator has in the selection of dependent variables and the extent to which the selection is guided by the investigator's hunches, insights, and hypotheses rather than by convention.

Nor does the selection/filtering process end at the point at which the data are collected. Unless the investigator has been narrowly restrictive at the first stage of coding, additional decisions must be made in the course of data analysis. The investigator should not feel compelled to analyze all of the data collected. The selection process can continue by posing particular questions and by selecting data appropriate to that question (see Chapter 4, by Castellan, and Chapter 5, by Patterson, this volume).

On the Role of Hypotheses

A third proposal that emerges in virtually all chapters is that the investigator should specifiy the nature of the question to be answered and the assumptions that underly it before the study is conducted. The research question has implications for all major decisions affecting the design, data processing, and interpretation, including category breadth, timing of observations, and statistical treatment of data.

A common pitfall is to assume that the data will "speak for themselves" in revealing the important structures of social behavior and that the research investigator can take a passive role in the discovery process. The flaw in this assumption is that the very formulation of a system of coding and scheduling of observations is shot through with prior assumptions about the structure and functions of social interactions. What one gets out of interactional observations is in a real sense dependent on what one puts into them.

On Observer Agreement

No single issue has produced more hesitation and concern about the validity of interactional methods than has the problem of observer agreement. If one has difficulty in translating a single "stream of behavior" into categorical units, how can it be possible to record reliably the confluence of two streams? The guides with respect to this issue are straightforward because a great deal of attention has been given to the problem. As Yarrow and Waxler discuss in Chapter 2, "observer agreement" itself is a relative index.

Descriptions of the level of observer agreement are necessarily relative to: (1) the persons who observe; (2) the subjects who are observed; (3) the specific categories that are used; (4) the statistic employed in the description; and (5) the nature of phenomena under investigation. It was once believed that the essential problem was to determine "category" reliability, independent of who does the observations and who is observed. The methodological work cited in this volume shows that this simple view of the problem of reliability is in error—that the categories interact with who is observed and who does the observation. On the basis of our present information about the process of observation, the following guidelines are proposed:

1. Behavior observation is a highly skilled endeavor, and concerns about the "reliability" of observations are sometimes overstressed. Simply because naive and untrained persons do not obtain the same categorical reports as persons who are intimately acquainted with the phenomena and are disciplined in the observation does not mean that the observational scheme is "unreliable." The pitfall is analogous to expecting a hunt-and-peck typist to operate at the same level of typing proficiency as a 100-word-per-minute

secretary. Indeed, as investigators have noted, it may be that it takes several weeks or months of experience to make the subtle distinctions that are required. And, as Yarrow and Waxler observe, not all persons are equal to the task. Nor are all individuals equally easy to observe. Concerns about code "reliability" (a) have often forced investigators to be overly cautious in what phenomena they are willing to explore, and (b) have led to the adoption of exceedingly simple and trivial recording patterns. This hesitation seems to reflect a misunderstanding of the relationship between the coding process and the research task. The observational skills required for interactional research are in their way just as demanding as the technical skills required in other forms of psychological and biological research. Nevertheless, the investigator has a continuing responsibility to make sure that his observations are (a) veridical, and (b) correspond to the results that might be obtained by other persons who are similarly trained.

2. "Agreement" concerns should not be limited to the first level of coding (that is, the translation of the observation of behavioral streams into some behavioral code). The careful investigator is equally concerned with second- and higher-level judgments. To ensure that the findings are replicable across the several levels of observation and analysis, it is useful to report agreement at each of the several levels separately. As a further check, it is desirable to report the outcomes obtained by analyzing separately the results of independent observers, taken across the several stages of the experiment (see Chapter 2, by Yarrow & Waxler, this volume). The issue of "reliability" then becomes one of whether the same conclusions would have been reached by treating the data of the two observers independently.

3. The level of "agreement" is relative to the statistics employed to describe similarity/dissimilarity. Different impressions may be communicated about the overall level of agreement depending on whether a correlation coefficient is reported (which can mask different propensities of observers to make use of categories), how the percentage agreement is reported (which categories are included in the numerator and denominator), and the criteria for determining individual counts of "agree" or "disagree" (the envelope of error permitted in adjacent time intervals). Furthermore, agreement on a particular category may not be sufficient to deal with the analysis of sequences. Hence the guidelines: Until a common standard is agreed upon, it is advisable to present information regarding levels of agreement in the assessment of particular observations in both percentage and in correlational form. When feasible, report whether the outcomes (i.e., conclusions) based on the analysis of the data of independent observers differ.

On the Design of Coding Systems

There are no "universal codes" that apply with equal power across settings, subjects, and issues—at least not yet. There is some question as to whether there ever will be, if it is the case that the "code" is an integral feature of the observation-discovery-hypothesis process. There is merit to the view that categories are "discovered," not generated or constructed. The essential idea is that the solution to a research issue depends on what is observed and how these observations are translated into codes.

Certain guidelines are useful to follow when confronted with the task of determining, say, how coercive sequences evolve or how sharing develops:

1. *Breadth of definition.* For interactional observations to be used in a powerful and precise fashion, it is often useful to avoid defining a category broadly at the first level of coding. Hence, as Eckerman discusses, it is more informative albeit more difficult to record acts of single individuals instead of relational categories dependent on two persons. "Imitation" or "matching" would be more economical than recording the acts of the individuals separately, but the economy has a dear price (in terms of arbitrariness, constraints, and capability for the discovery of new relationships). We must emphasize again, however, that the judgment with respect to category breadth and inclusiveness depends heavily on the nature of the questions to be answered.

2. *Length of time intervals.* For parallel reasons, most experienced researchers in interactional methods tend to prefer first-level recording systems that employ short time intervals. The advantages of multiple recordings with each covering a short-time period (e.g., 5–6 seconds) include enhanced observer attention, precision of definition, and facilitation of statistical analysis. Again, the decision is relative to the question under investigation and the nature of the phenomenon to be explained.

3. *The relativity of categorical systems* cannot be overstressed. Although a system appropriate for analyzing the social behavior of rhesus monkeys would seemingly apply with equal power to the social behavior of preschool children, for example, there are serious hazards in the direct adoption. One problem is that the essential means of communication in children (i.e., verbal) plays only a negligible role in primates. Hence the major sources of social control in one form may be of less significance in the other, but the differences are masked by the similarity of the coding systems adopted.

On the Multiple Levels of Analysis

A decision that confronts virtually all researchers in social behavior concerns the issue of how "molar" or "molecular" their observations should be. At one extreme of the "molar" level would be ratings of the individual's performance over a given time span (e.g., one year) and over a variety of settings. The other extreme of the "molecular" dimension would be observations of interactions that are coded each 16 milliseconds from a single-frame analysis of a high-speed video tape, or a detailed analysis of the sound properties of the maternal call of ducks (via a sound spectograph or frequency analyzer). Which is the most profitable strategy to follow?

The pitfall would be to view these procedures to be inherently incompatible. The advances possible by the employment of both molar and molecular codes have been demonstrated nicely in studies of animal behavior, where sophisticated procedures for the analysis of olfactory, auditory, and visual events are combined with the study of social interchanges of dyads and social structures of societies. In the study of child social behavior, however, the several levels of analysis have sometimes been viewed as competing instead of complementary.

1. *Observations vs. ratings.* A particular problem has been the failure of attempts to "validate" observations by demonstrating their correspondence with ratings that others have formed of the nature and content of relationships. Not infrequently, "ratings" of relationships have been shown to be negligibly associated with the direct observation of the same relationships (see Chapter 2, by Yarrow & Waxler, this volume, and Appendix A, this volume). Why the difference? One proposal might be that the two methods reflect different sources of variance and that both are "valid." On the one hand, ratings eliminate variations in the child's behavior that might be attributed to the setting, peculiarities in the acts of other persons, and other novel sources of environmental variance. Hence the rater acts as a computer in arriving at a judgment on the variance that may be attributed to the child's unique contributions to the relationship. On the other hand, direct observations of interchanges preserve the powerful effects of setting, the influence of the ongoing acts of the other person, and variations in immediate bodily states, as well as the child's unique and enduring contributions to the relationship. Observations thus may retain major sources of variance that are eliminated in ratings. Explicit recognition of the different kinds of information yielded by these techniques should sharpen one's use of them.

2. *Sociometric and sociobiological techniques.* A similar case can be made for the use of procedures that provide information about the nature of the social organization in which individuals interact. There is no theoretical requirement that interactional analyses remain at the level of two-person interchanges. On the contrary, analyses of the structure of the larger social unit can yield significant information about the compelling controls of the context in which the dyads are embedded (see Chapter 3, by Bekoff, this volume). By the same token, studies at the dyadic level can provide essential information for understanding the contributors to social structure.

3. *Thematic analysis.* One of the more pressing immediate problems in behavior coding is to devise useful intermediate and higher levels of classification that would permit the investigator to identify interpersonal "themes" (i.e., integrated patterns of behavior). This step is required to bridge

the gap between discrete "molecular" classification schemes, on the one hand, and molar personality descriptions, on the other. It is also required in order to identify recurrent interpersonal social strategies (or "games"), a point that has been recognized both by students of infant relations as well as the biological theorists who are concerned with the evolutionary control of social patterns (Dawkins, 1976; Maynard Smith, 1974). One pitfall in early interactional analyses was the implicit assumption that the behaviors are not structured or organized, or that patterns are so inherently complex that they cannot be classified on other than an atomistic level. Recent work permits us to reject both assumptions. However, the steps for classifying acts into integrated themes have been, at the present, worked out for only a limited range of interactions, age-levels, and species. The major work remains to be done.

On Development and Interactions

There has been a failure among contemporary workers to attend to the intra-organismic and age-related contributors to interchanges. This lack of knowledge about developmental controls has seriously handicapped attempts to formulate ideas on how interchanges are established and are changed in the course of ontogeny. The mere study of children of different ages will not in itself solve the problem unless explicit attention is given to how developmental differences and expectations associated with those differences serve to maintain and change relationships. This shortcoming, which is possibly the most glaring failure of contemporary interactional research, demands immediate attention.

On Analysis

Recent advances in contingency analysis permit powerful and appropriate ways to analyze interchanges (see Chapter 4, by Castellan, this volume). These include: techniques for dealing with changes in dyadic contingencies over the course of the relationship, procedures for estimating error reduction in prediction when one knows the actions of the "other" member of the dyad, and safeguards for combining observations across dyads. In addition to the contingency models, time-series and probability lag techniques are often appropriate for interactional problems.

The choice of analytic technique typically carries with it assumptions about the nature of the relationships to be identified. Hence it is imperative that research investigators become knowledgeable about the special characteristics of the analysis that they adopt instead of relying on convenience, prior familiarity, or convention.

On Pitfalls in Analysis

The statistical analysis of interchanges is not necessarily complex or even difficult. Because the territory is often unfamiliar, there are a few common problems that one should be aware of, including:

1. *Data tyranny.* Because interactional techniques are open-ended with regard to dependent variables, enormous amounts of data are generated in even small scale studies. The compulsion to attempt to analyze all of the data all of the time has tyrannized virtually all researchers who have explored the method. The tyranny should be resisted. If it isn't, numerous problems are created with regard to interpretation, description, and analysis. This pitfall can be avoided by the testing of hypotheses that have been formulated beforehand or, in some instances, during the course of the data analysis itself. In the latter case, one must recognize the possible confounding of expectations with results and, when appropriate, specify the need for replication and cross-validation.

2. *Violations of independence.* This problem crops up when one collapses data across observations, across subjects in dyads, across "others" in dyads, or across contexts. Unfortunately, the implications for the violation of independence have not yet been clarified for the tests that are typically employed in interactional analyses. The investigator who is sensitive to the issue has a number of techniques available to guard against the violation of the assumption. It should also be observed that the question may involve logical and theoretical considerations as well as statistical ones.

3. *Correlated outcomes.* Given the large number of measures derived from the same individual(s), it is likely that some proportion will be associated with the remaining measures. The investigator should therefore consider the meaning of any given relationship in the light of the total pattern of the results. For example, a characteristic such as "activity level" could be the common thread that accounts for a wide range of "significant" relationships among summary dependent variables (such as altruism, agonistic acts, and sharing). In this regard, the analytic strategy proposed by Campbell and Fiske (1959) might be employed to advantage. Furthermore, the collection of multiple dependent variables and their analysis may yield "chance" or fortuitous relationships. The investigator must be sensitive to these pitfalls in the interpretation of interactional data.

4. *Changes in patterns.* Interactional statistics typically assume that information obtained in the initial stages of a session (or series of sessions) will yield the same patterns as information obtained later. The pitfall is that systematic patterns that are modified over time or over contexts may be obscured. Changes in patterns may be brought about by learning or state factors (including changes in emotional states, diurnal cycles, hunger, etc.). In human social development, such dynamic changes in patterns are probably the rule instead of the exception. Castellan's chapter describes procedures

whereby the investigator may directly explore the temporal stability of the patterns that have been identified.

On Technological Advances

Two technological developments have been central to the advancement of interactional research: (1) the advent of inexpensive electronic systems for recording and analyzing what is observed; and (2) the accessibility of computers for storing, describing, and analyzing data.

Of the two developments, the advances in the systems for recording (as by TV and audio records) are the more fundamental for interactional study. They permit the research investigator to develop precise measurements of interchanges at the first level of analysis and to thereby provide an alternative to the use of summary trait constructs or measures at the initial stage of recording. In particular, interchanges can be disentangled by repeated scans of the records in order to identify the acts/statements of each person and how they occur in the sequence (Hall, 1973; Sherman, 1975). Advances in the technology of electronic recording (e.g., ability to impose digital times on each frame; capability to record simultaneously through three or four camera stations on one tape) have made TV techniques even more versatile and valuable.

But the technique will not in itself solve the difficult problems of interactional analysis. Some of the problems associated with its use were discussed by Yarrow and Waxler. The analysis of TV and audio records demands discipline, training, and skill. Of particular interest have been attempts to use direct observations and TV records in a complementary fashion (e.g., Holmberg, 1977).

Computer technologies permit one to store and process large amounts of information that can be handled in no other way. Although computer procedures seem uniquely suited for the analysis of interactional data, there are pitfalls for the unwary. At each stage of the treatment of the data, the investigator must consider which computer programs are likely to yield interpretable results and, on the basis of the information obtained, determine what is the next logical step in the analysis. This analytic strategy can produce significant and meaningful results (see Chapter 5, by Patterson, this volume). But such outcomes are not guaranteed. The pedestrian and routine use of preexisting programs to "discover" patterns can also yield trivial and/or misleading findings.

CONCLUDING COMMENTS

Most of the guidelines may not appear to be especially novel or revolutionary, nor are they intended to be. Nonetheless, certain points depart from intuition and from what appears to be conventional "common sense" in research. We would emphasize that the statements are offered as proposals rather than as rigid prescriptions, to guide further work rather than constrain it. Finally, we might raise again the question of "why interactional procedures?" The matter is nontrivial because there are other methods for studying social development (e.g., monadic observation, interviews, traditional experiments) that are more familiar and do not seem to pose as many obstacles. Our answer can be succinct: It is that the phenomena of social development demand multiple levels of analysis. Interactional methods are not merely an option available for the contemporary study of social patterns: they are required. It is our hope that these guides will facilitate their application to the questions identified some 80 years ago by J. M. Baldwin.

REFERENCES

Campbell, D. T., & Fiske, D. W. Convergent and discriminant validation by the multitrait-multimethod matrix. *Psychological Bulletin,* 1959, *56,* 81–105.

Dawkins, R. *The selfish gene.* Oxford: Oxford University Press, 1976.

Hall, W. M. *Observational and interactive determinants of aggressive behavior in boys.* Unpublished doctoral dissertation, Indiana University, 1973.

Holmberg, M. C. *The development of social interchange patterns from 12–42 months: A cross-sectional and short-term longitudinal analysis.* Unpublished doctoral dissertation, University of North Carolina at Chapel Hill, 1977.

Maynard Smith, J. The theory of games and the evolution of animal conflict. *Journal of Theoretical Biology,* 1974, *47,* 209–221.

Sherman, S. J. *Social interchanges in children: Formation, stability, and contextual constraints.* Unpublished doctoral dissertation, University of North Carolina, Chapel Hill, 1975.

IV APPENDICES

A How to Assess Personality and Social Patterns: Observations or Ratings?

Robert B. Cairns
James A. Green
University of North Carolina at Chapel Hill

INTRODUCTION

This appendix is concerned with an issue of methodology that has the potential of befogging contemporary understanding of how to approach the problems of behavioral analysis. The issue concerns the relative virtues and pitfalls of two major means of social and personality assessment: behavior ratings and behavior observations. The problem is not a new one, having been explored in some depth in the early years of social behavior assessment (Allport & Allport, 1921; Norsworthy, 1908; Rugg, 1921, 1922). Our aim in this note is to outline the current status of the problem and to provide a preliminary analysis of the recent advances that have been made toward its resolution. Finally, we offer some suggestions as to when the procedures are applicable and relevant, and when they are not.

THE PROBLEM

As other chapters in this volume demonstrate, there are multiple techniques available for the study of social patterns and the interactions between children. In the recent literature, increasing use has been made of behavior observation methods or behavior ratings or of some combination of the procedures. Which technique is to be preferred?

A direct answer to this question might be, simply, "The technique that works." Although the pragmatic solution provides a guideline, it does not solve the matter, simply because both procedures have been shown to "work."

For some applications, judgments by raters are most effective. Those applications appear to include the classifications of the maternal–infant relationship (Waters, 1978), certain predictions of individual differences in classroom behavior (Schaefer, 1975), and the identification of cross-situational stabilities in personality (Mischel, 1973).

For other purposes, behavior observations have been seen as the method of choice (e.g., Patterson, 1977). Observations preserve the precise actions of individuals and those with whom they interact, and it is assumed that the analysis of such contingencies will be critical for understanding the processes of interactional regulation and development. Illustrations of their effectiveness in the study of human and nonhuman behavior can be found in the chapters of this volume, including the study of aggressive behaviors, peer relationships, and prosocial actions. Despite the apparent lack of individual-difference consistency, precise behavioral analyses have been influential in the formulation of questions and the solution of problems of social development.

But is it not the case that both ratings and observations aim to obtain assessments of the social functioning of children in the context in which they behave? Yes, except that they differ markedly in the steps that are taken to gain that information and the assumptions that are made about the measurement, scaling, and transformational processes. They also differ in terms of the information that is provided. Recognition of these differences can help to solve the problem of which method should be preferred and when.

ASSUMPTIONS UNDERLYING THE METHODS

It is helpful at this point to identify some of the differences in the assumptions involved in the use of ratings and observation.

Ratings

The distinguishing characteristic of rating scales is that they involve a social judgment on the part of the observer, or "rater," with regard to the placement of an individual on some psychological dimension.[1] To illustrate, consider the problem of how to determine a 9-year-old child's placement on a dimension of "aggression." In a well-designed rating scale, the several points fall on a single dimension and, typically, are given clear definition in terms of the behaviors or properties associated with the several points. The rater must assign the child to a place on this dimension on the basis of intensity, quality, frequency, or some combination of the characteristics of the child's actual behavior.

---

[1]Here we discuss only psychological characteristics: Obviously ratings can be used to evaluate nonpersonal attributes and qualities, including those of context, era, or culture.

Despite differences in the psychometric properties of the various kinds of rating scales, they share in common the property that they *begin* with the complex information-processing capabilities of the rater.[2] The problems of measurement, scaling, and transformation are critical to all techniques of behavior assessment. In ratings, at least some of these steps—sometimes all of them—are taken by the rater privately, prior to recording the judgment.

The following assumptions about the abilities of raters seem to be commonly held:

1. The rater is assumed to share with the investigator, and with other raters, a theoretical concept of the quality or attribute to be rated. Many personality concepts are based on common experience and involve terms borrowed from everyday language. To the extent that we communicate effectively with colleagues and nonprofessionals, we might expect a reasonable consensus on what is meant by these concepts. For the most part, there is. Despite the degree of abstraction involved, most persons seem to agree (within tolerable limits) on what is meant by "intelligence" and "aggression," and, to a lesser extent, "dependency," "attachment," and "altruism." Why the agreement? At least one factor seems to be that judges have been highly "trained" by their experiences in living prior to participating in the research.

2. The rater is assumed to share with the investigator and other raters a concept of which behaviors of the subjects-to-be-rated reflect the quality or attribute. The relevant behaviors may differ according to the age-level or sex of the subject, the conditions under which the subjects are observed, the social class of the subject, or the cultural group of which he or she is a part. In any case, the rater must not only share with other raters the theoretical concept of the attribute but also the methodological concept of how variations in the attribute can be determined empirically. Again, the judge is the beneficiary of both the special training that he may be given by the investigator and by his experiences in living. Idiosyncracies among raters can arise by virtue of variations in such "training," in the rater's private definitions of the abstract concept of the attribute, or in the rater's notion of what behaviors "index" the attribute.

3. The rater is assumed to be able to detect information relevant to the attribute in the stream of the everyday life activities of the person-to-be-rated. This is no small order. Not only must raters determine whether or not a given

---

[2]There are several variant procedures that involve social judgments of an observer. These include ranking techniques (where children are ordered relative to each other on the dimension), dichotomous decisions (where a child is judged to be "aggressive" or not), and multiple-decision measures (where an inventory or "Q-sort" technique is employed and often factor-analyzed). Although there are important differences among such procedures, we focus here on their common elements, most of which reflect the judgmental nature of the initial classification.

act occurred, but whether it met the criteria for inclusion in the concept. Hence, raters must determine whether action patterns were intentional or accidental, justified or unwarranted, "jokes" or "deadly serious," and so on. The rater then offers a judgment that takes into account, and *discounts*, situational, relational, and ephemeral sources of variation that may be responsible for the observed behavior. Because most social attributes involve a fusion of properties of the person as well as events in the setting, the rater must both abstract information about whether or not particular acts occurred and interpret the causes and meaning of the acts.

4. The rater is assumed to share with other raters the same underlying "scale" on which the attribute will be judged. If, for instance, the rater believes that most people in the population have the attribute in abundance, the hypothetical distribution for this rater presumably will be negatively skewed. Alternatively, the rater may assume the attribute to be evenly distributed (rectangular) or normally distributed (bell-shaped). Presumably, the scores assigned to the sample that the rater observes should reflect the implicit distribution. The placement of a given subject on a scale requires, as well, assumptions about the "average" or mean level of the characteristic and what is an extreme level. Hence, the rater must perform a transformation on "raw scores" in judging whether the observed attribute differs from the mean level expected for the reference population, and if so, the direction and magnitude of the difference from the mean. The extent to which these scaling and transformational steps are left up to the rater (are internal and "private") or are kept under the direction of the investigator (external and "public") varies across procedures. In addition, significant advances have been made in understanding how to "rescale" the information provided by raters and thus to standardize their judgments (e.g., Schaefer, 1975).

To summarize the foregoing analysis, the rater is assumed to be a competent personality theorist, methodologist, observer, and psychometrician. The rater thus becomes a full collaborator in the investigation, sharing with the investigator the burden for determining how the major concepts are defined in theory and in practice and how the data analysis proceeds.[3]

---

[3]Although the early writers who were concerned with the use of ratings did not identify the assumptions of the procedures in this form, the guidelines that they offered reflected some of the practical implications of these assumptions. Accordingly, Rugg (1921) indicated that the following steps should be taken to achieve useful ratings: (1) the use of three independent raters to arrive at an average judgment; (2) the use of scales that are "comparable and equivalent" for all raters (i.e., which have similar end anchor points and distributions of the trait among the scale items); and (3) the use of raters who have a thorough knowledge of the subject. The distinction between the methodological techniques necessary to achieve reliable and valid ratings (Points 1–3) and the theoretical assumptions made about the rating process (Points 1–4 in the text) is necessary when comparing ratings with observational procedures.

Rating procedures take advantage of the ability of human beings to take into account multiple sources of information and to abstract and integrate relevant bits. But to what end? Such abstraction and integration permit raters to focus on the "enduring" properties of the person being observed. Ephemeral and irrelevant ("uncharacteristic") behaviors of the subject are eliminated in the first stage of the analysis. In order to arrive at a judgment, the human observer must weigh the significance of an entire series of action patterns by taking into account cultural, interactional, and situational norms and expectations, and by referring the subject's behaviors to those of the appropriate reference group of which he or she is a part. Typically, these are private, internal operations. The remarkable thing is that two or more raters can often agree within tolerable limits in the performance of this task. The convergence of ratings by three or more raters speaks well for the capabilities of human beings as information processors and analysts.

Observations

The distinguishing property of behavior observations is that they involve an attempt to record the actual activities of children as opposed to offering a judgment about children's personal dispositions or the quality of their relationships. Interpretations about the "nature" of the child or of behavioral organization are *not* made at the first level of data recording; these are to be made—if at all—in subsequent analyses of the data. Later analyses may include nonobservational data from the interchange.

Because of the focus of observations on behavioral events as opposed to qualities and enduring dispositions of children, less emphasis is placed on the observer as a theorist and psychometrician than as a "recorder." Hence, the problem of how to transform ongoing behavior into recorded information comes to the forefront. The corollary issues of categorization (how to lump observations together into a category) and breadth of observation (what to select out of the stream of activity for recording) are raised. Accordingly, the following assumptions are made in observational analysis:

1. Observers are assumed to have a clear idea of which events to record, so they know which acts "fit" the particular categories. In general, the more precise the distinctions (in terms of the specificity of the category and in the narrowness of the time intervals covered), the higher the level of agreement among observers when categories are summed.

2. Observers are assumed to have the ability to record accurately the acts of the subject-to-be-observed. To meet the requirement of interactional analysis, observers are also assumed to be able to record accurately the acts of *other* persons in the interaction, the sequential nature of the acts and interacts, and the context in which the relationships occur. To satisfy this

assumption, it is often necessary for the observer to have semipermanent audio or audiovisual records of the activity available for repeated observation. Such tape or videotape records permit multiple scans and help human observers to transcend their normal attentional and perceptual limitations.

In contrast to ratings, no special knowledge by the observer seems required with regard to the behavioral norms of the sample, or variations among the several age, sex, and ethnic groups within the society with regard to the frequency or normalcy of particular acts. Nor is a conceptual understanding required about the personality variable or the theory to which the information may be applied. What is presumed to be necessary, however, is that the observer has the ability to recognize and record accurately the relevant actions in the behavioral stream as they occur. Observers qua observers typically are not required to form a theory of the attribute-to-be-explained or to perform statistical transformations on the information at the first level of recording, except in the most elementary meanings of theory and analysis. On the contrary, theoretical and statistical preconceptions are sometimes assumed to interfere with precise observations. Accordingly, most investigators attempt to shield their observers (or themselves, if they act as observers) from the theoretic and analytic aspects of the investigation during the course of data collection. Despite such attempts, observer biases persist. They influence both what is "seen" and what is recorded (Yarrow and Waxler, Chapter 2, this volume).

GOALS OF THE METHODS

Perhaps the most important, and the least understood, functional difference between rating procedures and behavioral observations is that they differ with respect to the information that they aim to provide. What has made the matter slippery to grasp is that the two procedures do not merely complement each other (i.e., the information derived from the two methods is not independent) and are not merely different ways to abstract the same information.

Raters must filter from the mass of information gathered by virtue of "knowing" another person the particular information that is pertinent to the quality of attribute under investigation. The filter is not just a passive one. The rater must have sufficient knowledge about the comparison population or reference group to transform the relevant information to a new distribution, and to scale the individual's score in terms of that distribution. Such internal (private) computations of the rater presuppose the ability of judges to equate for circumstances and skills across children. They also presuppose the ability to refer the qualities of a given child to the distribution of these qualities in the relevant population.

Behavioral observations also impose a filter on the information that is attended to and recorded. This filter, however, is not as heavily influenced by the internal weighting systems, implicit personality constructs, and memory of the observer. Rather, the filter concerns what the observer must attend to (as determined by the nature of the categories employed) and what action patterns are actually perceived by the observer. Hence, selective attention and limitations of perception are key elements in observational methods.

The difference between observations and ratings in terms of their goals can be stated in statistical terms as well. Table A.1 shows the potential sources of

TABLE A.1
Potential Sources of Variance for Each Assessment Technique

Symbol	Ratings	Symbol	Observations
s_R^2	Characteristics of the rater: Idiosyncratic interpretations of the construct or dimension; Idiosyncratic interpretation of the relevant activities; Scaling of individual onto the group distribution; Knowledge of the individual child; Limitations of perception; Personal biases toward subjects (halos); Biases toward groups (stereotyping); Knowledge of reference population; Dispositions of rater (optimistic, etc.); Selective memory factors.	s_O^2	Characteristics of the observer: Selective attention factors; Limitations of perception; Personal biases toward subjects (halos); Biases toward groups (stereotyping).
s_{CS}^2	Characteristics of the child—Stable: Enduring dispositions and style of interchange.	s_{CS}^2	Characteristics of the child—Stable: Enduring dispositions and style of interchange.
s_{CT}^2	Characteristics of the child—Temporary: Fatigue, illness, momentary mood, etc.	s_{CT}^2	Characteristics of the child—Temporary: Fatigue, illness, momentary mood, etc.
s_S^2	Characteristics of the setting: Physical setting (classroom, home, etc.); Cultural or institutional setting.	s_S^2	Characteristics of the setting: Physical setting (classroom, home, etc.); Cultural or institutional setting.
s_I^2	Characteristics of the interchange: Behavior of the interchange partner; Relationship of partner to child (age, sex, past history, etc.).	s_I^2	Characteristics of the interchange: Behavior of the interchange partner; Relationship of partner to child (age, sex, past history, etc.).
s_e^2	Other sources of fluctuation: Errors of recording, mistakes in analysis, etc.	s_e^2	Other sources of fluctuation: Errors of recording, mistakes in analysis, etc.

variance among scores when either observational (behavioral) or rating methods are used. In both measures, six possible major sources of variance can be identified:

1. Characteristics of the rater (s_R^2) or observer (s_O^2).
2. Characteristics of the child that are stable (s_{CS}^2).
3. Characteristics of the child that are temporary (s_{CT}^2).
4. Characteristics of the context or setting (s_S^2).
5. Characteristics of the social interchange (s_I^2).
6. Miscellaneous sources of variation (errors of recording, etc.)(s_e^2).

The two procedures differ in what sources of variance they aim to capture and, potentially, in what sources of variance they actually reflect.

In the case of ratings, the aim is to assess the characteristics of the child that are relatively enduring or stable across settings and across specific interchange partners. This is s_{CS}^2 in Table A.1. The "ideal" rating of personality will (1) identify enduring and idiosyncratic features of the child, and (2) control for or eliminate sources of variation that are specific to settings, raters, and interchanges, and errors of memory and/or recording. Hence, it is expected that:

Rating = f(enduring characteristics of child)

or

$$R = f(s_{CS}^2).$$

For observations, the goal is to record accurately and precisely all relevant behavioral events of the child and those with whom the child interacts. Hence, no distinction is made with respect to sources of variation—whether interpersonal, intrapersonal, contextual, cultural, or ephemeral—while the observer is recording data. Efforts are made to eliminate two of the major potential sources of variation in observational scores. These are: (1) stable characteristics of the observer that may influence the recording; and (2) other sources of error, including lapses of attention, mistakes in coding, "category drift" (changes in what is recorded), and so on. But no attempt is made in the initial recording to determine whether and to what extent the actions are stable or temporary, determined by interpersonal or intrapersonal factors, context-bound or context-free, age-appropriate or age-atypical, or sex-appropriate or sex-atypical. Hence, the information retained in observations is, by design, inclusive, and:

Observational scores = f(enduring characteristics of child; temporary states of child; interpersonal acts; fusion of settings and institutional norms, and so on)

or

$$R = f\,(s^2_{CS} + s^2_{CT} + s^2_I + s^2_S + s^2_{CS \times I} + s^2_{CT \times I} + \ldots).$$

In most observational techniques, the sorting out of the various sources of control and regulation occurs in subsequent stages of analysis, not in the initial recording.

Why is it likely that direct observations of behavior and ratings will yield different results? The answer from the foregoing and Table A.1 is that relational, contextual, temporary, etc., sources of variance will ideally be retained in the observational scores in addition to "stable" qualities of the child. Ratings will ideally reflect variance due exclusively to such stable qualities.

These are the goals of the two procedures. But what sources of variance do they actually reflect? From our consideration of the assumptions that underlie the use of the two procedures, we might reasonably expect a differential contribution of the idiosyncracies of the rater or the observer. In particular, these "personal constants" or qualities of the human observer/ rater seem likely to play a larger role in the determination of rating scores than observation scores. Hence, we might anticipate that ratings will in fact be determined mostly by the first *two* factors in Table A.1 (stable characteristics of the child and the rater), whereas observations will be determined primarily by the *second through fifth* factors and their fusion (statistical interaction). We now turn to a brief overview of the empirical literature relevant to these expectations.

WHAT DO RATINGS AND OBSERVATIONS ACTUALLY MEASURE?

Up to this point we have identified what the two procedures typically aim to assess and what they potentially assess. Now we can comment briefly on what empirical studies suggest that they actually measure. It is beyond the scope of this note to cover systematically the massive literature that has accumulated over the past 70 years in studies that have used these methods. Our aim is more modest. We wish to selectively draw hints from that literature about what weights should be assigned to the sources of variance identified in Table

A.1. Happily, the picture provided by the research is reasonable, consistent, and coherent (although we offer only a preliminary view).

Consider first the question of whether or not rating scales succeed in their aim of identifying stable characteristics of individual children. In some conditions, they do. In cases where clearly defined rating scales are employed, where the children are observed in the same general setting, and where all raters are well acquainted with the children they are asked to judge, rating procedures have been moderately successful in identifying stable individual differences in personality characteristics. E. S. Schaefer's work illustrates the point. After extensive pretesting and evaluation, Schaefer developed rating scales that were employed in regular classrooms from kindergarten through sixth grade. Interrater agreement (between teachers in the classroom) was reasonably high (see also Olweus, 1977): The median correlation for seven different scales, such as extraversion, industriousness, hostility, was $r = .57$. Furthermore, ratings after 1 to 2½ years indicated similar statistical levels of prediction, even when new raters supplied the information on the retest. (These correlations are not high enough to warrant predictions for individual children—Schaefer, 1975—although they are high enough to permit one to use the procedures for the study of individual difference phenomena.)

In the foregoing illustration, all children were observed in the same general setting—the school. To what extent is the stability of rating scores dependent on the maintenance of the same context? One way to estimate variance due to changes in settings and relationships would be to compare the ratings on a given child by independent judges in two settings (say, at home and at school). The empirical evidence suggests that a generous estimate of the magnitude of such a correlation is about $r = .50$ (Bem & Allen, 1974; Magnusson, Gerzen, & Nyman, 1968; Yarrow & Waxler, Chapter 2, this volume). A less generous estimate would be $r = .30$ (Mischel, 1973; Rose, Blank, & Spalter, 1975). So relationships and contexts make a difference in the magnitude of the ratings. Nonetheless, the finding of significant correlations indicates that at least some "stable" characteristics of the child are captured by some rating procedures across time and space.

These findings are consistent with the results of validity studies, where ratings of the child (or of relationships) are used to predict some later behavior pattern. For instance, Bakeman and Brown's (1977) recent success in predicting features of the later mother–child relationship on the basis of the ratings of early mother–infant interactions indicates that the ratings were measuring some enduring features of the child and/or the mother. In overview, the findings of recent as well as early studies of ratings tend to support G. W. Allport's (1937) faith in the procedure as a primary means for identifying stable individual differences.

We can summarize the variance estimates graphically, if it is recognized that the estimates are a rough first approximation, and that they vary according to the design of the instrument and the parameters of the study (see Fig. A.1, left column). The evidence tends to confirm that the goals of rating scales are usually fulfilled, at least in part. The evidence also supports the expectation outlined previously—namely, that ratings are greatly influenced by the idiosyncratic characteristics of the persons doing the ratings. This is the "cost" of abstracting individual-difference variance at the first stage of analysis.

So much for the relation between aims and outcomes in the use of rating scales. What about observation techniques—what determines variations in observational measures of social behavior? First, it should be observed that observational methods have *not* achieved notable success in identifying individual differences among children that are stable across settings, relationships, and time. The failure to achieve such success should not be wholly surprising, since that was not an explicit goal of the methods in their design. Nonetheless, the failure has been a source of some disappointment—even disillusionment—for some users. Depending on the variable assessed in direct observations, the generalization of individual differences across contexts and relationships ranges from modest to nonexistent, with correlations ranging typically between $r = .30$ and $r = .00$.

Do persons who independently observe the same child at the same time obtain similar scores? The answer depends on what is observed, how the

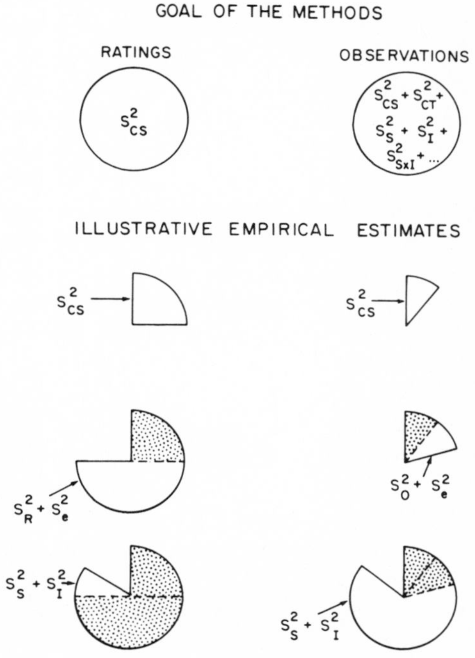

GOAL OF THE METHODS

FIG. A.1. Schematic diagrams that partition variance of rating and observational measures in terms of (*upper row*) goals of the techniques as they are frequently used, and (*lower rows*) empirical estimates of the weight that may be assigned to the several potential sources of variance. (See Table A.1, p. 215, for an explanation of the symbols.)

"similarity" is computed, and how many persons are being analyzed at one time. In "real-time" observations, the levels of agreement can range from extremely high ($r = .99$) to moderate or quite low ($r = .60$). Even in those instances where low levels of agreement are found in direct observation, the use of audio or audiovisual records that are repeatedly analyzed permits observers to reach the highest levels of agreement. Hence, refinement of the procedures for data gathering can greatly extend the perceptual and discrimination capabilities of the observers.

The ideal and empirical outcomes can also be summarized graphically (Fig. A.1, right column). No "ideal" weight is usually assigned a priori to the several sources of variance in observations except that the errors of memory and recording should be negligible. In actual practice, the proportion of variance to be assigned to the "stable" characteristics of the child (independent of context and setting) is rather modest (ca. 1% to 10%), as is the variance assigned to idiosyncratic differences among observers (ca. 1% to 30%).

The upshot of the preceding discussion (and illustrated in Fig. A.1) is that: (1) ratings should be relatively useful in the study of stable characteristics of children; and (2) observations (as normally employed) are unlikely to be useful for that purpose. Why? As shown in Fig. A.1, ratings assess a significant amount of individual difference variance, as they were designed to do. The procedures have also been shown to be greatly influenced by individual differences among the raters themselves. But this source of variance (due to rater characteristics) can be reduced by using two or more raters, thus canceling out idiosyncratic "rater" contributions.

Observations can also be used for the prediction of individual differences, but only under restrictive conditions (see later). Ordinarily, observations capture only a modest amount of stable individual difference variance. It is also the case that differences among observers can be reduced to negligible levels. The problem is that a large portion of variance in observations is left unaccounted for by these two sources. This 80% to 90% of "unexplained" variance has sometimes been considered "error" variance when it appears in test–retest observational studies. The observational measures are then considered "unreliable" or "invalid." We now look at this key issue more closely.

RELIABILITY, UNRELIABILITY, AND ADAPTATION

Can "unreliable" measures be useful for anything? The answer to this question depends on whether we can account for a major part of the variance that has been considered "error." Evidence on this matter has been obtained recently in studies of interchanges that permit us to identify what appears to be a major source of variance in observations of social patterns. Specifically, it has been shown that the immediate actions and responses of other persons in the relationship have a profound influence on the nature and direction of the child's behaviors.

To illustrate, consider D. J. MacCombie's recent dissertation (1978), for which he observed pairs of children (from 2 years to 9 years of age) in a standard setting. MacCombie found that children's acts (what they say and do and how they express their emotions) are typically closely synchronized with and responsive to the acts of their partners. The degree of correspondence within pairs was very high relative to the correspondence between pairs of children *in all age groups studied*. MacCombie found, for example, that median correlations were high ($r = .70$ to $.90$) between the acts of one child and those of the other child. Such correlations were obtained among children in middle childhood (years 6–9) as well as in younger children (years 2–5), with a modest reduction in correlation across ages. These findings are not limited to laboratory observations; similar contingencies have been reported in natural settings as well (see Bott, 1934; Holmberg, 1977). As Parke (Chapter 1, this volume) has shown, studies of context indicate that the setting has a strong influence on behavior, and, presumably, contextual and relational effects are fused in everyday life. These findings permit one to identify interactional–contextual factors as a major source of variance.

The finding, then, is that much of the information in the direct observation of interchanges can be "explained" if one takes into account the actions and reactions of other persons (see diagram at bottom of right column, Fig. A.1). This empirical outcome is, of course, what the interactional orientation is all about. The apparent "unreliability" arises because observational techniques accurately preserve the precise behaviors and actions of the children. Observations indicate that children respond flexibly to the changing social and contextual influences to which they are exposed.

To identify individual stabilities in observations, it may be necessary to move to more abstract or summary measures, including the number of interchanges or their duration or length. But even these measures are influenced significantly by interactional and contextual factors. "Reliability" (i.e., individual-difference prediction) is enhanced by controlling the sources of regulation (by holding the relationship or situation constant in the two observations) or by eliminating its influence by multiple observations in a wide range of contexts and relationships (hence, reducing these sources of variance relative to intrapersonal sources; see Cohen & Beckwith, 1976; Green, 1977; Gustafson, 1977; Sherman, 1975).

But to come back to the quesion raised earlier, can "unreliable" observations be useful for anything? The answer is strongly affirmative, *if* it can be shown that the scores are not merely produced by errors of the observers or by entirely private observer processes. Hence, they reflect real interpersonal, contextual, and intrapersonal controls. Accordingly, *direct observations of behavior can be the key for identifying how actual behaviors are elicited, maintained, and organized.* Such information may be critical for explaining the processes that regulate social patterns, as opposed to describing the social patterns. Both goals—description of individual differences and explanations of how differences arise—are worthy goals, but they are different. Accordingly, observation techniques are "useful"(or, even, indispensible) for identifying the dynamic controls that operate during the course of social development.

Conversely, ratings would not be useful in yielding information about contextual, interpersonal, and developmental processes. Why not? Because these sources of variance are typically eliminated at the first stage of data recording; ratings summarize over diversity in behavior to arrive at a judgment. It is ironic that the very factors that give the appearance of "reliability" and "predictability" in ratings preclude their usefulness as a method for the investigation of most processes of change and development.[4]

ARE THE PROCEDURES
DICHOTOMOUS?

Up to this point, we have treated the two procedures as if they were entirely nonoverlapping and shared few characteristics in common. It would be more appropriate to view the procedures as occupying different places on a continuum. Observations of behavior sometimes employ categories that require judgments with regard to the intentions and interpretations of subjects and others with whom the relationship occurs. Furthermore, there are important individual differences in attentional factors, personal biases, and perhaps stereotypes that affect the recording of behaviors.

The breadth of the categories employed in observations and the time interval across which information is integrated determine to what extent the observations approach ratings or vice versa. Typically, these parameters are in the public record in observational studies; this may not be the case with

---

[4]If ratings eliminate developmental changes at the very first stage of recording, they cannot, obviously, prove helpful in tracking developmental changes. Developmental variance may be reduced, or eliminated, if raters refer the child to the norm for his or her age group. For parallel reasons, parental ratings of boys and girls on such measures as aggression and dependency often have few differences (Sears, Maccoby, & Levin, 1957), whereas direct observations typically have found large differences (Feshbach, 1970). It is probably the case that boys and girls differed in actual behaviors relevant to these constructs but that these differences were eliminated by within-rater transformations. Behavior observations, however, fail to make such adjustments, and they faithfully preserve developmental and sex differences that exist in actual behavior, if such differences exist. Ratings show few *age-related* differences in, say, attachment, when the measures are taken at 6-month intervals on children from 1 to 3 years of age. Behavior observations, in contrast, show vast age-related differences when repeated measures are made over the same period.

rating procedures. In view of the range of possibilities regarding the time intervals of the observations and the narrowness of the behavior category, it seems appropriate to view "observations" and "ratings" as occupying the ends of a continuum as opposed to being qualitatively different means of assessment.

Some of the new multiple-measure rating techniques seem to stand in the middle of this continuum. A good sampling of these techniques is found in a recent issue of the *Journal of Abnormal Child Psychology* (1977, 5) devoted to assessment. For example, successive factor analyses and scale item deletions can be used to develop a set of items that achieve high levels of discrimination among individuals, even though raters are given minimal instruction about the nature of the variables. However, the generality of those techniques to other settings may be quite limited (e.g., Behar, 1977). Thus there may be a trade-off between situational specificity of ratings and the degree to which the characteristics and tasks of the raters must be made explicit or standardized.

SOME CONCLUSIONS

In concluding this note, it should be observed that the points we have covered constitute, in some respects, a new interpretation of the differences between ratings and observations. We cannot agree with Mischel's (1973) suggestion that ratings provide more information about the cognitive ability of the rater than of the dispositions of the child (see also Newcomb, 1937). True, the cognitive activity of the rater is intimately involved in all ratings or judgments that are produced. But the judicious use of several raters should control for idiosyncratic biases and thereby enhance the contribution of the information provided by the child's behavior.

On the other hand, we cannot accept the proposal that studies of behavior have outlived their usefulness. It is accurate that they are often "unreliable" in repeated observations, but the "unreliability" occurs primarily because behavioral measures are indeed precise and sensitive to powerful effects of interactional and contextual controls. In fact, *the abilities of the child to adapt to changing demands of the social and nonsocial environment constitute the central foci for a developmental analysis.* Washing out these adaptive capabilities, either by controlling them through statistical transformations on the obtained data or by requesting "raters" to control for them in the first stage of analysis, precludes an understanding of how accommodations are made and how behaviors change over time and space.

The main lesson to be learned from an anlaysis of the properties of these methods is that each may be useful but for different purposes. For those investigators who aspire to describe individual differences in behavioral style, or distinctive properties of interactions between two or more persons, ratings can be most useful. They help to quantify the everyday judgments each of us makes about other persons in classifying them, their behaviors, and their relationships. Such classifications are indeed useful in everyday experience (1) in developing expectations about behaviors of others, and (2) in scientific research, where the goal is to achieve significant predictive statements about individual differences in social and nonsocial behavior.

But for purposes of understanding the mechanisms of social patterns (how they are maintained and changed and how new patterns are brought into the repertoire of individuals and groups), there can be no substitute for the direct analysis of the activities to be explained. The very habits of perception and categorization that are useful in everyday life may work to the disadvantage of the investigator who aspires to identify the processes of behavioral control and regulation. That which is implicit in ratings processes becomes explicit in observational procedures.

Finally, the issues that are raised by ratings and observational methods are general ones, a point that was recognized early by Binet (see Cairns & Ornstein, 1979) and G. W. Allport (1937), and, more recently, by Cronbach (1957) and Wohlwill (1973). The techniques that are most effective in *describing the outcomes* of development may not be effective in *analyzing the processes* by which social patterns arise and are maintained or eliminated. Problems have arisen when the different functions served by the methods have become confused. Floyd Allport stated the matter clearly in his 1924 text, *Social Psychology*. After four initial chapters that introduced social psychology and described the determinants of human behavior in the nervous system, he began Chapter 5, entitled "Personality—The Social Man," in the following manner:

> Our method in the preceding chapters has been mainly analytical. We have attempted to reduce human behavior to its fundamental terms, and have found these terms to include prepotent reflexes, habit formation, thought, and emotion. These mechanisms furnish us with suitable principles of explanation. It is now desirable to shift our emphasis from explanation to description, and to study, not the mechanisms themselves, but the character and efficacy of the adjustments which they produce in operation.... These aspects may be called *traits of personality* [p. 99, Allport's italics].

It now appears that we have the methodological tools for closing the gap between these two levels of analysis.

REFERENCES

Allport, F. H. *Social psychology*. Boston: Houghton Mifflin, 1924.
Allport, F. H., & Allport, G. W. Personality traits: Their classification and measurement. *Journal of Abnormal Psychology and Social Psychology,* 1921, *16,* 1–40.

Allport, G. W. *Personality: A psychological interpretation.* New York: Holt, 1937.

Bakeman, R., & Brown, J. V. *Mother–infant interactions during the first months of life: Differences between preterm and fullterm infant–mother dyads from a low income population* (Tech. Rep. No. 5). Atlanta: Georgia State University, 1977.

Behar, L. B. The preschool behavior questionnaire. *Journal of Abnormal Child Psychology,* 1977, *5,* 265–275.

Bem, D. J., & Allen, A. On predicting some of the people some of the time. *Psychological Review,* 1974, *81,* 506–520.

Bott, H. McI. *Personality development in young children.* Toronto: University of Toronto Press, 1934.

Cairns, R. B., & Ornstein, P. A. Developmental psychology. In E. Hearst (Ed.), *The first century of experimental psychology.* Hillsdale, N.J.: Lawrence Erlbaum Associates, 1979.

Cohen, S. E., & Beckwith, L. Maternal language in infancy. *Developmental Psychology,* 1976, *12,* 371–372.

Cronbach L. J. The two disciplines of scientific psychology. *American Psychologist,* 1957, *12,* 671–684.

Feshbach, S. Aggression. In P. H. Mussen (Ed.), *Carmichael's manual of child psychology* (Vol. 2). New York: Wiley, 1970.

Green, J. A. *A developmental analysis of mother–infant interactions: Changes in infant behavior and capabilities.* Unpublished master's thesis, University of North Carolina, Chapel Hill, 1977.

Gustafson, G. E. *A longitudinal study of infants' interactions with their mothers: Some contributions of locomotor and social development.* Unpublished master's thesis, University of North Carolina, Chapel Hill, 1977.

Holmberg, M. C. *The development of social interchange patterns from 12 to 42 months: Cross-sectional and short-term longitudinal analysis.* Unpublished doctoral dissertation, University of North Carolina, Chapel Hill, 1977.

MacCombie, D. J. *The development of reciprocity in children's social interchanges.* Unpublished doctoral dissertation, University of North Carolina, Chapel Hill, 1978.

Magnusson, D., Gerzen, M., & Nyman, B. The generality of behavioral data I: Generalization from observations on one occasion. *Multivariate Behavioral Research,* 1968, *3,* 295–320.

Mischel, W. Toward a cognitive social learning reconceptualization of personality. *Psychological Review,* 1973, *80,* 252–283.

Newcomb, T. An experiment designed to test the validity of a rating technique. *Journal of Educational Psychology,* 1937, *22,* 279–289.

Norsworthy, N. The validity of judgments of character. In *Essays philosophical and psychological (In honor of William James).* New York: Longman, 1908.

Olweus, D. Aggression and peer acceptance in adolescent boys: Two short-term longitudinal studies of ratings. *Child Development,* 1977, *48,* 1301–1313.

Patterson, G. R. Naturalistic observation in clinical assessment. *Journal of Abnormal Child Psychology,* 1977, *5,* 309–322.

Rose, S. A., Blank, M., & Spalter, I. Situational specificity of behavior in young children. *Child Development,* 1975, *46,* 464–469.

Rugg, H. Is the rating of human character practicable? *Journal of Educational Psychology,* 1921, *12,* 425–438.

Rugg, H. Is the rating of human character practicable? *Journal of Educational Psychology,* 1922, *13,* 30–42; 81–93.

Schaefer, E. S. *Major replicated dimensions of adjustment and achievement: Cross-cultural, cross-sectional and longitudinal research.* Paper presented at the annual meeting of the American Educational Research Association, Washington, D.C., April 1975.

Sears, R. R., Maccoby, E. E., & Levin, H. *Patterns of child rearing.* Evanston, Ill.: Harper & Row, 1957.

Sherman, S. J. *Social interchanges in children: Formation, stability, and contextual constraints.* Unpublished doctoral dissertation, University of North Carolina, Chapel Hill, 1975.

Waters, E. The reliability and stability of individual differences in infant–mother attachment. *Child Development,* 1978, *49,* 483–494.

Wohlwill, J. F. *The study of behavioral development.* New York: Academic Press, 1973.

B

Note on Describing and Analyzing Interactional Data: Some First Steps and Common Pitfalls

Roger Bakeman
Georgia State University

Robert B. Cairns
Mark Appelbaum
University of North Carolina at Chapel Hill

INTRODUCTION

The purpose of this note is to offer preliminary guidance to researchers who want to describe and analyze their social interaction data. The first section presents a simple typology for describing the kinds of data typically encountered in studies of social interaction, followed by a catalog of techniques useful in the analysis of such data; the second section comments on some pitfalls that may be encountered during data analysis.

Interactional data may not be as diverse as they often seem at first. A common vocabulary for describing such data may bring common concerns and interests into sharper focus and may make for easier communication with other people (e.g., computer programmers). Furthermore, investigators in quite different content areas may have logically equivalent kinds of data or data structures and so should be able to benefit from data analytic strategies, including computer programs, developed by others. Still, a main problem is to describe the data in simple and meaningful ways. A variety of techniques, none of them especially complicated or even new, are surveyed here. Our cataloging of techniques should not obscure the fact that no mere technique can compensate for conceptual clarity. If data complexity seems overwhelming, then probably a clear idea, and not a correct technique, is lacking.

INTERACTIONAL DATA DESCRIPTION
AND ANALYSIS

Data Terminology

The first step in data description is to recognize the nature and characteristics of the data that are recorded. Its form places certain constraints on the types of description and analyses that are permissible. Hence, we offer a typology for the sorts of sequential data typically encountered in studies of social interaction.

Before considering this typology, it is necessary to clarify the distinction between the behavior and the record thereof. The actual *behavior* may be a continuously varying attribute such as blood pressure, heart rate, or virtually any other measure of physical extent, or it may be a binary or discrete process that at some periods in time is in an "on" state and at other times is in an "off" state. In the case of a discrete variable, the individual may be in one of several recognizably different states as a function of time. Time is, of course, a continuous attribute.

Our *recording* of the behavior may or may not reflect the continous or discrete nature of the behavior, but certainly the "natural" character of the behavior must, in the final analysis, be reflected in our statements. Our protocols may approach a continuous recording as in the case, say, of videotaping, where the frames appear each 16 milliseconds; or it may be essentially discrete, as in time sampling. The size of the window we use in time sampling may vary widely from study to study and may indeed vary within a single study as a function of the way we choose to code our data (see, for example, the following distinction between event sequence data and timed-event sequence data).

Finally, we need to distinguish among the ways we may treat our resulting measures. It is sometimes the case that we may, for the purpose of analysis, take continous records of a continuously varying behavior and treat it as discrete, or, more commonly, we may treat discrete data recorded in a discrete manner by models assuming continuously distributed attributes solely because the mathematics of continous sytems are so much easier to handle (as in the case of ANOVA and Pearsonian correlational techniques).

Following the standard textbook dichotomy, the simplest and clearest distinction is between sequences of contiuous and sequences of discrete data. Here we distinguish two types of continuous data and three types of discrete series; it is our belief that most examples in the literature will fit one or the other of these categories:

1. A *continuous series* results when the score for some continuous variable (such as blood pressure) is recorded at each successive time interval.

a. Such data are simply a string of scores, are often represented as a line graph, and are usually termed *time-series* data.

b. If more than one variable is recorded, then *multiple time-series* data result.

2. *Discrete sequential* data could be categorized in several ways, but three kinds occur most commonly in the literature.

a. The first we term *event sequence* data which result when the stream of behavior is encoded as a sequence of events or behaviors usually defined so as to be mutually exclusive and exhaustive. Such data are simply a string of codes or symbols.

b. The second type we term *timed-event sequence* data, in which duration, and not just sequence, is recorded. Such data can also be represented as a string of codes, but each code would represent not just an event but an event associated with a given time interval. For example, imagine four behaviors coded 1 to 4. A behavior stream recorded as event sequence data might look like "24213," whereas the same stream recorded as timed-event sequence data might look like "224222111133."

c. The third type of discrete series we term *multiple timed-event sequence* data. Imagine that we observe the following: At Time 1, the mother holds her infant, the infant vocalizes, and the mother vocalizes; at Time 2, the mother continues to hold her infant, the infant vocalizes, and the mother rocks her infant; etc. We could consider each unique combination of codes as a new code as animal behaviorists often do (see, e.g., Altmann, 1965), but this becomes unwieldy if more than a few behaviors are under consideration. Alternatively, such data could be represented as a sequence of *sets* of codes; each set then represents behaviors occurring within a time interval.

The different kinds of series should not be thought of as immutable, and rarely would there be much reason for degrading time series into event sequence data. But the reverse process is appealing because the investigator could then apply time-series techniques to previous categorical data. This transformation could be affected for multiple timed-event sequence data in at least two ways:

1. We could assume that the number of concurrent behaviors indicate activity or intensity of a behavioral system (as do Brazelton, Koslowski, & Main, 1974) and then categorize each successive interval with the number of those behaviors occurring in each interval yielding time-series data.

2. Or we could select one behavior of interest and code its presence with "1" and its absence with "0," yielding a binary time series (as do Jaffe & Feldstein,

1970). Selecting multiple behaviors would result in multiple binary time series (this is an analytic strategy recommended by Kaye, chap. 14, n.d.).

Analytic Techniques

How does one describe and test interactional data for statistical significance? Happily, most of the issues of interactional analysis can be approached with familiar parametric and nonparametric procedures. Indeed, the studies of interaction typically involve the report of means, percentages, and proportions. The analyses are similarly straightforward in that standard statistical models of analysis of variance and correlation can be employed if one is careful not to violate the assumptions underlying these procedures (see the following).

With the recent dominance in applied statistics by computer-generated analyses and multivariate statistics, much of the traditional wisdom resulting from description has been lost. With the publication of Tukey's *Exploratory Data Analysis* (1977), it is hoped that there will be at least a partial return to description as a beginning point in the treatment of experimental data. Due to the unusual data conditions encountered in interactional analyses, researchers in this area would be well advised to acquaint themselves with some of Tukey's techniques.

In addition, there are procedures that are particularly suited for describing concurrent and sequential patterns. Conditional probabilities, for instance, may be assembled in ways that are especially informative with respect to the problem of mutual contingency identification. Such techniques are hardly an innovation (see, e.g., Thomas, Loomis, & Arrington, 1933) but have received renewed attention recently. For specific examples and additional references, see Castellan (Chapter 4, this volume), Bakeman (1978), Bakeman and Brown (1977), Bakeman and Dabbs (1976), Sackett (1978, in press), and Stern (1974).

In addition to identifying behavioral contingencies, investigators may also be concerned with the orderliness or patterning of a stream of behavior viewed as a whole. That is, how predictable, on the average, are behaviors in a sequence? Would we enhance predictability appreciably by knowing just the previous behavior, the previous two behaviors, etc.? Among the methods that can be used to answer these questions are log-linear models (see Bishop, Fienberg, & Holland, 1975) or measures derived from information theory (for examples and references, see Attneave, 1959; Gottman & Bakeman, in press; Miller & Frick, 1949).

A third kind of question asked is whether an observed process can be adequately predicted by its own past, a particular intervention, or from the past of another series. Such questions are addressed by time-series analyses (e.g., see Glass, Willson, & Gottman, 1975; and Gottman & Glass, 1976).

One final point: None of these techniques are automatic avenues to the truth, and all can be abused. In no case should they dictate the course of data analysis. They are not masters, only tools to be masterfully used.

SOME COMMON PITFALLS

We have encountered some problems in our own work and the review of the studies of others that are of the garden-variety nature—pitfalls that are normally avoided when on familiar ground but that are subtly woven into the treatment of interactional data. It seems useful to include in this note some comments on the problems that are likely to be encountered and on how to avoid them (when possible).

Data Tyranny

Observations of interactions typically produce great volumes of data. For instance, a single 30-minute observation of a child will yield 360 5-second intervals. If 72 children are observed, about 25,920 observation blocks are generated. Depending on the coding system employed, scores may be generated on 5, 50, or 500, variables. Virtually all investigators have felt, at some point in their study, tyrannized by the vast amounts of data that flow in, and they feel under some compulsion to analyze it. Underlying the compulsion is a vague uncertainty of the consequences of ignoring some of the information, because one might be guilty of having selectively interpreted the data. At this point, certain of the techniques discussed by Tukey can serve us quite well.

There are at least three pitfalls when one atempts to analyze all of the data collected, if the original coding system was nearly exhaustive. First, there is a high likelihood that the results of the multiple analyses are themselves intercorrelated; hence, the interpretation of the outcomes would be less than clear and the operational level of the set of tests beyond determination. A second and associated problem is that "chance" associations are likely to appear in any large batch of data that is analyzed according to all possible outcomes and relationships. Finally, there is the sheer expense of attempting to order the data in such a way as to conduct the analysis. One becomes overwhelmed with data.

How does one avoid being tyrannized? The solution turns out to be less a statistical one than a logical and theoretical one. Because of the open-ended nature of interactional designs with respect to dependent variables, the major decisions made by the investigator involve selection. Hence, filters occur at three major stages: when decisions are made on how to code the stream of behavior; when one collapses, combines, and classifies the coded information; and when one selects data for analysis. At the third level, that of analysis, one may attempt to analyze all of the information (e.g., factor analysis), or one may test particular hypotheses. The latter choice may be dictated by the nature of the research question and/or the form of the data, or it may merely reflect the investigator's research style and preference. All things considered, there are significant gains for the investigator who states questions clearly and precisely prior to the third stage of selection/analysis, regardless of the technique employed.

Violation of Independence

As we observed earlier, familiar parametric and nonparametric procedures can be effectively applied to the analysis of interactional data. A recurrent problem that is encountered in these applications is the possible violation of the assumption of independence. This condition may occur in a variety of circumstances such as when one collapses across the interactions of subject, across observation blocks, across settings, or across partners.

Much is known about the problem in regard to the t-test and the analysis of variance. Little, however, is known about these effects on chi-square and correlational analysis. N. J. Castellan considers this problem in Chapter 4, and the reader is referred to pp. 90–112 for possible solutions when lack of independence is suspected.

A special problem of independence is encountered in interactions in natural settings. Individual children may be focused on at any time, and all interactions between those children and other members of the class and teacher are recorded. Hence, "subjects" may be independent, but their partners may not be. For example, one rowdy boy (or girl) may be over-represented as a partner in virtually all of the interchanges that are analyzed. Or a teacher may be the ubiquitous controlling force that influences all interchanges. How independent, then, are the results of the subjects under such conditions, and can standard parametric analyses be employed?

Investigators must proceed cautiously in the interpretation of information derived from multiple observations of a single social system, whether it is a classroom, family, or colony of animals. Even when it is possible to identify what appear to be single dyads within a system, one cannot assume that there is not an interlocking network of relationships. Hence, the investigator should typically consider the system as the unit of analysis in addition to whatever descriptions are offered of component dyads.

Conditional Probabilities and Their Properties

Conditional probability analysis has become a strategy of choice in describing and analyzing interactional data. Certain elementary errors are made when insufficient attention is given to the unconditional probability (base rate) in the interpretation. Three other pitfalls in the use of conditional probability analysis include:

1. the failure to recognize that the events that initiate about (activity pattern) may be different from those that maintain it; and
2. the failure to recognize that collapsing data from an entire session or series presupposes stable contingencies that exist throughout the session or series (stationarity assumption). This presupposition of stablility is a peculiar one for interactional analyses because it would not appear to permit learning or dynamic changes in interpersonal control properties.
3. the failure to consider patterns of acts ("themes" or "episodes") as units of analysis, in conjunction with atomistic descriptions of discrete acts. The information yielded by a contingency analysis of discrete acts may not be the same as an analysis of patterns, simply because the events that *elicit* patterns may not be the same as those that *maintain* their internal organization.

These problems are discussed in detail by Castellan (Chapter 4), along with suggestions on how they can be solved.

CONCLUDING COMMENT

This appendix was intended, as its title indicates, to provide some 'first steps" in interactional data and description. Those planning to take further steps are advised to become acquainted with the sources cited in our references and Chapter 4 of this volume.

REFERENCES

Attneave, F. *Applications of information theory to psychology.* New York: Henry Holt, 1959.
Altmann, S. A. Sociobiology of rhesus monkeys. II. Stochastics of social communication. *Journal of Theoretical Biology,* 1965, *8,* 490–522.
Bakeman, R. Untangling streams of behavior: Sequential analyses of observation data. In G. P. Sackett (Ed.), *Observing behavior: Data collection and analysis methods.* Baltimore: University Park Press, 1978.
Bakeman, R., & Brown, J. V. Behavioral dialogues: An approach to the assessment of mother–infant interaction. *Child Development,* 1977, *48,* 195–203.
Bakeman, R., & Dabbs, M. M., Jr. Social interaction observed: Some approaches to the analysis of behavior streams. *Personality and Social Psychology Bulletin,* 1976, *2,* 335–245.
Bishop, Y. M. M., Fienberg, S. E., & Holland, P. W. *Discrete multivariate analysis.* Cambridge, Mass.: MIT Press, 1975.
Brazelton, T. B., Koslowski, B., & Main, M. The origins of reciprocity: the early mother–infant interaction. In M. Lewis & L. A. Rosenblum (Eds.), *The effect of the infant on its caregiver.* New York: Wiley, 1974.
Glass, G. V., Willson, V. L., & Gottman, J. M. *Design and analysis of time-series experiments.* Boulder: Colorado University Associated Press, 1975.

Gottman, J., & Bakeman, R. The sequential analysis of observational data. in M. Lamb, S. Suomi, & G. Stephenson (Eds.), *Methodological problems in the study of social interaction.* Madison: University of Wisconsin Press, in press.

Gottman, J. M., & Glass, G. V. Analysis of interrupted time-series experiments. In T. Kratochwill (Ed.), *Strategies to evaluate change in single subject research.* New York: Academic Press, 1976.

Jaffe, J., & Feldstein, S. *Rhythms of dialogue.* New York: Academic Press, 1970.

Kaye, K. *CRESCAT: Soft ware system for analysis of sequential real-time data.* Unpublished manuscript, University of Chicago, no date.

Miller, G. A., & Frick, F. C. Statistical behavioristics and sequences of responses. *Psychological Review,* 1949, *56,* 311–324.

Sackett, G. P. A taxonomy of observational techniques and a theory of measurement. In G. P. Sackett (Ed.), *Observing behavior: Data collection and analysis methods.* Baltimore: University Park Press, 1978.

Sackett, G. P. The lag sequential analysis of contingency and cyclicity in behaviorial interaction research. In J. Osofsky (Ed.), *Handbook of infant development.* New York: Wiley, in press.

Stern, D. N. Mother and infant at play: The dyadic interaction involving facial, vocal, and gaze behaviors. In M. Lewis & L. A. Rosenblum (Eds.), *The effect of the infant on its caregiver.* New York: Wiley, 1974.

Thomas, D. S., Loomis, A. M., & Arrington, R. E. *Observational studies of social behavior: Volume I—Social behavior patterns.* New Haven: Institute of Human Relations, Yale University, 1933.

Tukey, J. W. *Exploratory data analysis.* Reading, Mass.: Addison-Wesley, 1977.

Author Index

Subject Index